PRAISE FOR *Brown and Gay in LA*

"The intersections of race, immigration, and queerness are as much at the core of Ocampo's book as bigger-picture analyses of masculinity. This book is the best platform to dive into the matter and reemerge feeling inspired and motivated to just be and become one's unique self, the person one was always meant to be."
—*Library Journal*

"[Ocampo] writes about the joy of discovering oneself but also about the hard journey it is to get there; the challenge of feeling like you don't fit in or that you are disappointing your parents because you are not who they want you to be. . . . The triumphs are real too; those nights on the dance floor or hanging in a kitchen—with pure community."
—Brian De Los Santos, *LAist*

"Ocampo analyzes with great empathy the struggles of his informants as gay children of immigrants, often with non-English-speaking families, conservative values, and Roman Catholic mores. Thoughtfully evoked and beautifully narrated.'"
—Vernon Rosario, *The Gay & Lesbian Review*

"In *Brown and Gay in LA*, Ocampo provides a wonderful description of the journeys that the gay sons of immigrants embark on as they explore their sexual and gender identities in Los Angeles. . . . This is the kind of academic book that successfully reads as both an ethnographic description and an extremely personal account that reflects Ocampo's own life as the gay son of Filipino immigrants in Los Angeles."
—Héctor Carrillo, *Social Forces*

"Navigating the pressures placed upon them by the older generation, the men included in this study are celebrated for their strength and the community they build together. At the heart of the book is a questioning of the concept of Americanness in the face of difference—whether racial or sexual."
—Anne Mai Yee Jansen, *Book Riot*

BROWN AND GAY IN LA

Brown and Gay in LA

The Lives of Immigrant Sons

Anthony Christian Ocampo

NEW YORK UNIVERSITY PRESS

New York

NEW YORK UNIVERSITY PRESS
New York
www.nyupress.org

References to Internet websites (URLs) were accurate at the time of writing. Neither the author nor New York University Press is responsible for URLs that may have expired or changed since the manuscript was prepared.

Library of Congress Cataloging-in-Publication Data
Names: Ocampo, Anthony Christian, 1981– author.
Title: Brown and gay in LA : the lives of immigrant sons / Anthony C. Ocampo.
Description: New York : New York University Press, [2022] | Series: Asian
    American sociology series | Includes bibliographical references and index.
Identifiers: LCCN 2022001983 | ISBN 9781479824250 (hardback) | ISBN 9781479898138
    (paperback) | ISBN 9781479806614 (ebook other) | ISBN 9781479837366 (ebook)
Subjects: LCSH: Gay men—California—Los Angeles—Social conditions. |
    Asian American gays—California—Los Angeles—Social conditions.
Classification: LCC HQ76.2.U52 C263 2022 | DDC 306.76/620979494—dc23/eng/20220217
LC record available at https://lccn.loc.gov/2022001983

New York University Press books are printed on acid-free paper, and their binding materials are chosen for strength and durability. We strive to use environmentally responsible suppliers and materials to the greatest extent possible in publishing our books.

Manufactured in the United States of America

10 9 8 7 6 5 4 3 2

Also available as an ebook

For those who had to fight

for love they always deserved.

Home is not something I should have to earn.

—Jose Antonio Vargas, *Dear America*

CONTENTS

A NOTE ON LANGUAGE

This book chronicles the life experiences of young adult men who have roots in the Philippines, Mexico, and Latin America. All of the men I interviewed are cisgender, meaning they identify with the sex they were assigned at birth: male. They are sons of immigrants. Most were born and all were raised primarily in the United States, which means they are "second generation" Americans.

The men who trace their roots to Mexico and Latin America generally identified with the ethnic designation related to their parents' home country: Mexican, Salvadoran, Cuban, Nicaraguan, Panamanian, and the like. They also referred to themselves as Latino and, less often, Hispanic. Within the last decade, queer activists have popularized the gender-inclusive term *Latinx* to resist the gender binary and privileging of the masculine designation. In the years I conducted my research, however—from 2012 to 2016—my interviewees referred to themselves as Latino; as such, I use that designation when referring to them in the collective.[1]

The men who trace their roots to the Philippines mostly referred to themselves as Filipino. Many of the student organizations they were members of, however, opted for the non-Anglicized spelling: Pilipino.[2] Only a minority of Filipinos referred to themselves as Asian, as they associated the label with East Asian ethnicities, namely Chinese and Korean.[3] In the late 2010s, queer activists and writers began referring to themselves as *Filipinx*, in a similar vein as Latinx.[4] Throughout the book, I mostly stick to Filipino, as this is how my interviewees self-identified.

When referring to Filipino and Latino men collectively, I use the term *Brown*, which has been used by writers to racially describe people of color who are neither Black nor White.[5] In his posthumously published book *The Sense of Brown*, José Esteban Muñoz notes that Brownness encapsulates "people who are rendered brown by their personal and familial participation in South-to-North migration patterns." *Brown* is not a fixed racial label, but rather an indexing of a shared relationship to a dominant order. It not only captures the experiences of people whose being and belonging is called into question by White nativists but also draws inspiration from the activists and academics who have historically used it as a term of empowerment in social movements and communities.[6]

With respect to capitalization, I capitalize the *B* in *Black* to recognize the unique racial history, social movements, and intellectual labor advanced by enslaved Africans and their descendants. While *Brown* is not employed as a racial identifier in the same way as *Black*, I opt to capitalize the *B*, as Brown has been used by Chicanos and Filipinos to mobilize decolonial and antioppressive social movements.[7] In this book, I capitalize the *W* in *White*. Some scholars argue that not capitalizing it helps to "decenter whiteness";[8] sociologist Eve L. Ewing argues that capitalizing the *W* forces people of European descent to reckon with themselves as racialized subjects instead of race-neutral actors.[9] Given my desire to shine a light on the racial exclusion perpetuated by White people and institutions (including White gay men), I opt to capitalize the *W*.

I grappled with how to describe the men when it came to their sexuality and sexual identity. The men generally referred to themselves as gay, and a handful identified as queer. Yet some would switch back and forth between the terms *gay* and *queer* indiscriminately; some used *queer* as a shorthand for the broader LGBTQ community; and some resisted *queer* altogether.[10] A few invoked the term in the same politicized spirit as queer studies scholars: as a way to disrupt categories of sexual identity and gender.[11] When describing my interviewees, I mainly refer to them as gay sons of immigrants or second-generation gay men. I will use *queer*, and related terms like *queerness* and *queer sexuality*, when highlighting moments when the men challenge heteronormativity and heterosexual privilege, as well as commonplace understandings of what it means to be Filipino or Latino. These men identify as gay and queer because they are sexually attracted to men, but they are also *queering* what it means to be a son of immigrants, a Filipino or Latino person, a man of color, and ultimately, an American.

Naming matters. In her book *Call Them by Their True Names*, the feminist historian Rebecca Solnit writes, "Precision, accuracy, and clarity matter, as gestures of respect toward those to whom you speak."[12] I am a scholar of race, immigration, and sexuality, and as such, every iteration of ethnicity, race, and sexuality entails careful reflection. There will be moments when I do not get it right, but I want the reader to know that I'm perpetually trying to do so.

Language evolves. As the reclamation of the term *queer* and the popularization of the term *Latinx* and *Filipinx* show, marginalized people are often the driving force of change. The naming conventions I use in this book will continue to evolve after it is published. As anthropologist Jonathan Rosa explains, "A new label is not a solution in itself. It's a strategy or a tool for framing a broader dialogue."[13]

Speaking of names, I use pseudonyms and make slight changes to the names of organizations and schools to protect the privacy of my interviewees. It is their stories that matter most, and it is the storytelling that will change hearts and minds, and later, hopefully, communities and societies too.

PREFACE

"We need to talk," my partner Joe tells me the night after the 2016 election. "If something happens to us, we need to figure out what we're gonna do."

Between the two of us, Joe's the lighthearted one, the one who never sweats the small stuff. I, on the other hand, am the overthinker, the worrier, the anxious one. Classic Virgo.

That night though, he's the one who's overcome with worry.

"What do you mean, 'If something happens to us'?" I ask.

"If *something happens* to us," he repeats, unwilling to say more.

"Like if someone tries to murder us?" I laugh. I laugh to diffuse tension. I laugh whenever he gets mad. It usually works, but not today.

"I'm serious," he says. "If something happens to us, I want you to run."

"No way. I'll fight with you."

Joe can't mask his incredulity. "Babe, you can't fight," he says, gently enough so as not to bruise my ego.

He was right. I'd never thrown a punch in my life. Never liked roughhousing with my cousins. Always tapped out if ever friends tried to wrestle me.

"I need you to run," Joe says. "I need you to tell the story of what happened. Besides, you fight better with your words." We've been together for nearly a decade now; it's the saddest, most loving thing he's ever said to me.

I wonder sometimes whether we were being paranoid, but then I remember what happened in 2016. Hate crimes were on the rise, fueled by a presidential campaign built on racial resentment and xenophobia.[1] There were too many violent incidents that felt too close to home to ignore. In June of that year, my graduate school alma mater went on lockdown, and several friends barricaded themselves in classrooms for hours because of a murder-suicide on campus.[2] Eleven days later, I was scheduled to give a commencement speech a few buildings away from where the murder-suicide took place.[3] The morning of the ceremony, I picked up my phone and learned that a mass shooter had killed forty-nine people, mostly Latinx and queer, at Pulse, a gay nightclub in Orlando, Florida.[4] They had attended Pulse's Latin Night, the same kind of queer POC party I'd frequented in Los Angeles. The same kind of queer POC party where I'd met many of the men whose stories are featured in this book.

Joe and I had planned to attend the Los Angeles Pride celebration in West Hollywood after my speech, but we ultimately opted out because of the shooting. Minutes after we made this decision, a news alert popped up on our phones: the police had arrested a man—driving a car with guns, ammunition, and explosives in his trunk—on his way to West Hollywood. They later reported that the man was heading there but was not planning to attack the Pride celebration.[5] Still, for Joe and me, this information did little to assuage the fear already firmly implanted.

The Monday after the shooting, I attended a vigil at Grand Park in Downtown Los Angeles for the Pulse victims. I got dressed and looked in the mirror. I saw that I was wearing a white shirt, and my morbid mind imagined it bloodied. I changed. For months, I would steer clear of light-colored clothing, just in case *something happened*. When I drove to Downtown, I circled the vigil a few times as I was looking for parking; instinct had me strategizing a good place to be standing if it came time to run. I worried that Grand Park would be next on the forever growing list of mass shootings: a college campus in Isla Vista, California; a Black church in Charleston, South Carolina; an elementary school in Newtown, Connecticut; an office building in San Bernardino, California; and days prior, a gay nightclub in Orlando, Florida.

As a queer person of color, ambient terror wasn't an entirely new feeling. I came out at the age of twenty-two, which means I have lived more years in the closet than I have out. The fear that took hold of my body for most of 2016 felt unique (it's a fear, by the way, that many Black and Muslim Americans have faced for most of their lives). But it wasn't totally unlike what I'd experienced before: the times I was called a faggot in school; the times I was made to feel "less than" in predominantly White spaces; the times I worried about being defriended or disowned if loved ones were to learn I was gay. Dress-rehearsing for tragedy felt normal.[6]

Whenever I'm afraid, I look to others who aren't. For example, after the 9/11 attacks, I developed a fear of flying. For years, before boarding a flight, I'd anesthetized my anxiety with alcohol, or an Ambien if it was really bad. But then, on one especially turbulent flight, I heard the flight attendants laughing behind me. I felt my pulse slow and my grip on the armrests soften. On another bumpy flight, I turned around to look at the flight attendant near the rear bathrooms. She was calmly texting on her phone, unbothered by the turbulence. By watching flight attendants—who, I knew, spent countless hours in rough air all year round—my fear of flying eventually disappeared.

I've learned to apply the same strategy to my Brown queer existence. From kindergarten through college, there weren't many people I knew who were going through what I was. Not in my school. Not on television. Not in books. But when I started graduate school at UCLA, I suddenly had no shortage of people who looked like me whom I could watch from a distance. I remember that queer Filipino twenty-something who'd sashay along the sidewalk in front of my apartment on his way to class. On weekend nights I'd occasionally hear him coming home from some party, buzzed, greeting passersby with a "Hey girl!" no matter their gender. I remember the first time I saw a crowd of Brown men sporting jerseys and white tees, men who grew up in neighborhoods like mine, grinding up on each other on a dance floor while the DJ was spinning hip-hop and reggaeton. I remember walking up to Grand Park in the days after the Pulse shooting and seeing queer people embracing, crying, and honoring the dead. Watching these moments, these people—*my* people—became my antidote for fear. Watching them allowed me to reimagine another way of being.

I started this project on gay sons of immigrants to tell a story that doesn't often make its way into books, television, or movies. But if I'm being honest, this book stemmed too from my need to see a blueprint for my queer Filipino American life: to see how others who looked like me and grew up like me navigated their social worlds across different chapters of their lives. The second-generation gay men I interviewed often remarked how they rarely had opportunities to talk about what it was like to grow up gay in an immigrant family, to be the one gay person in their schools and ethnic communities, to be a person of color in predominantly White gay spaces. Like them, I spent so many years navigating gay identity on my own, but with every interview, I came to feel like I was part of something much larger than myself.

Despite the damage done to LGBTQ communities by Republican lawmakers across the country, I can appreciate how the country has changed its tune about LGBTQ people since I began this study a decade ago. Parents are supporting their gay and transgender children.[7] Teachers are inviting students to share their pronouns.[8] Queer and gender-transgressing teenagers are influencing across the country—and across the globe—through their social media platforms.[9] Television shows featuring Black and Brown transgender women are earning nominations and wins for major awards.[10] Of course, these advances don't always lead to major structural or policy changes that benefit all queer people of color. Still, if queer people of color are able to see themselves in stories—ones that help them reimagine possibility—then it's a step in the right direction.

Ultimately, my fear gives way to optimism when I remember: those who have been forced to navigate racism, sexism, and queerphobia all their lives end up sparking the greatest societal change—throughout history and in the present. We see this in the Stonewall Riots.[11] We see this in the fight for immigrants' rights.[12] We see this in the Black Lives Matter movement.[13] And I see this in the everyday acts of resistance from the second-generation gay men I interviewed for this book.

In 2020, the COVID-19 pandemic shut down schools, restaurants, and businesses in the United States and across the world. As I write this, in early 2022, over fifty million Americans have been infected, and over eight-hundred thousand Americans have died—and Black people, Filipino Americans, Latinxs, and Native Americans are dying at disproportionally high rates.[14] A year into the pandemic, Joe and I attended a funeral for his uncle, one of the 95,458 Americans who died in January of 2021 alone. Even though there is a vaccine, there is no end in sight to the pandemic. It remains a question whether life will ever get back to "normal."

Over the past year, many of the spaces where gay sons of immigrants found refuge—classrooms, campuses, clubs—have closed their doors. Some have shut down indefinitely, others permanently. I worry often about the trauma that queer youth of color, especially, are facing during the pandemic.[15] When I'm most worried though, I remember a tweet from the comedian Jaboukie Young-White, a gay son of Jamaican immigrants: "Being a gay teen really prepared me for all of my closest relationships to exist entirely online during quarantine."[16] Pandemic life is a daily struggle, but Young-White's tweet reminded me that, even through the most constrained of circumstances, queer people manage to find connection when connection seems impossible. The need for connection with people who share my story was what drove me to write this book, and I hope these stories provide the bit of oxygen you need to keep on keepin' on.

1

The Gay Second Generation

One sunny afternoon in November 2016, sometime between the election and Thanksgiving, I was with Franklin Flores (b. 1992), drinking overpriced Americanos at a coffee shop in Koreatown, an ethnically diverse, densely populated neighborhood a few miles west of Downtown Los Angeles. It had been four years since I'd first interviewed Franklin, when he was a twenty-year-old sophomore at UCLA. Though he hadn't aged a day, a lot had happened in four years. Franklin was elected student body president of his campus—one of only three Filipino Americans and the first openly gay man to accomplish this feat. He completed his bachelor's degree. He was now working in philanthropy with a focus on civil rights advocacy. At the time of our second meetup, Franklin had just finished the grueling process of applying to graduate school. A lifelong Southern Californian, he was eyeing Ivy League programs in the Northeast.

One aspect of his life hadn't changed, however: Franklin had yet to come out to his mother.

"I do want to," he said. "I am ready to. I was thinking of coming out to my mom this past weekend. It's coming, I can tell. I'm actually hoping that when I get my grad [school] letters of acceptance, fingers crossed, I can just be like, 'Mom, here's my Harvard acceptance letter. By the way, I'm gay.'"

Franklin's portfolio of accomplishments was the kind of success story that immigrant parents long dream of for their children—hopes that predate their children's birth, perhaps even their own arrival to the United States. And yet, here he was, anxious about revealing a part of himself to the person he felt closest to in this world.

Unstated truths, Franklin knew, had a way of creating emotional distance. When he was a teenager, he learned that his father had another family back in the Philippines that he had kept secret. Looking back, he realized that this secret was the root of almost every conflict between his mother and father, who were now separated. Of course, Franklin's secret was nothing like his father's; still, he knew it was a rift that hindered his ability to fully know his mother—and himself.

"I want to have a closer relationship with my mom," he told me. "I think there are parts of me I won't be able to understand until I come out, until I can have conversations with my mom about her relationships, or where I can open up to my mom about what the meaning of love is. Or how you know that you are in love. When I can have those conversations with my mom, I think I will better understand my own history."

Coming out as gay is sometimes framed as a personal journey. But like the journey immigrants make, it's hardly an individual act. For Franklin, being gay was something to be negotiated alongside being Filipino American. He very much understood everything about himself—including his gay identity—in relation to his family's immigration story. He had come to more fully embrace his sexual identity during his undergraduate years; his desire to do so was why he decided to attend college ninety minutes away from his hometown in Riverside, a racially diverse, mixed-income city seventy miles east of UCLA. Still, Franklin worried that his being gay would signal the end of his parents' immigrant dreams.

"To be the first generation of kids born in the United States, we are basically living proof of what that sacrifice meant," he explained. "That was a big part of why I went to college. That was also a big part of why I didn't want to come out. To be thinking that my parents came over here to plant their roots and have a family and sacrifice so much, and I'm going to kill that. It was this idea that I'm not continuing the family because I'm never going to pass down my family name. I'm never going to have a son. Those were the ideas that would go through my head, ever since I was in middle school." Franklin was hardly alone. This long-held worry—that being gay was inherently incongruent with the hopes of immigrant parents—was one shared by many of the second-generation gay men I interviewed.

This worry drove Franklin to curate an identity that he felt his parents would be proud of, "in spite of" being gay—a college graduate at the number-one ranked public institution in the country, elected by his peers to be student body president, and on his way to the most prestigious university in the world.

Similarly, academic excellence was a survival strategy that was familiar to Armando Garza (b. 1985). Armando grew up in El Monte, a predominantly working-class Latinx city fifteen miles east of Downtown LA. To an outsider, his neighborhood looked like a scene out of *The Wonder Years*, rows of single-family homes with front yards big enough for kids to play, situated on a quiet street where neighborhood children could ride their bikes unsupervised. But beyond the idyllic facade, gang and drug activity were everyday realities mere blocks away from where his family lived—not surprising for a city where the poverty rate is almost double the national average.[1] It's why Armando nicknamed El Monte "the ghetto suburbs."

For Armando, school was a means to stay out of trouble. Spending time in the library meant less foot traffic with peers who were involved with gangs. But, like Franklin, Armando approached school as a sort of immigrant family obligation. Both of his parents were immigrants from Mexico and mainly spoke Spanish. His mother was a homemaker; his father worked as a mechanic. Neither of them had attended college, but they hoped Armando would.

Growing up, Armando felt that Latinos weren't expected to go to college—and especially not Latino boys. In El Monte, only 7 percent of residents had a bachelor's degree. His older brothers hadn't gone to college; most of the other Latino boys in high school hadn't either. In Armando's high school, where eight out of every ten students were Latinx, over 95 percent of students qualified for free or reduced-cost lunches.[2] For many of his classmates, making ends meet was a more pressing concern than higher education.

And yet, at seventeen, Armando had earned admission to Georgetown University in Washington, DC, alma mater to state governors, members of Congress, a Supreme Court justice, and a US president. He had also been selected for the highly competitive Bill and Melinda Gates Millennial Scholarship, which covered his tuition and housing for all four years of college. He chose to double major in English and Theater, an homage to his mother's knack for narrative.

"My mom's really smart but didn't have the opportunities for education," Armando said. "I think she could have been a writer. She loves telling stories." On some level, he felt his mother could live her dreams vicariously through him. Among his brothers, Armando was his mother's favorite. He'd be the one who'd accompany her to the grocery store or to the mall while his brothers were at baseball or soccer practice. He thought of her as his best friend.

The hardest part of leaving for college was leaving her. Armando remembered how much he cried when they parted ways at the airport. Many of his future classmates would have their parents helping them set up their new dorm rooms. But like many first-generation college students, Armando's goodbyes with his family would take place at the airport. When he landed on the East Coast, he had only his two suitcases, a twenty-dollar bill, and a bottle of liquid detergent that his mother had packed so he wouldn't have to buy it for himself.

Of course, attending college wasn't just about making his parents proud. "I wanted to get good grades so that I could get a scholarship and get the fuck away from my family," he quipped. "I wanted to go to college and explore and find out who I am. So typical!" We both knew right away what he meant, and we laughed. For people who spend most of their lives on the outside looking in, inside jokes are life.

Almost three thousand miles from home, Armando experienced all the firsts he'd been denied during his adolescence. First flirtation. First relationship. First love. First kiss. But the more he embraced being gay, the more compartmentalized his life became. "There was a divide," he confessed. "In college, I was gay Armando, and when I would go home and see my parents, I was straight Armando or asexual Armando." Besides school, the East Coast weather, and the obligatory I-miss-yous, there wasn't much to talk about with his parents. Before his senior year, he decided that he needed to at least come out to his mother. "I was going to graduate the following year, and I had to know if she was going to accept it or not."

In the summer of 2006, Armando was in El Monte after having spent a semester studying in France. He sat his mother down for a heart-to-heart conversation.

"Mom, I'm gay," he told her.

"Really?" She laughed, assuming he was joking.

"I might marry a man someday. I want to make sure you're okay with it."

"Are you sure? Because I gave birth to a boy. I don't remember giving birth to a girl."

"Mom, I'm gay," he repeated, this time more firmly. "That doesn't make me a girl. I'm still a guy. I'm a guy who likes guys."

"That's not normal! That's not the life I had envisioned for you. Out of [your brothers], I would expect you to be the one who goes to college, meets a nice girl, gets married, and has kids."

Armando's mother kept pushing back, wishing he would retract what he'd shared. He tried his best to stay composed. But then she started to cry, which in turn caused Armando to cry, heartbroken *for* her as much as he was *by* her.

As he recounted their conversation, my palms grew sweaty, a knot in my throat tightened. I was transported to my own version of this moment, which coincidentally happened around the same time, during a family vacation to New Jersey.

"Telling her this completely shattered her world," he said.

Encountering Gay Sons of Immigrants

When I entered the sociology PhD program at UCLA, in the fall of 2004, I set out to become an expert on immigration and race. In my statement of purpose, the essay in which applicants propose their future research ambitions, I wrote that I wanted to study how race shapes the lives of children of immigrants, a group that sociologists call the "immigrant second generation." I read hundreds of research studies about their everyday experiences with their families, and in their neighborhoods, schools, and workplaces. As the son of Filipino immigrants who arrived in this country in 1980, I was especially interested in the "new" immigrant second generation—the children of Latin American, Asian, African, and Caribbean immigrants who migrated after the passage of the Immigration and Naturalization Act of 1965, which opened US borders to immigrants after a four-decade hiatus.[3]

All the while, there was another world beyond academia into which I was being socialized, mostly between the hours of 10:00 p.m. and 3:00 a.m. A few miles east of my UCLA apartment was West Hollywood, a two-square-mile strip of bars, clubs, restaurants, coffee shops, adult stores, and health service organizations that catered to gay clientele throughout Southern California. As early as the 1920s, West Hollywood was a safe haven for queer men and women relegated by society to the closet. By the 1970s West Hollywood "had come to epitomize a new gay lifestyle," write historians Lillian Faderman and Stuart Timmons in their book *Gay L.A.* "The residents of West Hollywood became emboldened, expressing gay freedom not just after dark, but brazenly in the sun: holding hands, flirting, and cruising all over the district."[4] West Hollywood was the site for landmark moments in gay history. It became home for gay people seeking refuge from other countries, other states, or even other neighborhoods in LA. It was the site for gay-owned businesses and gay activist movements. It was the first American city to have a free health clinic for gay people, to have a majority-gay local government, and to legally recognize same-sex relationships and offer medical benefits to same-sex partners.

In 2004, I knew none of these things, despite being a lifelong Los Angeleno. I grew up in Eagle Rock, a racially diverse middle-class neighborhood in Northeast Los Angeles, but for most of my life, my family and friends rarely went west of the 101 Freeway, which runs north and south and splits the city in half. As Faderman and Timmons point out, "L.A.'s distinct ethnic neighborhoods, spread out over 450 square miles, and its clogged freeways and inefficient public transit system have created de facto segregation."[5] Anyone who has grown up or lived in LA knows it's a place where decisions about one's social life are dictated by race, class, and a willingness (or lack thereof) to sit through traffic.

But that year it was my budding queer sexuality that led me to venture to West Hollywood. After graduate school seminars, writing sessions, and happy hours, I'd make my way to the two-mile stretch of bars and clubs along Santa Monica Boulevard, at least three or four times a week, if not more. The residents of West Hollywood are mostly White and affluent, but the events I attended catered to gay men of color.[6] There were Latinx nights, which drew crowds of immigrant and US-born Latino gay men. There were also hip-hop nights, which drew mostly Black but also Latino and Asian American gay men. There was GAMeboi, which drew Asian American gay men of different ethnicities, mostly US-born Filipino, Chinese, Korean, and Vietnamese patrons. (The *GAM* in GAMeboi was short for "Gay Asian male," a nod to the AOL chat rooms of the 1990s).[7]

For the most part, these men were not West Hollywood residents; they came from surrounding neighborhoods, cities, and counties across Southern California, where the majority of residents were people of color (POC). Within a few months, the gay men of color I met at these parties introduced me to a broader circuit of queer POC party scenes beyond the main boulevard—in Hollywood, Silver Lake, the San Fernando Valley, the San Gabriel Valley, and the Inland Empire. In a region where Latinxs, Asian Americans, and African Americans collectively make up 70 percent of the population, there was no shortage of gay bars that catered specifically to gay men of color.[8] Historically, many of these clubs—Circus Disco in Hollywood, Catch One in Arlington Heights, and Chico's in Montebello—became the primary nighttime gathering spots for gay people of color who encountered racial discrimination in the predominantly White social scene of West Hollywood.

Straddling the worlds of graduate school and gay POC nightlife positioned me to see a major shortcoming in how sociologists were discussing immigration: they presumed that immigrants and their children were heterosexual. In my seven years of graduate school, I spent countless hours in seminars, lectures, and conferences learning about how the lives of children of immigrants were shaped by a constellation of factors—their parents' socioeconomic status, the demographic makeup of their neighborhoods and schools, their language abilities, their connections with the ethnic community, their racial identity, their gender, and their religion.[9] Throughout these conversations, the topic of sexuality rarely came up.

All the while, several nights a week, I was drinking, dancing, and socializing with second-generation Filipino and Latino gay men. Some of the men grew up in racially diverse neighborhoods like mine. Others grew up in working-class Latinx neighborhoods in East LA or Southeast LA. Others came from the multiethnic suburbs surrounding Los Angeles County. Others had migrated to Los Angeles from other parts of California or from the East Coast. We found our way to each other's company because whom we desired and how we expressed ourselves were incongruent with the rules of a heteronormative society. We were bound together by both our Brownness and our queerness.

It was through these men that I discovered renderings of gay second-generation lives. There were essay collections curated by queer Asian American and Latinx academics who study literature, culture, and HIV/AIDS activism.[10] There were documentary films and plays produced by LGBTQ students of color at local universities. Most of what I learned came from the people who existed at the intersection of immigration, race, and gay identity. Beyond academia, I learned so much from gay second-generation men of color who shared their lives online—on message boards, blogs, social networking sites, and social media. At the club, we'd dance, shedding the shame we'd all grown up with, basking in the longing and acceptance denied to us for most of our lives.

From the Margins to the Center

When you turn on the television or watch the news, immigration, race, and LGBTQ issues are often talked about as if they are separate, unrelated matters. Beyond queer digital media or a queer studies class in college, it's not often that we hear stories of people who exist at the margins of all three issues.[11] It's no wonder then that Franklin and Armando, men of color who grew up in immigrant families and communities, had such difficulty coming to terms with being gay. Society presented them with no models of people whose lives resembled theirs.

Brown and Gay in LA offers a corrective to this erasure. This book bridges the conversations around immigration, race, and sexuality by centering the narratives of second-generation gay men. Over the course of five years, I interviewed over sixty Filipino and Latino gay men living in Los Angeles. Most were sons of immigrants from the Philippines and Mexico—respectively, the largest Asian American and Latino ethnic groups in LA—but a handful had parents who migrated from countries in Central America and South America, including Colombia, El Salvador, Guatemala, and Honduras.[12]

By interviewing second-generation gay men of different ethnic backgrounds, I was able to see how their experiences varied depending on how they were racialized by others. Plus, I was able to understand their experiences in relation to each other. As the historian Natalia Molina has argued, even when people of different ethnic and racial backgrounds don't reside in the same neighborhood or attend the same school or live in the same historical moment, their experiences are still affected by what she calls "racial scripts"—"the ways in which we think, talk about, and act toward one racialized group based on our experiences with other groups whose race differs from our own."[13] For example, when Filipino and Mexican American men reminisce about high school, their experiences may differ because of how their teachers view Asian American and Latinx students in relation to each other.[14] As I'll discuss in a later chapter, the difference in their racial experience during high school will affect how they navigate gay identity during their adolescent years.

I started the research for this book in 2012. By then I had been a part of the gay POC scene for close to a decade. If I showed up to La Cita in Downtown LA on a Monday, or Mickey's in West Hollywood on a Thursday, or Circus Disco in Hollywood on a Friday, I'd know more than a few people there. It was my intimate familiarity with the gay POC scene (and my identity as a gay man of color) that allowed me to connect with many of the men I ended up interviewing. Conversations about our first time going out to a gay Latino club or the bar where we'd met our first boyfriends or where we'd had bottomless mimosas on a Sunday fun-day helped break the ice. Most of the men I approached for a sit-down interview agreed because they'd seen me around. Of course, I didn't just want to interview gay men who were active in gay nightlife. Later, I connected with others through college student organizations, local art and music events, and word-of-mouth referrals from those I'd already interviewed.

I opened our conversation with themes seemingly unrelated to sexuality. I asked the men: What was it like growing up in an immigrant family? What was it like growing up in your neighborhood? What were your interactions like with your classmates and teachers in school? Who were your friends during your elementary school, middle school, high school, and college years?

Eventually we started talking about how they came into their gay identity. The men shared their first memories of realizing they were "different" from other boys. They recounted the disparaging comments their family members, classmates, and members of the church made about gay people. They recalled story lines on television shows and movies in which gay people were belittled—or, worse, beat up and killed. They remembered their parents watching alongside them and saying they deserved it. They spoke about strategies they developed to conceal their queerness at home and at school, the places children are supposed to feel most safe. They talked about the fear of being, as the late queer scholar

José Esteban Muñoz once put it, a "spy in the house of gender normativity."[15] Many recounted these painful moments with such vivid detail and emotion that you would think they had taken place last week instead of years or even decades ago.

The men also talked about how their gay identities evolved across the different chapters of their life. As much as being gay was a struggle, it was also a source of connection, joy, and liberation. They formed friendships and chosen families with other gay people of color. They organized for immigrant rights. They broke gender norms. They made art. They danced. They found gay POC role models who showed them how to navigate their families, ethnic communities, LGBTQ spaces, and society at large as Brown men who were openly gay. Being in community with other gay Filipinos and Latinos allowed them to see that their sexual identity need not be at odds with their racial identity, nor—as Franklin and Armando feared—at odds with being "good" children of immigrants.

Many spoke about what it was like growing up in a time when being gay was associated with an untimely and tragic death. For the men born in the late 1970s and early 1980s, the AIDS epidemic loomed large in their childhood and adolescent years.[16] This was a period when almost every story line in the media equated AIDS with a death sentence. The men born in the late 1980s and early 1990s did not witness the devastation of the epidemic; by the 2000s, because of advances in research, the medical establishment was approaching HIV/AIDS as a treatable, if chronic, disease.[17] Still, this younger cohort was well aware of the other dangers of being gay; they learned of the brutal murder of Wyoming teenager Matthew Shepard and the tragic suicide of Rutgers University student Tyler Clementi.[18]

By the time they were young men in their twenties and thirties, the national pulse on LGBTQ issues was rapidly shifting. States began legalizing gay marriage in 2004.[19] To borrow the words of queer Latinx writer Carmen Maria Machado, they came of age "in a culture where gay marriage went from cosmic impossibility to forgone conclusion to law of the land."[20] After a decade of heated legal battles at the state level to define marriage as the union between one man and one woman, the US Supreme Court—in a five-to-four decision—declared marriage equality a federal law in June 2015.[21] This legal victory wasn't simply about the material benefits of marriage; it was about "the fundamental human desire for love and commitment," as journalist Molly Ball writes in the *Atlantic*.[22] Of course, for major segments of the LGBTQ population, such as Black and Brown queer and transgender people, there are other priorities besides gay marriage. Workplace discrimination, health inequality, housing insecurity, and violence (particularly against transgender Black women and women of color) are more pressing issues.[23] Nonetheless, that acceptance of same-sex marriage doubled within a decade and a half—from 30 percent in 2004 to 60 percent in 2019—indicates that the cultural landscape is tipping in the direction of LGBTQ acceptance.[24]

Even with these metrics of progress, however, the truth remained: growing up gay, especially as a person of color and a son of immigrants, was hard. The majority of the men said they'd been a target of *both* racism and homophobia at some point in their lives. They were called faggots—behind their backs, to their faces, and in multiple languages. They held memories of being barely tolerated or outright rejected by members of their family and community. Manny Roldan (b. 1991), a Filipino American college student, shared his mother's heartbreaking reaction when she discovered he was gay. "It got to the point where, when we were eating, I would drink from my mom's cup, and she would throw away the cup," Manny said. "If I sat on her bed, she would change the sheets. It was emotionally devastating. Like not feeling welcome in my own home." Societal attitudes toward gay people may have been shifting, but for Manny, this did nothing to ease the tension between him and his immigrant parents.

In the era of marriage equality, I've encountered more than a few straight people who tell me that being gay is "not that bad" because being gay is "more accepted now," as if the increasing acceptance of gay marriage could erase the trauma experienced by men like Franklin,

Armando, and Manny. They conveniently ignore the labor and every-day acts of resistance it took for gay people to exist in a heteronorma-tive world. Throughout the writing of this book, I kept returning to a question posed by Imani Perry, professor of African American studies at Princeton University, in her book *Breathe: A Letter to My Sons*: "How do you become in a world bent on you not being, and not becoming?"[25] Perry is not writing specifically about queer experiences; she is writing about the challenges Black boys face growing up in a society where Black boys and men are routinely and unjustly criminalized, imprisoned, and killed. The men I interviewed are not Black, nor do they experience race and racism in the same way. But by virtue of their Brownness and their queerness, they, too, know what it feels like to be a "problem," to riff off the classic question raised by sociologist W. E. B. Du Bois.[26]

In many respects, *Brown and Gay in LA* is an acknowledgment of—and a tribute to—the labor of becoming. The chapters that follow chronicle how second-generation gay men "become" in a society that unapologetically privileges, normalizes, and centers Whiteness and straightness.

Centering the narratives of gay sons of immigrants isn't merely about filling a gap within sociology and public conversations about immi-gration, race, and LGBTQ issues. Taking a cue from the long tradition of Black feminist writers who coined and advanced the concept of intersectionality, *Brown and Gay in LA* shows that much can be learned from the people who exist at the intersection of racism, sexism, and homophobia. As the scholar Keeanga-Yamahtta Taylor writes in her book *How We Get Free*, "if you could free the most oppressed people in soci-ety, then you would have to free everyone."[27]

The stories of second-generation gay men are a window into under-standing how inequality happens—within families, schools, ethnic com-munities, and queer spaces. In history, it has been those least served by racist, patriarchal, and heteronormative systems who have unearthed the possibilities for social change. For example, the modern gay liberation movement owes a great debt to Marsha P. Johnson and Sylvia Rivera, the gender-transgressing queers of color who organized and supported gay and transgender people of all races.[28] As the scholar Roderick Ferguson argues, these "drag queens of Stonewall were denied the presumed privileges of normativity . . . they illuminated the ways in which non-normativity might be used for revolutionary shifts in the social order."[29]

In chronicling the experiences of Filipino and Latino gay men across different arenas of their lives—in the immigrant family and community; in elementary school, middle school, and high school; in college; in gay spaces (both virtual and in-person)—each chapter offers insights for reimagining these spaces so that they are less exclusionary and more inclusive.

As *Brown and Gay in LA* focuses on Filipino and Latino second-generation gay men in Los Angeles, it's not meant to be representative of all queer POC experiences. The intersection of race, gender, and sexuality shape the experiences of Afro-Latinx and Black children of immigrants, queer and transgender daughters of immigrants, transgender sons of immigrants, and nonbinary and intersex children of immigrants in different ways. One book cannot fully capture the rich mosaic of second-generation LGBTQ experiences. In my choice to pan in on the particular, I hope you catch glimmers of the universal. As my friend, the Filipina American scholar Carolina San Juan once told me, in a moment when I was struggling to write, "Your book is about the queerness in all of us that wants to be loved."

Indeed, it is.

2

Lessons in Manhood and Morality

I could feel the word "gay"—or maybe the word's conspicuous absence—
floating in the air between us.
—Saeed Jones, *How We Fight for Our Lives*

Despite what many people believe, boys aren't born masculine; they are
socialized to be masculine. This is a process that usually begins with
family. Before they can speak in complete sentences, boys are indoctri-
nated by parents, siblings, and other family members with the rules of
masculinity—the set of behaviors that demonstrate to others that they
are "real" boys and, later on in life, "real" men. Whenever I explain gender socialization to my students, I tell them a story about my nephew
Rich.

It was 2008, Christmas Eve at my cousin's house. Rich was six years
old at the time. The family Christmas gathering was always a multigenerational affair: there were around sixty people, ages two to seventy-two,
packed in one house. There were the grandparents, aunts, and uncles
who'd grown up in the Philippines and migrated to the United States as
adults. There were their US-born children and grandchildren. There
were family members who shuttled between the Philippines and Los
Angeles. As with every Filipino get-together, the house was filled with
chatter and gossip, a harmonious blend of English and Tagalog.

When midnight hit, everyone crammed into the living room. My
aunts whipped out their digital cameras, and my uncle placed his cam-
corder on the tripod—ready to capture the moment the kids opened
their presents.

Rich's mother handed him and his older sister Raya two identically
sized boxes. As everyone watched, Rich opened his present first and saw

that he'd received a pink Nintendo DS, a handheld video game console. Raya opened her box and received the same gift, but hers was blue. Their mother had mislabeled the presents.

Rich's face went blank. Then he burst into tears. Everyone started laughing, which, of course, made him cry louder. Raya, being the good big sister, tried to explain to Rich that their mom had made a mistake; their presents were switched by accident. She offered the blue Nintendo DS to him, but he kept right on crying. The damage was done.

I share this story of my nephew's reaction to receiving the "wrong" present to underscore how early on boys are socialized to follow gender norms.[1] There is nothing inherently wrong with young boys liking pink. In fact, in the early twentieth century, pink was considered the "sex-appropriate" color for boys by *Time* magazine and popular clothing retailers. "The generally accepted rule is pink for the boys, and blue for the girls," wrote one publication in 1918. "The reason is that pink, being a more decided and stronger color, is more suitable for the boy, while blue, which is more delicate and daintier, is prettier for the girl."[2] The gendered association of the colors switched by the 1940s—blue for boys, pink for girls. Rich was born well after that, in 2002.

By the age of six, Rich had learned that boys aren't supposed to like pink. When he found himself with the pink toy, he was dumbfounded, and the entire family laughed at him, reinforcing the notion that it was "wrong" for him to possess anything pink. His big sister Raya instinctively came to the rescue by offering him the blue toy, the "correct" color for boys. She was only a few years older, but she already knew how to repair the situation, illustrating how girls, too, engage in gender socialization from a young age. This family story illustrates what sociologists have long argued: that masculinity is a performance, and the rules of masculinity are maintained by the interactions between people within a specific social context.[3] More often than not, this is a process that happens unconsciously.

I know this because when I asked Rich and Raya about this story a decade later, in 2018, they didn't remember it. Their mother barely remembered it. Only one of my cousins could corroborate the story, probably because she was, at the time of the incident, a college student majoring in sociology. I remembered because I too was studying sociology, and so I was trained to take stock of such moments.

At the same time though, this incident reminded me of moments in my own childhood when my family let me know, by scolding or deriding me, that I was breaking the rules of masculinity: Watching *My Little Pony* on TV instead of *G.I. Joe*. Singing "Material Girl" by Madonna. Walking on my tiptoes. Flailing my hands when I talked. Opting to watch gymnastics and figure skating over basketball and football. I learned early on that violating these unwritten rules of gender would compromise my sense of belonging—and safety—within my own family.

Different from Other Boys

Franklin Flores had his own story of receiving a Christmas present he didn't want. Except, unlike in my nephew's case, Franklin got a gift that young boys were supposed to cherish.

"There was one Christmas, my godfather gave me a huge car set," Franklin remembered. "And everyone was like, 'Wow!' I tried to be grateful, but I think my excitement wasn't there." Even at a young age, he knew boys were expected to like cars. He knew it was "wrong" to dislike the gift he'd received.[4]

As a child, Franklin much preferred to do the things his older sister Eleanor did. When Eleanor started dance lessons, he wanted to dance too. When she joined the color guard team at school, he insisted on playing with her flags. His father would come home from work and see them playing, and he'd scold Franklin: "Why are you playing with the flag? Why aren't you playing basketball like your [male] cousins?"

Franklin learned early on that he wasn't allowed to like the things his sister liked or, worse, to act the way his sister did. "When I was a kid, I might have the faintest of feminine voice inflections or my hand might move like this," he explained, daintily waving his wrists. "My dad would be like, 'Don't do that!'"

What intrigued me most about this part of our conversation wasn't Franklin's answers; it was the question he was responding to. I had asked him, "How early did you know that you might be attracted to boys instead of girls?" I had inquired about his sexual orientation, and he instinctually responded by talking about his gender expression as a young boy. From an early age, the men I interviewed learned to conflate gender and sexuality; to like the things girls like, to act the way girls act, is to *be* gay. This was an association that many had difficulty unraveling, even as they grew older.[5]

Franklin realized he had to hide his "girly" interests from his parents, especially from his father. He'd still dance, and still play with his sister's flags, but only if his father wasn't home. When his father was home, Franklin would switch over to playing video games like *Street Fighter* and *Mortal Kombat*. But his small act of resistance against his father's policing was to pick the female fighters like Chun Li and Kitana. "I always gravitated toward the female characters," he said. Franklin was also drawn to strong female characters on television; he and his sister were fans of *Sailor Moon*, an anime series about a group of teenage girls who were "fighting evil by moonlight [and] winning love by daylight." When I asked Franklin if he'd felt comfortable watching *Sailor Moon* (once dubbed by BuzzFeed "the gayest cartoon on television") in front of his father, he flinched. "I felt like I had to hide it, for sure," he said. One thing he definitely hid from his father was the crush he'd developed for Darien, the male love interest of *Sailor Moon*'s title character. "I was falling in love with this dream guy in a tuxedo." Franklin knew never to let anyone in his family in on *this* secret.

To be clear, there's nothing inherently wrong with young boys enjoying the activities or interests of young girls. There's nothing wrong with them acting like a girl or pretending to be a girl or even wanting to be a girl. There's nothing wrong with them having crushes on other boys. And yet, all of the second-generation gay men I interviewed learned early on that to act effeminately and to even hint that one might be gay was strictly forbidden.

These lessons in manhood and morality were plentiful during their childhood and adolescent years. I would ask the men, "What kind of messages did you hear about being gay when you were growing up in your family?" Some would share a story like Franklin's, in which a father, uncle, or cousin would violently reprimand them for "acting like a girl." Others said the messages came indirectly: they'd overheard a family member make disparaging remarks about a gay person on television or a gay relative in the extended family, for example. These were the moments that ingrained a sense of shame and fear around being gay, a self-stigma that would take years for the men to unlearn in early adulthood. As gay sons of immigrants, they encountered these "lessons" about queer sexuality not only in their own homes but also at church, at family gatherings, in the ethnic community, and in their parents' home country.[6]

Censoring Queer Content on Screen

Rolando Aguirre (b. 1993), a Mexican American college junior, said he was around eight years old when he knew he was "different." "I had physical attractions toward the same gender when I was in fourth or fifth grade." At the time, he didn't have the words to articulate that he was gay, but he knew he felt drawn to other boys in a way that his brothers were not. By that age, he already knew that same-sex attraction wasn't something he could share with them or with his parents. I asked Rolando how he'd learned that he had to keep this part of himself hidden.

Rolando said "the lesson" happened in 2006 when he was thirteen. His mother had gone to a local video store to rent a movie for the family to watch. Since Rolando's father was fond of Western films, she chose a DVD that had two cowboys on the cover. She had no clue that the film she had selected, *Brokeback Mountain*, was about a forbidden love affair between two married men in rural Wyoming: Jack Twist, a rodeo cowboy (played by Jake Gyllenhaal) and Ennis Del Mar, a sheep herder (played by the late Heath Ledger).

Later that night, Rolando, his parents, and his brothers gathered in the living room to watch the movie. About a half hour into the movie came the infamous scene. Jack wakes up in the middle of the night and sees Ennis shivering under a blanket. He invites Ennis to sleep next to him in his tent. Jack wraps Ennis's arm around him as they sleep, and Ennis resists, but after a brief tussle, the two have sex. It was at this point in the film that Rolando's father became enraged.

"Get that shit out!" his father screamed, practically ripping the DVD from the player. The following day, Rolando accompanied his father to the video store. As soon as they walked in, his father berated the women at the checkout counter. "This belongs in the porno section!" he yelled, pointing at copies of *Brokeback Mountain* displayed in the front aisles. "This is wrong. This shouldn't be anywhere near [the front]. You should label this as a homosexual film!"

I asked Rolando how he felt after witnessing this exchange. "It was his reaction at the video store that really affected me," he said. "That's when I was like, I shouldn't say anything about myself now. It kind of actually depressed me for a while. Like his hatred toward homosexuals."

"Did you stop hanging out with your dad?" I asked.

"I just stayed in my room a lot," Rolando said solemnly. "Didn't come out for a while."

Many of the men I interviewed recalled moments when their parents reacted negatively if they saw gay people on television. Alvin Velasco (b. 1989), a Filipino American data analyst, was around seven when he began feeling an attraction toward the male characters on television shows. It was around this time, too, that he witnessed his parents getting angry whenever a gay person appeared on screen. "They'd say things like, 'Look at that *bakla!*' But in a tone of voice where you could tell something was bad," Alvin said.[7]

Alvin distinctly remembered his father's reaction to one particular episode of *Ellen,* an ABC comedy popular in the mid-1990s. Before Ellen DeGeneres was a daytime talk show host, she was the title character in

Ellen, a sitcom about a quirky thirtysomething bookstore owner and her group of friends. Ellen's coming out episode, which aired in 1997, was one of the most watched moments in television history. Alvin and his parents were three of the forty-two million viewers who tuned in for that episode.

"Cover his ears! Cover his eyes!" Alvin's father barked at his mother after Ellen uttered the words "I'm gay." After that episode, his family abruptly stopped watching *Ellen*, even though they had watched it religiously for years.

At seven, Alvin didn't understand why his father was upset; all that mattered was that he was. "I don't know if I was sad, but obviously it stuck with me," Alvin said. "I learned never to openly share my thoughts about other men."

Some of my interviewees remembered their parents expressing disapproval of television content that "seemed" gay, even if the central topic of the show wasn't about queer sexuality. James Rosario (b. 1991), a Filipino American preschool teacher, remembered his mother's disdain whenever she'd catch him watching *Project Runway*, a reality competition for aspiring fashion designers. *Project Runway* premiered in 2004 when James was thirteen, and every Wednesday night, James would be glued to Bravo. He remembered the first time she caught him watching.

"Can you turn that off?" his mother said. "You shouldn't be watching that anyways."

"I can watch whatever I want," James said.

"Guys shouldn't be watching that."

Whenever his mother voiced her objections, James pushed back. Occasionally, the discussion would get heated. "That's when I knew that I had to hide [being gay] from my mom. After that point, I knew what side she stood on. And I haven't brought up [my sexuality] since then."

It was disheartening to hear James speak about the emotional rift between him and his mother. But as Rolando's and Alvin's stories illustrate, fathers tended to react with more vitriol than mothers when seeing their sons consuming gay content on television. These are some of the remarks some of the men I interviewed remembered their fathers making:

If I ever found out my son was like that, I would beat him. I would kill him. I would disown him.

If you ever end up gay, I'll give you a gun, and you can just shoot yourself.

Someone should line up all the gay people against the wall and shoot them all dead.

The men I interviewed weren't just concerned about losing their parents' love and acceptance; some feared for their physical safety. For them, seeing their fathers' violent response to anything remotely queer made it difficult to be in the same room with them during their childhood and adolescence, so they avoided them at all costs.

On a different level, the juxtaposition of White gay people on television shows and unaccepting parents at home instilled the belief that White parents were more progressive than parents of color when it came to LGBTQ issues. "I saw the White community as more accepting of [gay people] than the Latino community," said one respondent who was an avid watcher of gay television shows and movies as a kid. When the gay men I interviewed talked about television content of their childhood and adolescence that featured gay characters or story lines, they often named majority-White shows like *Will & Grace* (an NBC sitcom about two gay men and two straight women living in New York) and *Queer as Folk* (a Showtime drama about the shenanigans of four gay men in Pittsburgh). The absence of gay people of color on screen may affect how second-generation gay men interact with family. As psychologist Kevin Nadal notes, "The consistent lack of LGBT people of color in the media may [be] discouraging LGBT people of color (young and old) in feeling comfortable coming out in their families and communities."[8]

Of course, there were other influences besides television and film that shaped the relationship between second-generation gay men and their families.

God-Fearing Gay Sons

In 2015, BuzzFeed released the short documentary *Coming Out to Immigrant Parents*, which featured the stories of gay Asian American and Latino millennials. One of the interviewees, Joel, a second-generation Mexican American, spoke about how religion shaped his experience growing up gay in an immigrant family. "My God, I was so scared," Joel said, emotional but measured. "I had feelings for guys. I repressed them. My parents grew up in Mexico. My mom, she's very religious. From a very conservative family." As Joel recounted the moment of coming out to his mother, his eyes welled up with tears. "I think you're gay because you haven't been going to church for four years," his mother told him. "You're a bad person." For Joel, the reception of his queer sexuality was shaped by his family's religion, which in turn was inseparable from the ethnic community in both Mexico and the United States. This collision of queerness, religion, and ethnicity was echoed by many of the Filipino and Latino gay men I interviewed.

Sociologists have written about religion's positive impact on immigrant life. For Filipinos, Mexicans, and other Latinos in the United States, the focus has been on the role of the Catholic Church given the influence of Catholicism in both the home country and in immigrant communities. (Though the majority are still Catholic, there has been a steady rise of Evangelical Protestantism among Filipinos and Latinos both here and abroad.)[9] Some immigrants have relied on their Catholic faith to help them endure the difficulties of crossing the border.[10] Many immigrants turn to their Catholic parish as a temporary refuge from the racism and socioeconomic challenges they face in the larger society;[11] masses and other church activities provide them opportunities to connect with other immigrants from their home countries. Many low-income immigrants rely on the church for assistance with food, clothing, and basic health services.[12] Through the church, children of immigrants can forge strong connections with immigrant and second-generation peers; as a result, they remain closely connected to their ethnic traditions.[13] When immigrants have been villainized, scapegoated, and harmed by xenophobic lawmakers, the Catholic Church has publicly voiced its support for immigrant communities.[14]

For gay sons of immigrants, however, the impact of religion can be far from positive. Some of the men I interviewed recalled sitting in Sunday Masses with their families and hearing the priest explicitly pronounce homosexuality as a sin. Others remembered church leaders speaking disparagingly about same-sex marriage in their presence. During the 2008 election, several of the men remembered their priests and congregation actively voicing support for Proposition 8 (which would ban same-sex marriage in California) during and after Sunday mass. These moments sent a clear message to gay people: You are not welcome here.

Franklin had a hard time wrestling with this contradiction—so much so that it affected his relationship with his family. His parents had long relied on the church, especially when they were experiencing economic hardships, housing insecurity, and marital problems; but for Franklin, a young man struggling with his sexuality, being in church made him feel like his entire existence was a sin.

"It was really hard coming from a predominantly Catholic family," he said. "I was really struggling with religion, and that put a big strain on my relationship with my dad. When I went to church, it just seemed that they would always tell us all the reasons we would go to hell. I really hated it. I hated going. I hated being Catholic. But it was really hard, because at the same time, my dad and mom really relied on religion. It was kind of like a crutch for them. 'Everything will be okay,' they'd say. 'Let's go to church and pray, and everything will be fine.' In my mind, I was like, 'No. God hates me. I am going to hell because I am gay.'"

The homophobic messages Franklin heard in church not only put a strain on his relationship with his parents and sister; they also adversely affected his relationship to Filipino identity. Many of the homophobic messages he was hearing came from other Filipinos in the congregation. "My church was really, really Filipino," he said. "The whole culture, I don't want to say it was hateful, because I don't think it was really hateful. [Being gay] was just so taboo, so forbidden. [Filipinos at church] implied you aren't going to heaven if you're *bakla*." Because Filipinos associated themselves so closely with the Catholic Church, Franklin felt reticent about forging relationship with other Filipinos throughout his childhood.

During our conversation, Dario Garcia (b. 1981), a Mexican American clinical social worker, reflected on how growing up in a devoutly Catholic family and community negatively impacted his mental health. When I asked him what messages he had heard about being gay when he was growing up, he answered, "I come from a Mexican background, and I was raised Catholic, so the message I got was that it was a sin." Most of the time it was other churchgoers, but on rare occasions, the priests at his parish spoke explicitly about being gay. The messages were mixed. "Sometimes I heard that just because you are gay, you are going to hell. Other priests told me that if you see someone of the same sex but don't have sex with them, then you won't go to hell. But if you do, you will." His parents' and siblings' connection to Catholicism was why he distanced himself from them during his adolescent years. "Specifically, because of religion, I hit a stage of depression."

For all the reasons mentioned, Joaquin Marquez (b. 1984), a Mexican American visual artist, hated going to church as a child. But after his great-grandmother passed away in 2008, his extended family started attending Sunday Spanish Mass regularly, and his mother asked if he would join them. Joaquin acquiesced to his mother's request.

On the very first Sunday he joined his family for Mass, the priest happened to bring up Proposition 8, but instead of focusing on the ballot initiative (which, in context, would already be inappropriate in its own right), he went off on a tangent.

"We're at this huge-ass church, and we're in the third row," Joaquin said. "Towards the end [of mass], the priest starts expressing his opinions about gay people, saying, 'They're going to teach your kids to be gay in school.'" As the priest was talking, Joaquin looked around at his predominantly Latinx congregation and saw people nodding in agreement. His leg started shaking, and his mother tried to restrain him.

"Don't," she whispered to him, anticipating an outburst.

"He's pissing me off," Joaquin responded. He would've stayed quiet, but then the priest kept on about how the parishioners, with their vote, needed to prevent the schools from teaching kids "how to be gay." Joaquin stood up and admonished the homophobic priest in front of the congregation.

"You're not God!" he said in Spanish. The crowd gasped, but Joaquin continued on. "Why are you spreading lies?" His mother tried quieting him down, to no avail. The priest, though shaken, didn't bother addressing him. Seeing his family and the largely Latinx congregation instinctually side with the priest was the last straw for Joaquin. "I walked out, and ever since then, I never went back," he said.

Often it was these displays of complicity that sent the loudest messages about whether gay people would be welcome in the family and the ethnic community. The story Joaquin shared was of his experience at church in his early twenties, but I couldn't help but wonder what it would've felt like for a younger queer or questioning Latinx to watch that exchange, to witness someone gay and Latinx have the courage to stand up in front of a predominantly Latinx congregation, publicly disagree with a homophobic priest, and be totally unsupported by members of his family and community. For gay sons of immigrants, it would be impossible to unsee such a moment.

Messages from the Homeland

In my interviews with second-generation gay men, many associated being Filipino or Mexican with being socially conservative. As Franklin's and Joaquin's stories show, part of this had to do with the close connections with Catholicism or some other form of Christianity. But part of this belief stemmed from their interactions with extended family and people in the home country.

During summers and holidays, Rolando and his family would travel to the rural town in Sonora, Mexico, where his father had grown up. Rolando recounted one Christmas when a tragedy struck the town. "One of the neighbors ended up hanging himself because he got caught sleeping with another man," he said. Though Rolando didn't know the man well, he'd seen him often whenever his family was visiting. Given how often they'd seen the man, I asked Rolando how his family reacted to the news. "They just brushed it off," he said. "It's a ranch. It's a really small, secluded area, and [the people there] are very narrow minded. It's very, very homophobic."

Some of the Latino men encountered homophobia more directly in the home country. Everardo Villar (b. 1980), a Mexican American teacher, was born in Los Angeles but spent several years of his childhood in a small town in Michoacán, located west of Mexico City. From a young age he could see how different he was from the other men and boys in his town. "I was kind of quiet," he said. "I was introverted. Feminine." While the other boys his age were playing soccer, Everardo preferred to reenact scenes from *The Little Mermaid* with his cousin Francisco, who also happened to be gay. "We used to play *Little Mermaid*. We didn't have dolls. We would use plants. We would hide, though. We would go somewhere where nobody could see us. Of course, people *did* see us, and they could tell we were different." The boys who played soccer would bully them and pick fights; Everardo and Francisco would fight back. "Sometimes I got beat up," Everardo remembered, "but I defended myself."

Filipino gay men were less likely than Latinos to describe the home country as homophobic, perhaps because they remembered gay and gender-transgressing people being omnipresent in the Philippines, both in everyday life and on television. Still, they felt that gay people, particularly gay men, were seen as one-dimensional caricatures. Chris Mojica (b. 1993), a Filipino American college student, was born in the United States but lived in the Philippines from age six to age eleven. At an early age he was aware of the gay men he would encounter when accompanying his mother to a hair salon or a boutique. They were unapologetically effeminate. "Growing up, it was embedded in my mind in the Philippines that being gay is being a cross-dresser," Chris said. "That whole stereotype of being flamboyant, always having a purse, or wearing makeup and women's clothing." While his mother and others were always friendly with these men, Chris also remembered the way they would whisper and poke fun of them behind their backs. "It made me see that being gay wasn't considered normal."

Not all of the men had had opportunities to travel back to their parents' home countries. Even so, they remembered seeing caricatures of gay people through transnational media outlets like the Filipino Channel (TFC). Xavier Navarro (b. 1994), a Filipino American college student, recalled that gay men were often the butt of jokes on Filipino television shows he watched as a child. "In Filipino media, [the shows] make jokes of gay people," Xavier said. "They are so extreme. Like, one thing that really upsets me is when I'm at home, and my parents are watching TFC, especially the game shows. They portray gay Filipinos as only being feminine or dressing in drag. I think what really upsets me about that is how the portrayal of that would affect my parents' view of me." Xavier later clarified that he saw nothing wrong with men being effeminate. In fact, as an adult, he would come to see embracing femininity as empowering and an act of resistance against the rigidity of gender binaries. Still, he was frustrated that such one-dimensional media portrayals made it difficult for his family to see gay people as anything more than a stereotype. Theo Espinoza (b. 1985), a Filipino American art director, echoed Xavier's worries. "I think the Filipino community might be becoming more accepting because we see gay characters on TFC," he said. "But sometimes I wonder, are they being accepted or are they being put on this show to be clowns?"

Fernando Serrano (b. 1993), a Mexican American college student, remembered seeing queer people on the Spanish channel at an age when he was still too young to understand his own sexuality. When he first saw a gay man on Spanish-language television, it confused him, and so he turned to his mother and grandmother for answers. "On the news or, like, in novellas, I remember I'd ask my mom, 'Oh, why is he like that?' My mom would just be like, 'Oh, they're born like that.' Perhaps she didn't see [queerness] in me. My grandma was like, 'Oh the devil is in them. They have demons inside of them.'" These interactions instilled a sense of fear in Fernando, who was afraid his family would reject him for being gay. The response from his grandmother also instilled the belief that homophobia was more prevalent among older generations than later ones.

Queer scholars of color have noted that while such thinking is commonplace, communities of color are not any more homophobic than White Americans. Such thinking reifies the problematic trope of immigrant cultures and home countries as "backward" and White Americans as more "enlightened" on LGBTQ issues.[15] While some of the men were quick to typecast their families and ethnic communities as homophobic, the stories of men with gay relatives revealed nuances in how gay people were received in Filipino and Latino social circles.

"Family" within the Family

When I spoke with Alfonso Ruiz (b. 1988), a Mexican American graduate student, one of the first things he mentioned was that he had two gay uncles, his Tío Tomás and Tío Antonio, both younger brothers of his father. "You're so lucky," I told him. "I'm jealous." While I have cousins around my age who are gay, there is no one in my parents' generation who is (at least not that I know of). My cousins and I never spoke to each other about being gay until we were in our twenties. In contrast, Alfonso said his uncles were the reason he was able to learn about gay relationships and communities at an early age.

During his childhood, Alfonso and his sisters would spend weekends at their uncles' homes, which gave them many opportunities to interact with other gay men in their social circles. Whenever his uncles were dating, they would bring their partners to family gatherings, which signaled to Alfonso that his family was accepting of them. When Alfonso was a teenager, his Tío Tomás would take him and his sisters to West Hollywood to grab lunch and stroll through the boulevard during the day. His uncle was the first person to explain that West Hollywood was a community that catered to gay people and that he and his friends would spend a lot of time there. "I saw the life my uncle lived," Alfonso said. "I saw that he had a fun life in LA." It was around this time that his Tío Antonio began taking him and his two sisters to the Pride parade that took place in West Hollywood every June. Years later, Alfonso would learn that it was his mother (suspecting he might be gay) who had encouraged his uncles to expose him to gay culture. "That was their way of helping me accept [my sexuality] a little more," he said. "I never officially told them I was gay, but I knew at some point they knew without me having to tell them."

Carlos Rivera (b. 1986), a Cuban American small business owner, saw his gay uncles and cousins as role models. "I had a crapload of people in the family that were gay," Carlos said. "My uncle is gay, my dad's favorite cousin, he's gay. And there were gay cousins all over the family." He appreciated how his family wasn't "just tolerant." His uncles and cousins never shied away from talking about gay-related topics, whether it was gay celebrities in pop culture or HIV/AIDS in the gay community. When they brought their romantic partners to family events, they would introduce them as partners, not as roommates or friends. "Every gay person in my family has been partnered, and I see gay men in relationships that last ten, fifteen, twenty years," Carlos said. "Because of this, there's never been a doubt in my mind that I can be in a long-term relationship."

Of course, not everyone had such rosy stories about their gay family members. Matt Mendiola (b. 1989), a Filipino American social worker, spoke about the complicated relationship his parents had with his Tita

Linda, his father's eldest sister. "Tita Linda is lesbian," he explained. "She [is] the eldest, so everyone respects her." It was Tita Linda who financially supported Matt's father when he first migrated to California from the Philippines.

Tita Linda commanded much respect from his parents, but Matt noticed they were cryptic about his aunt's personal life: "Tita Linda had a partner, but they never talked about her. If they did, they would just say, 'That's her friend.' But it was pretty obvious [that she was Tita Linda's partner]. I could tell even when I was young." Tita Linda's partner rarely attended family get-togethers, and when she did, she kept to herself. Even his parents barely interacted with her. In contrast, Matt had many fond memories of interacting with the partners of his aunts and uncles who were straight. He didn't think much about these differences when he was a kid, but when he reflected back on it as an adult, he felt it sent a message: No matter how much Tita Linda did for the family, she wouldn't be as wholeheartedly accepted because she was gay.

As Matt's story demonstrates, the presence of gay relatives didn't always mean families were more gay friendly. For example, having two gay uncles didn't hinder Alfonso's father from making homophobic remarks when those uncles weren't around. Echoing the experiences of the other men, Alfonso said his father would scold him if he were consuming queer content on television. "If there was something gay on television, like *Queer as Folk*, my dad would say, 'Why are you watching that shit?'" Alfonso acknowledged that his father had a good relationship with his gay siblings, but such remarks made it difficult for him to be as open with his father about his personal life as he would have liked to be. "It's one thing when your brothers are gay, but it's a totally different thing when your son is." Just because he had gay brothers didn't mean Alfonso's father was better equipped to parent a gay son.

While gay family members signaled the possibility of a future, sometimes that future wasn't always a positive one. Hugo Ortiz (b. 1985), a Cuban American fitness trainer, remembered attending the funeral of an older cousin, Amilcar, who died of complications from AIDS in the early

1990s. "I remember seeing Amilcar in this coffin with a glass case over it," he said. "This was back in 1992, so there was still a fear of the disease being airborne, and so you couldn't touch the body." When Hugo was a teenager, his parents sat him down and explained that the disease that took Amilcar's life was common among gay men. Around this same time, one of Hugo's uncles, who happened to be gay, shared that he was HIV-positive. His uncle showed him the daily medications he had to take. "That's what I associated being gay with," he said. "It made me wish so bad that I wasn't gay. That I wouldn't end up like that." With age and maturity—as well as advancements in HIV/AIDS research—Hugo came to learn how harmful this line of thinking was, especially since he had close friends who were living with the disease. Unfortunately, in his childhood, most conversations around HIV/AIDS framed the disease as a death sentence, not a treatable chronic condition, which sheds light on why Hugo and other men I interviewed tended to focus on the stigma, and unfortunately not the humanity, of gay men living with HIV.

Managing Masculinity at Home

The childhood and adolescent experiences that these men had within their immigrant families and ethnic communities shaped their conceptualization of gay sexuality.[16] As these stories show, the second-generation gay men I interviewed learned early on to associate gayness (and by extension, effeminateness) with immorality. They learned, too, that there were consequences to not adhering to the rules of masculinity prescribed by their families and communities.

Often the reprimands came from the men in their families. When he was growing up, Rex Pabalon (b. 1981), a Filipino American school counselor, felt like his father was always disappointed in him because he lacked athletic prowess. "He knew I was different," Rex said. "He was hypermasculine. He did boxing, and when he came here [to the United States] he did sports, he joined the military, and I was the complete antithesis to him. I didn't do sports or anything that was boy-like."

"Do you think that affected your relationship with him growing up?" I asked.

"I think he realized that I was not going to be into anything that he was into. Sometimes he would tell me to 'man up.' But I don't think he would do anything to disparage me. We did have a tough relationship, though. He knew I was smart, and sometimes if I would talk back at him, I think he was intimidated by how intelligent I was at a young age."

Hearing these remarks, I found it odd that Rex felt his father had not done anything to "disparage" him. Even if he never uttered harmful words, his father's actions made it clear that Rex was not the son he had hoped for. That Rex's father felt threatened by his intelligence spoke volumes about the way his conception of masculinity demanded that he remain dominant at all costs, even if it emotionally harmed his own son.

Rex also recalled the teasing that came from his older cousins. "They would call me gay at an early age," he recalled. "They were into sports. I wasn't. They would talk about girls. I didn't. And I wasn't roughhousing as much as they were. They pegged me as the gay one in the family early on." With the way he was being treated, Rex found it difficult to be around his family, especially his father. Every time he was around them he felt he had to "act straight" and "act like a boy." "I was so accommodating for the entire family," he said. As Rex grew older he distanced himself from his father and cousins as much as he could. But eventually, the isolation and rejection he felt from his family led to depression during his teenage years.

Many of the gay men I interviewed remembered being reprimanded if ever they were caught "acting like a girl" or "acting gay." Often there was nothing specifically girly or gay about the behaviors they were scolded for. "My dad was super homophobic," Fernando explained. "Even him showing affection to me or my brother, that was considered gay. Like hugging, that to him was very gay."

Other men echoed that they were berated for their supposed gay behaviors. Manny Roldan said, "When I was really little, I had this really loud laugh, and my grandmother would say, 'Don't do that. You're gonna sound like a gay!'" Similarly, Abel Perez (b. 1991), a Mexican American physician, also said he got in trouble if his voice sounded like one of his gossipy aunts. "I was talking to my mom and dad, and my mom made a joke," Abel recalled. "I said, 'Aaaayyyy,' but in a really feminine way. Then my dad's ears perked up, and he got really serious and said, in Spanish, 'Don't say it like that because that's gay, and you don't want to be gay.'"

These moments were traumatizing for Manny and Abel, who both said they started policing their behavior after they were admonished. "After that, I became super alert," Abel said. "I kept worrying, does [my father] think that I am gay? And after that, I just made sure to be extra cautious because I didn't want to be a disappointment. I just became alert and fearful that he would question my sexuality." In the moments when these men displayed the most vulnerability and joy, they were shamed by the people in their lives who were supposed to unconditionally love and accept them. Both Manny and Abel felt like their fathers prioritized the comfort of homophobic family members over their sense of safety and belonging.

The second-generation gay men I interviewed managed their behavior so that no one in their family would suspect they were gay. They were vigilant about monitoring their gender presentation so that they were seen as masculine—or, at least, not effeminate. They policed their voice inflections, their mannerisms, their clothing choices, their musical and television preferences, and even their friendship networks—not necessarily to pass as straight, but to be seen as not gay. They did so because they feared they would lose social and emotional support from their parents and other family members.[17]

Some of the men I spoke with said they hid their sexuality because they felt a deep sense of family obligation. On one of his summer trips to his father's hometown in Mexico, Rolando remembered his mother telling him to watch how he acted so that he didn't make the family "look bad." Although this was many years before he officially came out to her, the implication was clear: Rolando's mother worried that if other members of the extended family were to find out he was gay, it would reflect poorly not just on him but also on her and her husband.

The familial pressures these second-generation gay men faced were echoed by the gay children of immigrants featured in the BuzzFeed documentary. Andrew, one of the men in the video, framed his decision as an act of service to his immigrant parents: "I want to have a life that makes them happy. I didn't want to impose [my sexuality] on my parents at all. I didn't want to stress them out." Aware of the struggles his parents endured to leave their home country and create a life for him in the United States, Andrew felt his sexuality would somehow cancel out their hard work and sacrifices. "One of the biggest things you think and talk about and base your decisions [about sexuality] on is reputation," said Rashmi, a second-generation Indian featured in the video. "What will the family think?" Such remarks perfectly capture the sense of responsibility that gay children of immigrants feel: the notion that being gay is consequential not just for them but also for their entire family.

3

Surviving School

There is something about being queer that makes one more fastidious about learning. . . . The theme of being "different," "artistic," "creative," "having a drive," and being a "bookworm" comes up too many times for it to be a mere coincidence.

—E. Patrick Johnson, *Sweet Tea: Black Gay Men in the South*

More than algebra, English, or biology, there's a subject that boys master in school—a subject that never appears on any academic transcript, whose lessons occur mostly outside the walls of the classroom. Not a day passes where boys aren't tested on this subject, and so they study and they study—often without realizing they are studying—because proficiency means survival. If ever you were to ask these boys—who've since become men—about this subject they've worked so tirelessly to master, many will tell you about the painful moments when they failed, memories that haunt them well into adulthood.

The subject I'm referring to is masculinity. The often painful pedagogy of masculinity came up immediately in my conversation with Eugene Torres (b. 1981), a graduate student at California State University–Long Beach. The word he used to describe his elementary and middle school years: awful.

"In elementary school, I was a bit androgynous, and I was a bit chubbier, and I had a higher pitched voice, and I had no style," Eugene remembered. "People couldn't nail down my gender. There were times when people didn't know what gender I was, and for the people that knew my gender, I was effeminate. They would call me gay. I was teased so much and bullied so much in elementary and middle school for not conforming to the stereotype of a male."

Middle schools and high schools are hostile environments for boys who, as Eugene put it, "aren't masculine enough": the ones who joined the drama club instead of the football team, the ones who idolized pop stars instead of rappers, the ones who felt more comfortable befriending girls rather than other boys. According to a national school climate survey conducted by GLSEN, an educational outreach organization, boys who violate the prescribed rules of masculinity are violently bullied by their peers. Over 90 percent of the LGBTQ students that GLSEN surveyed reported that negative remarks were made about gay students' gender expression, and young men were targeted more often than women. Two-thirds of the students said they overheard a teacher or school counselor making homophobic remarks.[1]

When young men adhere to the prescribed rules of masculinity—that is, if they act, speak, and dress the way young men are "supposed to"—they're rewarded with social acceptance and a sense of belonging. But when young men violate gender expectations, they're publicly sanctioned by their peers—especially other boys. Often they hurl homophobic slurs—faggot, fairy, fruitcake, and the like—to keep each other in line.[2] Regardless of sexuality, many boys know firsthand the pain of being called a faggot in school, but for the ones like Eugene who were *actually* gay these insults cut much deeper.

Getting Schooled on Heterosexuality

Whenever I teach my class on gender and sexuality, I start the semester by asking my students, "Where did you first learn about heterosexuality?" Most are baffled by the question. Except for a few queer students in the room, most of the class has never conceptualized heterosexuality as something that is *learned*. I then ask a follow-up question: "Where do you get the message that heterosexuality is 'normal'?" The hands start shooting up. A couple of students will talk about heteronormative households (e.g., mom, dad, and children) in their own families or on television. Eventually, though, the conversation will segue to how heterosexuality is normalized in school. One student mentions how her biology teacher spent much of the year focusing on reproduction, the process of procreation between male and female members of a species. "Sexual diversity is made invisible in the curriculum and science textbooks by the heteronormative lens of Darwinian reproductive drive," write Vicky Snyder and Francis Broadway in the *Journal of Research in Science Teaching*.[3] Another student will note how the books assigned to him in his middle school and high school English classes almost always featured romantic relationships between men and women. Yet another student will highlight how the rituals beyond the classroom, such as school dances, normalize heterosexual relationships, including the hierarchical dynamic between boys and girls (i.e., boys are supposed to ask girls to prom, not the other way around).

In normalizing heterosexuality, schools also breed an allegiance to masculinity. In her book *Dude, You're a Fag: Masculinity and Sexuality in High School*, sociologist C. J. Pascoe writes, "The heterosexualizing process organized by educational institutions cannot be separated from, and in fact is central to, the development of masculine identities."[4] The process Pascoe describes often leaves gay students feeling stigmatized and silenced.[5] Already made to feel different in the context of their home lives, gay boys (and boys questioning their sexuality) are further marginalized by peers at schools.

Jesse Madrigal (b. 1984), a Mexican American graphic designer, told me he felt that being gay was more of a problem for him at school than it was at home. "I knew I was attracted to [boys] at age five, even though I didn't know what attraction was at that age," he said. "I went toward boys, and not in the way boys played with boys. It was something different."

"So how did you know something was wrong with that?" I asked.

"I didn't think it was bad. My parents never said anything bad [about being gay]. In elementary school, my friends weren't at that stage where they were gonna ask that girl out or gonna kiss girls. It was still very playful. It wasn't until junior high when everything got defined."

"Defined?"

"People grew up. I feel like that's when sexual exploration was happening, and guys are asking girls out. And I was like, 'I don't want to ask a girl out.'"

Franklin Flores also remembered the pressure to perform heterosexual attraction when he started middle school. He worried that if he didn't, his friends would label him a fag. During elementary school, Franklin had heard his friends hurling gay epithets at each other almost daily. Back then, though, they did so mainly to police each other's behavior. If you liked the wrong music, you were a fag. If you were backing the wrong sports team, you were a fag. If you watched a certain TV show that the other boys didn't, you were a fag. Before middle school, being called a fag had more to do with taste than it did with sexual attraction.

By the time he reached sixth grade, the words *fag* and *gay* landed differently. This was because Franklin was starting to feel an attraction to his male friends. He started to wonder whether the other boys in his class were in on the secret that he could barely admit to himself. "Thoughts [about attraction to other boys] would come up when we would wrestle or go to hot tubs together," Franklin recalled. "I think it was the transition from sixth grade to seventh grade when I finally started realizing I am just not attracted to women. I can't bring myself to do it."

School dances, and the courtship rituals surrounding them, exacerbated the anxiety that Franklin felt around his emerging queer sexuality. "Who are you going to ask to the dance?" his friends would ask each other. It was a question he dreaded every time he heard it, as he knew they would eventually get around to asking him. "You had to pick someone [to ask], and I always found it hard to pick someone," he explained. "I'd try to pick some girl who I was just friends with within the band." The stress of having to pretend to be straight became too much for him to handle at times. "Junior high was dark. That's when I started developing suicidal thoughts, because I was gay, actually." Psychologists have found that young gay men who are bullied for not "acting straight" are more likely to have suicidal ideations than those who "pass."[6] It is important to note that for Franklin (and many other gay sons of immigrants), sexuality wasn't the only source of struggle in their middle school years. As I will discuss later in this chapter, Franklin said much of the emotional stress he experienced on a daily basis had to do with his parents' marital conflicts and economic instability.

Throughout my conversations with second-generation gay men, it was clear that navigating the perception of their sexuality was a part of day-to-day life at school. But they also spoke about how their school lives were shaped by race; not surprisingly, Filipinos and Latinos told very different stories about the way teachers and peers typecast and stereotyped them. Because they were grappling with sexuality during their elementary school, middle school, and high school years, many of the men spoke about school as something they survived, but also as an outlet that helped them cope with the pressure they felt as gay sons growing up in immigrant families. As we'll see, the survival strategies available to them were very much shaped by how they were racialized in school.

Academic Covering

Manny Roldan told me he started pulling all-nighters in sixth grade. His parents, both college-educated health professionals who had migrated from the Philippines, had always encouraged him and his older sisters to do well in school. Even so, they were never helicopter parents who kept track of every exam or grade he earned in class. In fact, there were times when his parents would ask him to lay off the books whenever they saw him looking sleep deprived. "Anak, you have to sleep. You have to watch your health," his mother would tell him.[7] "You shouldn't study so much because you're going to stunt your growth," his father would say.

Manny didn't heed their advice. When he entered high school, he enrolled in every honors and advanced placement (AP) class his school offered. On top of his rigorous course load, he served as class president for all four years of high school. "Gay people love leadership positions," Manny joked.

"If your parents weren't pushing you, what pushed you?" I asked.

"I wanted to beat my sisters," he said, chuckling at his competitiveness. Moments later, and seemingly out of nowhere, his mood shifted. "Actually, sometimes I think I just did that to make up for being the son my dad wanted. I thought if I can't be the football son he always wanted, at least I could be the smart son."

Throughout his childhood, Manny worried constantly about not acting masculine enough. His father constantly questioned why he never wanted to play basketball like the other boys in his family and the neighborhood. As was mentioned in chapter 2, Manny's grandmother would scold him if ever he cackled too loudly. "She would legitimately get mad at me," he said. Even his sisters started to poke fun at him when he became more fashion conscious in middle school. "I'd was becoming more selective about how I'd dress, and my sisters would always be like, 'You're so gay.'"

"How would that make you feel?" I asked.

"It made me want to change," he said solemnly. "It made me want to be straight."

Manny tried. In his sophomore and junior years, he had girlfriends, but these relationships quickly fizzled as soon as the girl he was dating initiated anything sexual. He even tried getting drunk just so he could reciprocate their advances. It never worked. After his third relationship with a girl failed, he panicked. "I can't be *that* guy," Manny thought. "I can't be gay. My life will go down the drain if it ever gets out."

By the end of his junior year, Manny stopped trying to go out with girls in his class and instead doubled down on his academics and extracurricular activities. When his friends or family asked why he didn't have a girlfriend, he would tell them he was too focused on trying to become valedictorian so he could get into a top college. Becoming the star student became Manny's "cover."

The concept of "covering" refers to the way marginalized people amplify some other aspect of their identity as way to neutralize the impact of their marginalized identity. Covering was introduced by sociologist

Erving Goffman in his 1963 book *Stigma: Notes on the Management of Spoiled Identity*. Goffman writes, "It is a fact that persons who are ready to admit possession of a stigma (in many cases because it is known about or immediately apparent) may nonetheless make a great effort to keep the stigma from looming large. The individual's object is to reduce tension, that is, to make it easier for himself and others to withdraw covert attention from the stigma. . . . This process will be referred to as covering."[8]

Covering is a useful framework for understanding Manny's strategy. By frontloading his academic identity, Manny hoped to deflect questions and uncomfortable conversations about his sexuality. Covering wasn't about trying to pass as straight; it was about controlling the frame through which his classmates and others viewed him. Being the star student wouldn't make waves in the way being the gay student would.

Many of the second-generation gay men I interviewed, both Filipinos and Latinos alike, opted for a strategy like Manny's. The term I use to describe this practice—investing in academic achievement to distract others from one's queerness—is *academic covering*. Academic covering includes a variety of strategies: presenting oneself as an academic overachiever, enrolling in as many honors and AP courses as possible, staying in the good graces of teachers and school officials, and participating in extracurricular activities associated with high achievers (e.g., student government, debate team, orchestra, yearbook). For the gay men who adopted academic covering, this strategy proved functional in both their school and family lives.

Josue Pedroza (b. 1990), a Mexican American college student, said he turned to academics as an escape for the teasing he experienced in middle school. Classmates bullied him often because he was effeminate and because he was overweight. "I hated junior high," he said. "Probably my least favorite years of my life because I was teased a lot, not just for being queer but also for being fat. . . . I would try to hide [my queerness], but people were like, 'Oh, you're gay!'" Josue said the harassment from other boys occurred "always at lunch time or outside the classroom setting." When he wasn't in class, he often spent his free time helping teachers with whatever they needed—anything to avoid the lunchroom or the campus yard. Josue thought of his teachers as a shield against the harassment he faced among his classmates.

Many of the gay men I interviewed also felt that being academically excellent served a function with their families. Academic covering would allow them to win back points they would lose if their parents were ever to learn they were gay. Excelling in school fit squarely with the expectations of growing up in an immigrant family: immigrant parents of all ethnicities, socioeconomic classes, and educational backgrounds hold high hopes that their children will pursue higher education.[9] In the eyes of immigrant parents, earning a college degree rationalizes the sacrifices and hardships they have endured while trying to build a life in the United States.[10] From an early age, children of immigrants internalize the hopes and ambitions of their immigrant parents, and school becomes one way to fulfill their sense of familial obligation. "My dad and mom always wanted me to do well in school, and so I was always on the honor roll," Josue said. Other second-generation gay men I interviewed more explicitly linked their academic achievement to their parents' migration story. "My parents immigrated straight from the Philippines," said Carlo de Guzman (b. 1994), a Filipino American college student. "They moved here so we could get a better education and make a better life for ourselves."

Academic covering was a strategy that both Filipino and Latino gay men embraced during their primary and secondary school years to counteract the stigma of being seen as gay. As they recounted their educational experiences, however, it became clear that Filipinos were more easily able to adopt academic covering because of the way they were racialized in schools. Of course, there were Latinos who were able to engage in academic covering, but the ability to do so was predicated on their ability to counteract the negative stereotypes imposed on young Latino men in their schools.

Filipino Americans and the Model Minority Myth

Jerald Gutierrez (b. 1986), a Filipino American registered nurse, admitted he wasn't very studious in elementary and middle school. The youngest of four siblings, he arrived in the United States when he was just nine years old. Adjusting to school in a new country was an emotionally difficult experience. It wasn't that fourth grade in the United States was more academically challenging than it was in the Philippines (it was far easier, actually); it was socially adjusting that was hard. Even though at least one-third of his new American classmates were Filipino, they weren't at all welcoming of Jerald. They made fun of him for being from the Philippines, for speaking with an accent, and for dressing differently. They called him a "FOB"—fresh off the boat. His difficulty adjusting led to him earning mostly Cs and a few Bs on his report cards.

FOB wasn't the only pejorative Jerald's male classmates hurled at him. In middle school, they teased him for spending his recesses and lunches talking about anime with the girls instead of playing basketball with the boys. "[The boys] kept saying anime was gay," he said. "This was before anime was huge. All they saw were the male characters who, to them, looked like girls with their long hair." One time, in eighth grade, he managed to get invited to a sleepover at one of the other boy's houses. "Finally, I felt like I was fitting in," he said. The moment he arrived, however, his hope dissipated when he overheard some of the other boys whispering to each other. "Jerald's a fag!" he heard them say, not seeming to care that he was within earshot. The way they said it was different from how they yelled it at each other on the schoolyard. This time it didn't seem like they were joking; they seemed almost angry. Jerald didn't know what exactly prompted their taunts, but it didn't matter at that point. "I didn't even know for sure that I was gay," he said. That sleepover was a turning point for Jerald. He decided he'd stop trying to befriend the other boys and instead only hang out with the girls, with whom he felt safe.

High school was Jerald's chance for a fresh start. Many of the boys who teased him were attending the same school, but in a school of three thousand students, he'd more easily be able to avoid them. Like Josue, he found refuge in the honors and AP classes. "The guys who used to tease me were all in the regular classes. I only had to see them in gym," he said. "In honors, it was mostly girls, and mostly Asian. I didn't want to be in the regular classes with those guys, the ones who made fun of me. Getting into honors was a matter of survival."

Based on his middle school track record, I knew that Jerald didn't have the grades that one usually needed to be admitted into the honors and AP courses. I asked him how he was able to enroll in those courses having entered high school with a grade point average below 3.0. Jerald said his counselor automatically signed off on his request to be in the honors and AP track without bothering to check his transcript. In his school, the Asian American (mostly Filipino) and Latinx populations were roughly the same, at about 40 percent each. Despite their similar numbers, Asian American students were overrepresented in the honors track, while the Latinx students made up the majority in the "regular" track.[11] Though Jerald never said outright that he got into the honors courses *because* he was Asian American, sociological research suggests that his race played a role.

Sociologists Jennifer Lee and Min Zhou have found that "Asian Americans benefit from 'stereotype promise'—the promise of being viewed through the lens of a positive stereotype that leads one to perform in such a way that confirms the positive stereotype, thereby enhancing performance." As Lee and Zhou note, the stereotyping of Asian American students as inherently intelligent and hardworking occurs regardless of their *actual* academic performance.[12] In her book *Academic Profiling*, sociologist Gilda Ochoa conducted research in Los Angeles high schools where the student bodies comprised Asian Americans and Latinxs. She observed time and again how racial categories became synonymous with academic abilities—*Asian* became interchangeable with *smart* and *hardworking*.[13] These studies suggest that Jerald's Asianness prompted his school counselor to assume that he belonged in the honors and AP track.

Even though they attended different schools, many of the other Filipinos I interviewed shared stories similar to Jerald's. The academic racial hierarchy had Asian Americans (and Whites, if they were present) filling the honors and AP classrooms, while Latinxs and African Americans were the majority in the regular ones. When describing the racial landscape of his high school, Chris Mojica said, "We [Asian American students] can easily get into honors and AP. There were no White people there. . . . Everyone else was Hispanic. There were some high-achieving Mexicans, but there were also lots of low-achieving Mexicans." Michael Garibay (b. 1993), a UCLA classmate of Chris's, said, "It was predominantly Asian, South Asian, and Filipino in the AP courses. There were Black and Latino students, but not proportional to the size [of their population]." The fact that Filipinos were often typecast as "model minority" students in high school sheds light on why so many of the Filipino men were inclined to engage in academic covering. These remarks (Chris's especially) also illustrated how the academic tracking system prompted students to internalize negative stereotypes about other racial groups at the school.

For Franklin, academic covering allowed him not only to cope with the emotional stress of grappling with his sexuality but provided him with the stability he lacked in his family life. The second-generation gay men I interviewed weren't only struggling with sexuality during their childhood and adolescent years; many grew up in households that were experiencing financial struggles and domestic disputes. Franklin's story is an example of this.

Although Franklin's parents were both college-educated professionals, they struggled financially. For many years, his mother's disability made it difficult for her to hold down a full-time job; it took a number of years for her to secure disability benefits that would've kept the family afloat. On top of that, his father poured their family's savings into a business that unfortunately failed during the Great Recession. When those efforts failed, his parents turned to gambling, which sunk them further into debt. Franklin recalled his family being evicted from several different apartments during his middle school years. In the worst of times, his family would spend weeks or even months living in an extended-stay hotel. The instability of his home life was a major cause of the depression Franklin suffered in his middle school years.

Like Jerald, things changed for Franklin in high school because of the stereotype promise he experienced. In his hometown of Riverside, the high school he attended had students from what Franklin described as the "hood side" of the city (comprising mostly African Americans and Mexican Americans) and a smaller proportion of students from the more affluent parts of the city (mostly Asian Americans and Whites). Franklin had spent the last eight years attending school with the Black and Mexican American students, but most of his teachers and classmates assumed he was from the richer side of town. "[The teachers] thought I was part of that same group of rich Asians who didn't belong to the area but went to the school because of the International Baccalaureate program," he explained.

Although there were major economic and marital problems at home—which would have led Black and Latinx students to be labeled as "at risk"—his teachers assumed he came from a stable middle-class household. "They assumed I was smart, rich, and from a good family, and that wasn't the case at all," Franklin said. Even back then, he felt that this had something to do with his race. "I was Asian, so they saw me as model minority." Franklin noticed how the same teachers who supported him were the same ones who negatively stereotyped his Latino friends, many of whom, he pointed out, "had nicer houses and stronger families than I did."

Being in the good graces of his teachers allowed Franklin to become more comfortable with his emerging queer sexuality. In an essay for one of his English classes, he wrote about all of the difficulties he was facing—his parents' rocky marriage and financial troubles; his father's secret family back home in the Philippines; and his own struggles with his sexuality. For most of his life, Franklin had long kept these parts of his life secret, but his English teacher, Mrs. Lopez, encouraged him to draw on these experiences for his college application essays. It was one of the first times in his life that someone—and an adult, at that—had signaled that it was okay to be gay.

By his senior year, Franklin stopped caring whether classmates in school thought he was gay. "I had a more feminine gender presentation," he said. "I was in theater. I loved dance. I was doing color guard. I loved doing things guys traditionally didn't do. I was in the school musical, and I had a lead role, and for that role, I had to dress in drag and wear heels."

"Were you open about your sexuality back then?" I asked.

"No, I wasn't. But gender play was no problem. I think part of it was, I had a feeling everyone already knew."

"Did anyone ever give you shit for doing those things?"

"This is going to sound arrogant of me, but I feel like I had a support system. I was part of the student government. The principal and the teachers loved me. . . . At the same time, of course, I would walk down the aisles and people would whisper, 'That's the guy who dressed in drag.' But I didn't give a shit. I felt comfortable doing what I do."

In high school, Franklin may not have had a gay-straight alliance or a group of queer friends to help him grapple with his queerness, but having the support of at least one teacher was more than what most of the other men I interviewed had had. Out of the more than sixty second-generation gay men I spoke with, Franklin was one of the few who had come out to a teacher in high school. When he shared that he was gay with that teacher, she didn't ignore or shame him; rather, she showed him how to frame his sexual identity as part of his intellectual and personal development.

Franklin's ability to harness the support of teachers was predicated on being labeled as one of the "smart Asian kids." I wondered, though, if one of the Black or Latino boys he had grown up with had had the same struggles—with his sexuality and family situation—would he have been able to secure support from teachers and school officials in the same way Franklin had? No one can know for certain. But the stories of the Latino men I interviewed suggest that not all gay young men of color were afforded the same protection that Franklin was.

Stereotyping Latino Boys

I first met Jaime Avila (b. 1985), a Mexican American bank employee, in 2010 at Mickey's, a West Hollywood nightclub. It was a Thursday, Latin Night, and hip-hop and reggaeton were blaring inside. I went out to the second-floor patio to get some air, and Jaime happened to be smoking a cigarette next to me. We struck up a conversation, and when I mentioned to Jaime that I was finishing up a PhD program in sociology, his ears perked up. He was finishing his bachelor's degree at California State University–Los Angeles and had ambitions to pursue a doctorate in English. We spoke for more than half an hour, and for most of the time, Jaime was more inquisitive than I was. In the most charming of ways he asked me about my favorite books and writers—not the usual conversation I was used to having at a nightclub.

A few years later, when starting the research for this book, Jaime was one of the first people I contacted for an interview. We met at a coffee shop in Silver Lake, a few blocks from the apartment he shared with his partner. By then he had finished his bachelor's degree, and though he still had graduate school ambitions, he admitted that those plans were on hold because he had to work full-time.

Before we got to talking about his school years, Jaime shared his family's migration story. His family was from Guadalajara, the metropolitan capital of Jalisco, Mexico. His father migrated to Southern California first while Jaime, his mother, and four siblings stayed behind in Mexico. His father settled in Orange County because he found a decent job as a parking attendant at the local airport; by Jaime's fourth birthday, the rest of the family would follow. One of Jaime's first memories in the United States was the culture shock of attending a predominantly White school. "Me and my brother were the only two Mexican kids," he said.

I was curious to hear about the early school years of the person who had organically brought up Geoffrey Chaucer and the *Canterbury Tales* in our very first conversation at a West Hollywood club. Jaime said he had always been fond of literature, even when he was a kid. But in his elementary school years, his teachers—almost all of whom were White women—treated him like he was a troublemaker.[14]

"As a kid you don't really realize what's happening," he said. "When I think about it now, in retrospect, there was clear discrimination. I felt like teachers were always looking out for what I was doing wrong." Jaime remembered getting in trouble for the most minor infractions.[15] Whispering to a classmate during class? He was being disruptive. Sitting the wrong way in his seat? He was disengaged. Challenging a teacher to a discussion? He was being disrespectful.

And his classmates weren't any better. "I got bullied," Jaime said of his elementary and middle school years. "I wasn't, like, particularly effeminate, but I wasn't a macho boy either. I don't know if it had something to do with that or because I was the only Mexican. To tell you the truth, I don't really know if it was that or my budding gayness, but I definitely got bullied. I was definitely bullied by multiple kids." As Jaime's remarks show, it's not always clear why gay students of color experience bullying in school. It would be misleading to attribute the harassment Jaime encountered among his White classmates solely to sexuality or solely to race.[16]

I asked Jaime how he survived school given that he lacked support from both his teachers and his classmates. Since he didn't have anyone to turn to, he had to get creative. "I was on government assistance, so I would get free meals at lunch," he explained. "I was one of the few kids [in the free lunch program] because everyone else was from affluent families. On Fridays, we'd have pizza, and there would be Pizza Hut, so I would give out all my free tickets to all the kids so everyone would get free pizza." Jaime was in fourth grade at the time.

I took a moment to fully digest what Jaime was telling me. At nine years old, Jaime, one of the only Mexican American students in the entire school, was being harangued by his White teachers and harassed by his White classmates. The most logical strategy he came up with was to forgo eating lunch for several days, save his free meal vouchers, and give them away to the rich White kids who had been bullying him because he didn't look or act like the other boys at school. That Jaime had to resort to this was an indication of how much race, class, and sexuality constrain the everyday agency of gay students of color in school.

"So, did it work?" I asked. I hoped that maybe a teacher or classmate would've commended him for his ingenuity. Of course, that wasn't the case.

"No. I got in *a lot* of trouble for that. Just for giving out free pizza tickets. I remember it was Miss Miller who yelled at me."

"You still remember her?"

"Yeah, of course! She would always scream my name: 'Avila! Get your ass over here!' Those exact words. I'll always remember those exact words. You know you can't really say anything as a kid, but to tell you the truth, I didn't even know what the word *ass* meant. She always picked on me. In retrospect, I felt it might've had something to do with me being Mexican. The thing is, I was a really good kid. I've always been a good student, but I felt like I was always getting in trouble."

Some might be surprised that a student like Jaime was treated so poorly by his teachers, but researchers who study racial inequality in education wouldn't. Studies have documented time and again how White school officials treat Latinx students—especially young men—as if they are a problem. They assume Latinx students are less invested in education and have less academic potential than Asian American and White students.[17] Sociologists have shown how school authorities often typecast young Black and Latino men as troublemakers, criminals, and gang members.[18] Black and Latino boys tend to be policed and punished more harshly than White ones; they are more likely to be suspended, or even reported to police, for minor infractions or acts of insubordination.[19] In the context of his all-White school, it's not too farfetched to assume that a White teacher like Miss Miller targeted Jaime because he was Brown.

But Miss Miller wasn't the only White teacher who made Jaime feel like an outsider. Jaime remembered a middle school English teacher who was particularly dismissive whenever he spoke up during class discussions. "There was one teacher, Mrs. O'Connor, I remember her specifically," he said. "I remember she asked a question about a book we were reading. Some Michael Crichton book. I remember giving a really good answer, and then some other White kid gave what I thought was a dumbed-down version of the answer that I just gave, but he got extra credit points for it. I was just sitting there. I had to just let it go." No matter how much Jaime tried to display his studiousness, his teachers in elementary and middle school never seemed to invest in him as a student. Unlike the experiences shared by the Filipino gay men I interviewed, it seemed that academic covering was never an option for Jaime. In a school where teachers like Miss Miller and Mrs. O'Connor were policing his behavior and underestimating his academic potential, Jaime said, "I was always saw myself as an outsider."

Jaime's situation improved when he started high school. His family moved to a more racially diverse part of Orange County, and the high school he attended was majority-Latinx (about 75 percent), with a smaller proportion of Asian American and White students. He was bullied a bit at the beginning, but eventually he started playing sports. "I was a really good runner, and so I played soccer," he said. By joining the soccer team, he was able to fend off any rumors about him being gay. Plus, moving to a high school where most of the other students were from the same ethnic and socioeconomic background made it easier to come out of his shell. "I was a class clown, and I think that endeared me to a lot of people," he said. "I was able to get along with all sectors—the drama geeks, the athletes—so I was never suspected [of being gay]." While Jaime ultimately framed his high school years as a happy chapter of his life, his story highlighted how the survival strategies available to young gay men of color were shaped by their racialization within the context of school. Unlike with Filipinos, Latino gay men weren't always able to dive into their academics as a cover for their struggles with sexuality.

"Exceptional" Latino Boys

Not all the Latino men I interviewed had school experiences as negative as Jaime's. About half of the Latino interviewees spoke about their academics as an outlet for coping with their emerging queer sexuality. I noticed a pattern among the Latinos who engaged in academic covering. First, they attended schools where Latinxs composed the vast majority of the student body. Second, they often spoke about having a teacher, often a teacher of color, who helped them navigate challenges they faced in both their academic and home lives. Third, they felt that their academic success depended on their ability to distinguish themselves from other Latino boys at school.

Gay Latino men who adopted academic covering as a strategy often attended schools where Latinxs comprised more than 80 percent of the student population. These schools were located in predominantly Latinx regions of Southern California, such as East Los Angeles, Southeast Los Angeles, and select cities in the San Fernando Valley and San Gabriel Valley. In a school where practically every student was Latinx, it was commonplace for Latinxs to be well represented in the advanced academic tracks, such as Gifted and Talented Education (GATE) in middle school, and honors and AP in high school. In contrast, in schools with smaller number of Latinxs, the majority of Latinxs would be relegated to the "regular" track, which made it more likely that teachers and school officials would typecast Latino young men as underachieving—or, worse, as troublemakers, criminal, or gang affiliated.[20]

Many of these men also mentioned having a teacher—most often a Latina or other woman of color—who went above and beyond the call of duty to mentor them both academically and personally. In her book *Latina Teachers*, sociologist Glenda Flores refers to these highly committed educators of color as "cultural guardians."[21] In her research on Latina teachers, Flores describes many as cultural guardians because in addition to cultivating their Latinx students' academic potential, they also helped them navigate racist incidents that might have otherwise derailed their educational pathways (as was the case with Jaime). The Latinos who engaged in academic covering had teachers who volunteered to give them rides to and from school, paid out of pocket for their extracurricular activities and college applications, and took the initiative to build relationships and communicate regularly with their students' immigrant parents, often in Spanish.

Latinos who invested in the educational game remembered being labeled as the "good Latino" or the "nerdy Mexican" student. They often found that teachers and school officials considered them "exceptional" in relation to other young Latino men in their school. In Ochoa's research of a predominantly Latinx and Asian American high school, she observed how "Mexican" and "Latino" became synonymous with "ghetto" and "stupid." Many of the gay Latino men who embraced academic covering were aware of the negative stereotypes associated with Latino boys in their school. "A lot of us [Latinos] are not expected to graduate high school," said Fernando Serrano, who grew up in Cudahy, a working-class neighborhood in Southeast LA. In order to be seen as one of the "good students," some went so far as to alter their clothing style or musical tastes to demarcate themselves from the "typical" Latinos on campus. Others mentioned having friendship circles that were not predominantly Latino nor predominantly male.

This constellation of circumstances was why Armando Garza, a Mexican American city planner and Georgetown University graduate introduced in an earlier chapter, came to view academics as his primary strategy for surviving the hardships related to his queer sexuality. Armando grew up in a low-income neighborhood in El Monte. As a young man, he witnessed violence on his block and, on occasion, in his own home. School became his means of escape. "I was ten years old, and I thought I needed to get good grades so I can find a way to support myself if I want to be able to get out of my house," he said.

Growing up, Armando had a hard time fitting in with his older brothers. From a young age, his brothers had been involved in sports year-round, from baseball to soccer. "My dad wanted us all to be baseball stars, which my brothers were, but I was a clumsy person," he explained. "I was just not into sports."

Because of his lack of interest in sports, Armando's brothers teased him incessantly. "My brothers would call me 'faggot.' I think my brother Gustavo always knew I was gay, and I think he hated that about me. He called me 'faggot' before I even knew I was gay. What really messed me up was my bigger brother picking on me and making me feel like I was weak or that there was something wrong with me. I would try not to put myself in situations that would make me feel like that."

In elementary school, Armando's father tried to sign him up for the same sports leagues his brothers participated in, but he did everything in his power to avoid being in the same space with them, especially Gustavo. "My big focus became school as a form of survival because I didn't like the environment that I was in," he explained. Whenever his father would take his brothers to the park, Armando would beg his mother to drive him to the library—anything to avoid being around Gustavo. His mother was happy to oblige. (Years later, his mother disclosed that she and his father were dealing with marital problems, and so she was happy to get out of the house whenever she could. Accompanying Armando to the library was an escape for her as well.)

"I liked going to the library more than the park," Armando recalled. "I liked staying out, doing my homework, instead of going to hang out with my brothers and the kids who played soccer or baseball. I hung out with my mom a lot more than my dad. My mother would be the one driving me to the library. She would stay in the parking lot for three hours while I would be in the library reading and doing homework. I was kind of weird. I was super focused on school."

"That was weird?" I asked.

"Me liking school was girly in the context of how I grew up," he said. "Like my brothers, other boys at school, none of them were schoolboys. So, me liking school was weird." I was struck by Armando's choice of words here: *weird*. Embracing a schoolboy identity made him different from his brothers, as well as the other boys in school (who, in El Monte, were mostly Latino).

Even though Armando always thought of himself as "one of the smart kids," he recalled times in elementary years when teachers underestimated his academic abilities because he was Latino. When he was eight years old, his teachers placed him in an English language learners' classroom with students who were recent immigrants, even though Armando's primary language was English. Years earlier they had done the same thing with his two older brothers, even though they, like Armando, were born in the United States. "That messed my brothers up and made them lag behind in their English development and school skills," Armando said. Had his mother not advocated for him to be moved, Armando would have stayed on that academic track.

Several years later, when Armando was in middle school, he wanted to be part of the GATE program because it was more academically challenging than the regular track. When he approached his language arts teacher, Miss Parish, who happened to be White, she refused. "My teacher didn't want to put me in advanced classes. She wouldn't recommended me for it." When I asked Armando why she was so resistant, he suspected it might have had to do with Miss Parish's previous interactions with his two older brothers. "None of my brothers had ever done honors," he said. "They weren't the best students." This teacher's problematic assessment of Armando is what sociologist Victor Rios describes as a "courtesy stigma," a "stigma that develops as a result of being related to someone with a stigma."[22] Without Miss Parish's backing, Armando had no choice but to stay in the regular track. He wasn't particularly stressed out about his coursework; it wasn't very academically rigorous. He spent more time worrying about how he would fare socially with the other boys in the regular track classrooms. He was more anxious about the "tests of masculinity" that the other boys subjected him to than any test administered by the teacher.

Things changed for Armando when he met Mrs. Trujillo, his middle school science teacher. Mrs. Trujillo was the first Latina teacher that Armando had, and she was the exemplar of a cultural guardian. She wondered why Armando wasn't in the GATE program, even though he had straight As and excelled in her class.

One day, she pulled him aside to talk to him about his future. "You know, you're really smart and you're talented, and someday you're gonna go to USC [the University of Southern California]," she told him. "You need to be on the honors track." Armando informed her that he had tried, but his language teacher had different ideas. Mrs. Trujillo was incensed. She insisted that Armando march to the counselor's office and demand that he be in the GATE program. She even told Armando what to say: "You need to tell your counselor that you want to be signed up for honors."

The next day, Armando did as he was told. He told the counselor that he wanted to be enrolled in the honors track.

"Well, Miss Parish didn't recommend you," the counselor told him.

Armando asked her to review his transcripts and test scores. When the counselor peeked at his record, she changed her mind, albeit reluctantly.

"Looks like your test scores are good, and you speak differently, and your science teacher [Mrs. Trujillo] says you can handle it, so we'll let you in. Why not?" the counselor said somewhat passive-aggressively.

The interactions Armando had with Miss Parish and his counselor (who also happened to be a White woman) illustrated the uphill battle that Latino students often face in school. The counselor needed a mound of evidence to even consider that Armando was smart enough to be placed in the honors program. Beyond his test scores, grades, and a teacher's backing, the fact that Armando spoke "differently" from other young men also mattered. Echoing the research by Victor Rios, Latino young men like Armando must go above and beyond to prove their nondelinquency to White school authorities who assume the worst about them without bothering to get to know them.[23] "Looking back, Miss Parish—she was a White lady—I think she was kind of racist," Armando said. "There were other kids in her class who were smart, and she put them in regular classes. For those of us in honors, we had to fight for it." Armando's educational experience was very much unlike the Filipino gay men who said they were "automatically" placed into honors.

By the time he was in high school, Armando was certain that he was gay, and he doubled down on his efforts at school. His situation at home worsened. Armando witnessed physical altercations between his older brother Gustavo and his parents, and his parents' marital problems escalated to the point of violence. "All those things combined, and then with me subconsciously knowing that I was gay, and knowing my parents were probably not going to be okay with it, that's when school became my big focus," he said. "School was my way out of this madhouse."

Embracing academics in high school granted Armando more opportunities for escape. He attended a high school that was predominantly Latinx (85 percent), with a sprinkling of Asian American students (15 percent). Even though Latinxs were the majority, their representation in the honors and AP courses was disproportionately low. Still, because of Mrs. Trujillo, Armando knew how to advocate for himself to be in the advanced academic track. "I was usually one of, like, four Brown kids in the honors track, and the rest of the kids were all Asian," he said. By being labeled one of the "smart Latinos," Armando had access to activities and opportunities that distracted him from the struggles he was facing with his sexuality. One year he participated in the Upward Bound program, which allowed him to spend his summer months in Northern California. Another year he was selected by his teachers for a summer internship working at the state capitol in Sacramento. Another year he spent several weeks touring colleges along the East Coast. Armando was cognizant that each accomplishment inched him closer to his ultimate goal: to move as far away from his family as possible so that he could "finally explore" his gay identity.

Adopting academic covering came at a cost, however. Armando felt like his academic identity pulled him farther away from his Latino classmates. Being part of the advanced track in high school shaped who was part of Armando's social circle. "I tended to identify more with the Asian kids than the Latino kids, especially as I went further in high school, because I was in the honors track," he said. "No one really talked shit, but people always described me as the kid who was always hanging out with all the Asians. I felt like something was wrong with me because I had no Latino friends. I felt like I was Asian-washed." Beyond their academic connection, his Asian American friends influenced his cultural tastes too. "I'm Mexican, but I started watching *Dragon Ball Z*, wearing baggy pants, and I was even spiking my hair and dyeing it with frosted tips."

Even Armando's parents played a role in shaping his high school social circle. Because his older brother Gustavo had fallen into the wrong crowd during high school, his parents were much stricter with Armando. "For the longest time, my parents never let me go to anyone's house because they were really overprotective," he recalled. "I didn't go to parties. I didn't go to kickbacks. I didn't do drugs. They didn't want me to follow through the same kind of stuff my older brother did." Yet when it came to Armando's Asian American friends, his parents' rules went out the window. Unlike with his brother's friends, Armando's friends were allowed in the house. His mother was always hospitable whenever they came over. She would offer them water, soda, and arroz con pollo if it was dinnertime. As Armando remembered, "My parents loved my Asian friends because they thought they were all very school oriented. When they would come over, my parents would say, 'Oh they're good people. You're hanging out with a good crowd.'"

While Armando's parents were welcoming of his Asian American friends, the reception wasn't immediately reciprocated when he visited those friends' homes to study. "A lot of my friends were Asian girls," he said. "Their parents were a little wary of me because I was Mexican." The parents of his Asian American friends were suspicious about Armando's intentions—they worried that he might get them pregnant. In the process of reassuring their parents, the girls all but outed Armando to prove that he wasn't like the *other* Mexicans. "They had to convince their parents that it was okay for me to come over and study because we were *really* going to study. They'd be like, 'Mom, Dad, we are going to do calculus. Plus, he's gay.' Okay, no, they didn't say *that*, but they basically implied it." Armando's Asian American friends used his queerness as way to offset the negative stereotypes their parents held about Mexican American young men. Their perception of gay men as "effeminate and weak" offset their stereotype of Latino young men being threatening.[24] On another level, Armando's experience illustrates how his access to academic support—in this case, the ability to be part of a study group with the other honors and AP students—depended on his ability to demarcate himself from the "typical" Mexican American boys at his school.

The Limits of Academic Covering

For young men like Armando, Franklin, Jerald, and Manny, academic covering served a function. Investing in their educational lives provided a short-term escape from classmates and family members who marginalized them. By leaning into their academic identities, they had an alternative to the constant feeling of otherness. Excelling in school drew attention away from their bourgeoning gay sexuality, and it also became an insurance plan of sorts: being an excellent student could buffer the blow their immigrant parents might feel upon learning they had a gay son. If it didn't, then their academic achievements might help them escape a hostile living situation: Armando was able to travel almost three thousand miles away to attend Georgetown University, and Franklin and Manny both moved an hour away from their hometowns to attend UCLA. Though Jerald didn't move out on his own after high school, his nursing program gave him a legitimate reason to maintain a healthy distance from his family. These young men knew that doing well in high school would grant them admission to college, where they would have the autonomy to embrace who they "really" were. When I asked Franklin why he opted not to come out in high school given the support he had, he responded, "I figured, I'll just wait till college to explore my sexuality."

The problem with academic covering was that it was an individual-level strategy. The ability of Armando, Franklin, Jerald, and Manny to survive their middle school and high school years did nothing to transform the heteronormative aspects of the institutions they attended. Their teachers and classmates weren't suddenly less homophobic (or less racist, in Armando's case), nor did they commit themselves to transforming the school environment for other LGBTQ students. LGBTQ history and perspectives remained absent from the classroom curriculum, homophobic remarks continued to be said under teachers' watches, and the heteronormative rituals of high school, such as school dances and proms, were never interrogated. In short, their individual success stories didn't facilitate institutional change.

In fact, these instances of engaging in academic covering were predicated on the young men's ability to capitalize on racial stereotypes. Filipino American gay men who leaned into their schoolboy personas were benefiting from the model minority stereotype associated with Asian Americans. In contrast, Latino gay men who adopted this strategy had to distance themselves from negative stereotypes associated with other Latinos at their schools. At no point did any of the men who engaged in academic covering receive any significant support from teachers or counselors that was directly related to their sexuality. If anything, leaning into academic excellence as a survival strategy reinforced their belief that social acceptance—among teachers, classmates, and family members— was, at best, conditional.

Manny's story is a case in point. By his senior year of high school, he was in position to be the class valedictorian. Beyond having the highest grade point average in the school, he was well liked by his classmates, who elected him class president for all four years of high school. Outside his school life, however, Manny had a secret: shortly after being elected senior class president, he began dating Angelo, a junior from a nearby high school whom he had met on social media.

Excited about his new relationship, Manny began posting pictures of himself and his new boyfriend on an Instagram account he kept hidden from his classmates. Somehow though, one of these classmates came across a picture of Manny and Angelo sharing a kiss and took a screenshot. Within a day the photograph of Manny kissing his boyfriend was circulating around the student body via text message.

"That shit went fucking viral," Manny said, still traumatized by the incident. "People would bring out their cell phones and show it to others and say, 'OMG, Manny's gay!' People would bring it up on their computers."

"Did the teachers say or do anything?" I asked.

"They knew, but they didn't say anything."

After news of his sexuality spread like wildfire, Manny felt that everyone abandoned him. "I kind of fell into a depression," he said. "I just didn't want to be at school. And then my relationship went down the drain."

This was the moment when the people designated to protect Manny should've intervened. And yet, Manny's teachers, counselors, and supposed friends did nothing. With one Instagram post, the house of cards that Manny had built to distract everyone from his sexuality came tumbling down. All of a sudden it didn't matter that he was valedictorian or that he was the senior class president. It felt like the revelation of his sexuality got him canceled in the eyes of everyone who had once supported him at school.

Educators trained on how to support LGBTQ students would've prevented the harm Manny experienced. School officials could've reprimanded the students who circulated the screenshot in malicious ways. A teacher or counselor could've spoken directly with Manny about the struggles he was facing at home regarding his sexuality. They could've offered counseling. They could've reassured Manny that his newfound love was something worth celebrating, not something to feel ashamed about. Instead, Manny ended up ditching school for much of his senior year. He moved out of his parents' house. He became depressed.

"I would sleep over at UCI where my sister was attending college," Manny said. "I would skip school and just stay there because it was hard to go. It was hard to go to school and face people who were whispering about me behind my back. Some of the teachers were being a little homophobic. I just felt like a really big embarrassment."

Within a few months, Manny would have the chance to move far away from everyone he knew in high school. He would be attending UCLA, and he would have the chance to start a new life—on his own terms, openly gay. When I had the chance to sit down with Manny, he was wrapping up his first year of college. He was excited about having started a new chapter in his life, but uneasy about the fact that he would soon be vacating his dorm and spending his summer months back at his parents' house, a place that no longer felt like home.

4

Escaping to College

When the time came for me to apply to college, I kept everything a secret from my grandparents. I simply forged their signatures and sent the packet off. . . . When I received the notification of acceptance, I clasped the letter to my chest, feeling my heart implode. Finally, I had my ticket out.

—Rigoberto González, *Butterfly Boy: Memories of a Chicano Mariposa*

Omar Reynaga (b. 1981), a Mexican American counselor at a Latino LGBTQ advocacy organization, saw college as his chance to move out of Pasadena, California. Although the city evokes images of sprawling homes, White wealth, and Rose Parades, Omar joked that he was from the "slums of Pasadena," the part of the city where gang activity and drug dealing were omnipresent. In his neighborhood, being a young Latino man meant being typecast as a gang member. When he was in high school, Omar did everything in his power to distance himself from this stereotype. He was in every honors and advanced placement (AP) class and he earned top grades; he was the head of student government, a varsity member of the tennis team, and the editor of the yearbook. Part of his motivation had to do with his need for "protection" and "not wanting to feel threatened" by classmates who bullied him for being effeminate and hanging out mostly with girls; his academic and extracurricular life felt like a barrier against the bullying. Academic covering was Omar's strategy for escaping this chapter of his life.

There was one specific incident, Omar confessed, that convinced him he needed to move as far away as possible for college. During high school, he had a classmate, Narek, who teased him relentlessly from the time he was a freshman. Whenever they would cross paths, Narek would call him a *gyot*, the Armenian equivalent of "faggot." Each time he did,

Omar tried to brush it off. But by his senior year, Omar grew tired of the harassment and retaliated.

As the editor of the yearbook, Omar took the liberty of changing Narek's senior quote to read "I am a gyot." When the yearbook came out, Narek saw what Omar had done, and in the middle of class, physically assaulted him. The teachers, unaware of the ongoing harassment Omar had endured, took Narek's side. Omar had been slated to be the keynote speaker for the upcoming graduation ceremony, but the principal stripped him of that honor. In an instant, everything he had worked for in high school seemed like it no longer mattered. He felt abandoned by the same school officials who had supported him the past four years.

"I really wanted to get the hell out of here," Omar said. By then, he had received acceptances from several colleges, including Pepperdine University and four campuses in the University of California system— Irvine, Los Angeles, Riverside, and Santa Barbara. Everyone expected him to attend UCLA, but he opted for UC Santa Barbara. "Santa Barbara was far enough away for me. To get away from my neighborhood. To get away from my parents. To get away from the drama at school. I said I did it for the academics, but I really needed to get space and grow socially."

Omar's decision-making process illustrates how sexuality can affect the higher education pathways of second-generation gay men. While sexuality may not have been the only driving force to pursue higher education, it influenced many of the decisions these men made during their college years. They saw college as a means to an end: a way to carve out independence from the heteronormative family and friend circles they felt trapped by. For many, their college years were their first opportunity to break free of the social circles and daily routines they'd known since childhood. No longer would there be a predetermined schedule of what time to go to school, which friends to hang out with, or what time to come home.

As I was writing this chapter, I happened to be reading *No Ashes in the Fire*, a memoir by Black queer writer and activist Darnell Moore.

I came across a passage that captures the connection between higher education and queerness expressed by the men I interviewed:

> Graduating from high school was a necessary goal, but only so I could be free. Free to explore the world outside the alley-like streets I knew as home. Free to recreate myself into a young man bestowed with the gift of magic and not the burden that comes with the curse of pretending. Free so I would no longer need to act my way through the awkward popularity contests high schoolers create to survive scrutiny by peers. . . . I knew if I was going to live life on my own terms, it would have to be away from what I knew and away from the cage of cliched expectations, so I applied.[1]

The narratives of Omar Reynaga and Darnell Moore reveal how gay people of color can grow exhausted of the identities they have meticulously curated. By going off to college, especially to a campus that was far from everyone they knew, they have an opportunity to reinvent themselves—in a new place, with a new social network. With this newfound autonomy, the men I interviewed felt they could more freely explore their sexuality.[2]

It's worth noting that the men I spoke to were a highly selective group with respect to educational attainment. At the time of my interviews, around 85 percent of them were en route to finishing, or had already earned, their bachelor's degrees. In comparison, a study by the Williams Institute at the UCLA School of Law reported that 15 percent of LGBTQ Latinxs and 42 percent of LGBTQ Asian Americans and Pacific Islanders had graduated from college.[3] The men I interviewed who grew up in middle and upper middle class households and neighborhoods enjoyed certain privileges that facilitated their pathway to college. They attended well-resourced high schools where teachers and peers expected them to attend four-year universities. Their family's economic survival didn't depend on them entering the workforce full-time right out of high school. Their parents were college educated and had the financial means to pay for books, school supplies, computers, and college application fees.[4]

Omar and other working-class gay men who pursued college didn't share these privileges. Many had parents who hadn't finished high school and had grown up in households that were living paycheck-to-paycheck. But, as noted in previous chapter, these men benefited from having extraordinarily supportive teachers and counselors of color who helped them navigate the grueling college application process and secure financial aid. Many participated in extracurricular activities (e.g., student government, science clubs, speech and debate teams) and educational outreach programs (e.g., AVID: Advancement via Individual Determination or Upward Bound) with college-going cultures.[5] About one-tenth of the men did not pursue higher education. For these men, their queer explorations after high school took place in other arenas—at queer POC neighborhood parties (also known as T-parties), gay POC bars and clubs, and LGBTQ social networking sites—which I will discuss further in the next chapter.

Off to College

Arvin Salonga (b. 1982), a Filipino American community college counselor, spoke to me about the role that distance played in his decision of where to attend college. When Arvin was a senior in high school, he chose to attend UCLA, which was about twenty-five miles north of his hometown of Carson, a middle-class, racially diverse suburb that sits between Los Angeles and Long Beach. Even though his new campus was relatively close to home, Arvin joked that LA traffic provided an extra layer of protection between him and his tight-knit, gossipy Filipino family. When he moved to Westwood Village, it felt worlds apart from his old life in Carson. During rush hour, the commute could take up to two hours or more, which made it unlikely for his parents to drop in for a surprise visit and catch him "doing something gay."

Arvin was eleven when he knew he was attracted to men, but within his large extended family and friendship network in Carson, he felt Filipinos had to fit certain tropes of masculinity. Most of his Filipino male cousins and friends played basketball. Their clothing tastes aligned with an aesthetic popular among Black hip-hop artists: baggy pants, sports jerseys, mint condition Nike sneakers. Most of them had had girlfriends, and those that didn't passed the time pursuing girls. "In my family, you learned how to 'do' masculinity from the older [male] cousins," Arvin said. "They policed my behavior. They'd say, 'Why are you talking like that?' if I said something really femme." Beyond the anxiousness he felt among his cousins to adhere to the rules of masculinity, he also felt pressure from his grandmother to be straight. "My grandma would ask me when I'd get married [to a woman], and she even had a gay son!" he recalled. "Because I'm her favorite, she'd even say to me, 'You need to have kids before I die.'"

As much as he loved his family, Arvin knew he needed to leave in order to explore who he really was. Moving from his multigenerational household in Carson to the dorms of Westwood Village allowed him the freedom to stop pretending. "When I first got to college, I made the decision to not claim 'straight,'" he explained. It would be a few months before he would come out to his college friends as gay, but he remembered feeling lighter the moment he stopped trying to pass as heterosexual.

I interviewed several second-generation gay men who traveled much farther than Arvin to feel this same freedom. Some of the men grew up outside the Greater Los Angeles Area—in the San Francisco Bay Area, the Central Valley, San Diego, and as far away as the East Coast. Bernardo Lopez (b. 1993), a Mexican American college student, grew up in a low-income neighborhood in Bakersfield where "everyone knew everyone's business." In high school most of his male friends were becoming sexually active; he wondered why he lacked the sexual drive that seemed to be at the forefront of their minds. He hadn't realized how much he'd been suppressing his sexuality until he received his college acceptance letters. "Everything changed once I got into UCLA," he said. "I figured this is the time to [explore my queer sexuality], since I'm away from home." Michael Garibay, a Filipino American student at UCLA, relocated to Southern California from New Jersey so he could untether from family

and friends and explore his sexuality. In high school he hadn't yet figured out if he was gay or bisexual, and he thought moving across the
country for college would allow him to sort it out. "I wasn't really out to
my parents at the time," Michael said. "I felt that being somewhere far,
I could at least mull over [my sexuality] on my own while getting an
education." This was a major reason he chose to attend UCLA.

Some of the LA transplants spoke about their need to escape the conservative environment of their families and communities. Aldo Quijano
(b. 1985), a Filipino American graphic designer, grew up in the farm-
worker community in Delano, in the Central Valley. For his entire life
his family had been part of a Catholic parish and rosary group that was
"extremely conservative." The priests and parishioners would regularly
denounce homosexuality, same-sex marriage, birth control, and abor-
tion during Mass and even in casual conversations. "I felt like going
to a college in LA, where people would be more liberal than the
Central Valley," Aldo said. This was what drove him to attend California State Polytechnic University–Pomona, located about thirty miles
east of Downtown LA. Julio Marín (b. 1991), a Mexican American
medical student, grew up in Bakersfield, a suburb that "moves at a rural
pace [and] values rural culture."[6] He grew up in a predominantly Latinx
community, but spent his teenage years shuttling his disabled mother to
doctor's appointments in the other side of Bakersfield, which was "very
conservative, very Republican, very White, and very well-off." The con-
servativeness of the Central Valley was a big reason he chose to attend
college in Los Angeles.

For Phil Rosario (b. 1979), a Filipino American small business owner,
moving to LA for college wasn't about escaping a conservative family
or community; it was about untethering from the image he had manufactured within the Filipino American student activist community (as a
cover for his sexuality). In high school and in his first year of college at
San Francisco State University, he was a leader for the Filipino American
student organizations. He spearheaded social events, coordinated guest
speakers from the local Filipino community, and helped organize on

behalf of Filipino veterans who had served in World War II but still hadn't received government benefits.

"It was a whole scene—the Filipino scene—everyone knew me," Phil said. "Even though there were gay people in college, who sometimes asked me if I was gay, I'd deny it and people would defend me and say, 'No, he's not gay.' I felt like I was lying to people, and that made me feel bad. I knew I had to leave." The pressure to maintain his public image as a Filipino student leader became overwhelming, especially because most of the other Filipino men in the organization were straight. He filled out a transfer application for California State University–Fullerton, located about forty miles southwest of Downtown. "I just couldn't do it any-more," he told me, "And so, I made a plan to come to LA. I packed up my stuff in December, and I told my parents I was leaving." After the holidays, in his first year of college, Phil moved to Fullerton, months before he knew for sure that he would be accepted as a transfer student. Once he was accepted, he was thrilled to be starting life at a new campus where not a single person knew who he was.

Of course, not everyone has the means or opportunity to move out of his hometown for college. Eugene Torres, the Filipino American gradu-ate student whose story opened chapter 3, dreamed of moving to North-ern California to attend UC Santa Cruz. Eugene grew up in a Filipino Evangelical Christian family that had a fundamentalist interpretation of the Bible. "Our church was very fire and brimstone," he explained. "Being gay, I felt like I was perpetually sinning because in the Bible it says I'm not supposed to be, and it's an abomination. The fact that I knew it was an abomination at age eight was very telling of how our family's church was." Moving away to UC Santa Cruz was supposed to be his exit strategy, but unfortunately, even with financial aid, his mother—herself a single parent—couldn't afford to send him. "My mom didn't have enough money for me to go. UC Santa Cruz was the most expensive UC [campus] for housing, so it made more economical sense to go to com-munity college, right across the street from my house." Despite having been accepted to UC Santa Cruz and several other universities, Eugene opted to attend El Camino College in Torrance.

Even though Eugene was unable to relocate to Northern California, community college allowed him to explore his queerness in ways that felt impossible in high school. "High school was a very self-contained area, and rumors, even pre-internet on cell phones, moved pretty fast," he said. "At community college, no one really cares, so rumors never move that fast. It felt safer to come out in college." While attending El Camino, Eugene started dating without worrying about being questioned by his mother; when he was on dates, she assumed he was in a night class or studying. Unlike high school, his classes met just three times a week, and so he had more opportunities to meet up with other gay men for coffee or drinks. His campus may have been next door to where he grew up, but his social life there felt worlds apart from his family and the high school friends he hadn't yet spoken to about his sexuality.

Regardless of where they went to school, college granted second-generation gay men more opportunities to explore their sexuality and sexual identity. In the process, they reconceptualized their understandings of family and community. To put it another way, sometimes they had to *leave* home to *find* home.

The Unbearable Whiteness of Gay Spaces

Given that many of the gay men I interviewed went off to college to explore their sexuality, one might think that their first stop on campus would've been the university's LGBTQ student center (often called a Pride Center) or a gay student organization. For the most part, this was not the case for Filipino and Latino gay men, especially if they attended historically White colleges and universities.[7] When we got to talking about their college years, I asked them whether they'd attended meetings or events sponsored by their campus Pride Centers. These were some of their responses:

[The people at the Pride Center] just never really felt like my kind of people. (Edwin Perez, Salvadoran American media strategist)

There's this idea that White queers, specifically male individuals, are at the pinnacle. They're really just neglecting a lot of the issues that a lot of people of color face. (Julio Marín, Mexican American medical student)

I'd go in there, and everyone was White. To be honest, no one would ever talk to me. (Manny Roldan, Filipino American college student)

Although Edwin, Julio, and Manny attended different universities at different times, they shared a common experience when setting foot into a campus Pride Center: exclusion. The people who frequented the center and led the student organizations housed within them were mostly White, a stark contrast from the racial makeup of the neighborhoods and schools where my interviewees had spent their years before college. The culture shock of being in a predominantly White space deterred them from forming meaningful connections with other gay students at Pride Centers and in gay student organizations.[8] To borrow the words of sociologist Victor Ray, campus gay spaces were "racialized organizations" where Edwin, Julio, and Manny saw Whiteness as a necessary "credential" for membership.[9]

Some men spoke about the class differences they felt when in the presence of White gay students on campus. Armando Garza grew up in a working-class Latinx neighborhood in El Monte and attended Georgetown University, a predominantly White private college whose tuition was at that time about $30,000 a year (in 2022, the tuition is nearly twice that amount). He was on a full scholarship, but many of his classmates came from families that were wealthy enough to pay out of pocket. In his first year, he went to a meeting for one of the gay student clubs, and he felt the class differences right away. "I just didn't really feel welcome," he said. "A lot of them were rich White kids. They talked about not fitting in because they were gay, but they were still rich and White. It felt like they were looking at me because my jeans were baggy, and I wasn't wearing designer jeans like them." Armando's remarks illustrated how class identity on campus was so closely tied to racial identity: the White students were wealthy and the Brown students were broke.

For Armando, the racial and class distinctions he internalized influenced his interactions with the gay community beyond the Georgetown campus. Whereas his White classmates were socializing with other upper-class White gay men at predominantly White gay bars, he felt more comfortable in gay scenes where Latino gay men and other men of color comprised a majority of patrons. "I wasn't getting prettied up to go to the bougie White gay club in DuPont Circle," he said. "I didn't go to that. I would go to the Latino gay club that's a hole in the wall, and it's all these undocumented immigrants from Latin America. That was my scene. That was what I preferred. I wasn't with the uppity, rich White kids that were sucking cock on Capitol Hill."

Having grown up in a close-knit Latinx family and community in LA, Armando hoped that moving across the country would allow him the space he needed to explore his gay identity and become part of a gay community. Instead, the Whiteness and wealth of the gay students at Georgetown prompted him to lean into his racial identity. "TV was the only exposure I had to White people before then," he explained. Back in LA, he'd spent most of his time around other children of immigrants, many of whom were hyperconscious of how their actions—good or bad—were a reflection of their ethnic and racial communities, as well as their immigrant families. As he put it, "If I mess up, it'll make all Mexicans look bad." At Georgetown he was awestruck by the freedom and privilege with which his White classmates—including his White gay classmates—lived. Whereas Armando felt the pressure to maintain a level of respectability as one of the few Mexican American men on campus, his White gay classmates had the freedom to flaunt their sexual proclivities without consequence. Observing these differences on a daily basis affected how he related to his sexual and racial identities. "They [White gay men] were a different thing. I felt more Latino than gay."

Attending a more racially diverse college didn't preclude the other gay men I interviewed from experiencing what Armando had at a predominantly White campus. Bernardo Zamora (b. 1993), a Mexican American college student, moved fifty miles southeast from a low-income Latinx neighborhood in Oxnard to attend UCLA. When he entered college in 2010, the majority of the undergraduates were students of color: Asian Americans and Pacific Islanders (37 percent), Latinxs (16 percent), and African Americans (4 percent) collectively made up over half of the student population.[10] Yet when he attended an LGBTQ student center event, he noticed that the "main" gay student organization was mostly White, and queer students of color had their own, ethnic-specific, organizations. "I don't go to that space," Bernardo said in reference to the organization whose membership was mostly White. "There's a lot of ignorance there."

"Ignorance in terms of—?" I asked.

"People of color stuff."

Bernardo entered college just two years after California voters passed Proposition 8, the infamous ballot initiative that defined marriage as between one man and one woman. Ultimately, Proposition 8 was struck down by a federal court a month before his freshman year of college, but marriage equality was still at the forefront of people's minds on campus, especially among White gay students he met. Bernardo didn't shy away from critiquing the White gay students who seemed to only care about same-sex marriage while ignoring social and political issues that felt more urgent among LGBTQ people of color. "I hear them talk about politics and what we should be advocating for, and everyone was talking about marriage," he said. "Well, what about job discrimination? And people getting fired for being queer? What about undocumented queer folks? Homelessness? I feel like [marriage equality] shouldn't be the whole focus. I feel like that's a very middle-class White folks' focus. I feel like once that's granted, they'll step away, and they'll leave the rest of us [queer POC] to pick up ourselves."

Bernardo grew up poor, in a low-income mobile home community where young people worried more about police presence than school. During elementary school and junior high, he switched schools more times than he could count because his parents were separated, had difficulties making ends meet, and were regularly evicted from their homes. When he was in high school, he earned good grades, but had no intentions of going to college—that is, until one of his counselors took it upon herself to pay for his college applications and SAT exams out of her own pocket. Although his interactions with his teachers were positive, he still remembered how poorly other Latinx students were treated at his same school. "I would stop by my cousin's classroom to drop something off, and I'd see the environment he was in," he said. "The teacher's knocked out, there were students smoking [weed] in the back of the room, and then my cousin is laughing in the corner with the other guys and there's girls in the front doing their makeup. Not in homeroom. In an *actual* class, like English." Even though Bernardo struggled with his sexuality, being gay was hardly his only source of stress. This is to say, marriage was the absolute last thing he ever worried about as a gay man who was also Latino and low income.[11]

Bernardo's resistance to the middle-class concerns of his White gay peers in college had much to do too with a traumatizing experience he once had with his father, the parent to whom he was much closer. After Bernardo had spent a weekend in Oxnard, his father offered to drive him back to campus. At the halfway point, they stopped at a McDonald's, and Bernardo noticed his father was being especially inquisitive about his personal life. Bernardo assumed his father was hinting for him to come out. He had seen his father be friendly with gay people in the past, so he decided to tell him. To Bernardo's surprise, his father became enraged in the middle of the McDonald's.

"What about the Bible?" his father yelled, in Spanish. "Marriage is between a man and a woman! God's going to punish you for this." His tirade jolted the other customers, who turned to see what the commotion was about.

Bernardo did his best to maintain his composure. "I respect your opinion as of now because I know you don't know what I know," he said, calmly. "I'm not going to speak above you."

"Fuck you!" his father screamed back before storming out of the McDonald's.

When Bernardo walked outside, he saw that his father had thrown his backpack and travel bag out of the car. He picked up his belongings and ran to the sidewalk.

"I thought he was gonna run me over. He just drove away, and I didn't know where he went." Bernardo tried calling his mother, but she was with her boyfriend and so didn't offer to pick him up. He had no choice but to phone a friend at school, who drove thirty miles from UCLA to pick him up.

At the time of our conversation, a year and a half had elapsed since this incident had happened. Bernardo and his father hadn't spoken since. After he shared this story, it made sense why Bernardo didn't care about same-sex marriage. Marriage equality was the least of his problems. Had this fight with his father happened a year earlier than it did, when Bernardo was still in high school, he would've been homeless. Fortunately, he was on full financial aid and had a dorm where he could weather the storm.

* * *

Pride Centers and gay student organizations weren't the only campus spaces where the men I interviewed observed differences between themselves and their White gay counterparts. Franklin Flores, a friend and classmate of Bernardo's at UCLA, discovered these differences when he started dating River, a "tall White guy" from UC Berkeley. Franklin met River at a student government conference for undergraduates across the UC campuses. Although they lived hundreds of miles apart from each other, the relationship gave Franklin a "sense of security." Despite the distance, River found creative ways to express his affection. On Franklin's birthday, for example, he arranged for one of Franklin's favorite YouTube singers to send him a personalized video greeting. "I loved him, I did," Franklin admitted. "I thought he was a really great guy, even if I thought he was way too into PDA [public displays of affection]." Having only been out a year or so, Franklin wasn't yet at a place where he could reciprocate River's gestures, but he appreciated him, nevertheless.

The freedom with which River embraced his sexuality reminded Franklin of the White boys back in high school who were part of the color guard team. When he first saw them, he was envious. "I admired those guys who were dancing on color guard," he said. Sometime after that, Franklin became conscious of the latitude that Whiteness affords, in terms of sexuality and gender expression.

And therein lay the problem with River. Franklin, of course, didn't mind River's unapologetic embracing of his sexuality; what Franklin did mind was how unaware his White boyfriend was about the other struggles he faced in terms of race and class. Even though he was seventy miles away from his hometown of Riverside, Franklin carried his family's troubles with him. During middle school, his family bounced from apartment to hotel to apartment after each inevitable eviction. During high school, his father left the United States for "vacation" but ended up staying permanently, leaving his disabled mother as the sole guardian of him and his sister. Her disability made it difficult to make ends meet. When Franklin and his sister moved away to college, his mother had to give up their apartment and rent a room just to stay afloat.

As Franklin came to know River, it became harder to ignore the lightness with which he lived. River was gay, but he was still White, and with each passing month in their relationship, his privilege became more apparent.

Franklin recounted the time he accompanied River to visit his mother in San Diego. "He went to his mom's house, and I would make cookies with her," he recounted. "I kept thinking, 'This is fucking weird.' I would never. I don't even have a home to take [him] to. I told him, 'I am not even out to my mom, so I am not going to take you to meet my mom.'" What bothered Franklin wasn't so much that River was open about his sexuality to this mother; it was more that he sensed River felt his family was superior to his because of this fact. For young men of color like

Franklin facing racism and socioeconomic struggles, the potential fall-out of coming out is not the same.

At one point, it felt like River was trying to push Franklin out of the closet. On Valentine's Day, River penned a love letter chronicling the first day they met and other milestones in their eleven-month relation-ship. He emailed the editors of the UCLA student newspaper and asked them to publish the letter as a surprise. Franklin was not thrilled. "I was so fucking surprised," he said. "I wake up to an envelope under my door, and it's a note that says, 'Have you seen the paper today?' And I was like, Okay, what is this?"

Franklin left his dorm and scurried to find a copy of the newspaper. When he picked it up, he was horrified to find River's letter to him printed on the front page. "He didn't tell me," he said. "And this is what pissed me off too. It even had a picture. A fucking drawing of us. On the front page of the paper." Shortly after Valentine's Day, Franklin broke it off with River. "He was so White and privileged. I realized I couldn't be with him because we were in different places."

Throughout his teenage years, Franklin had imagined college as the chapter of his life where he could embrace his sexual identity without fear. His relationship with River was part of that project. But like many of the second-generation gay men I interviewed, Franklin also learned that the "gay community" doesn't always feel like a community at all. These men of color and White gay men may share a sexual identity, but when they occupy the same space—even a space as close as a romantic relationship—they can still feel worlds apart.

The Pressure to Choose Identities

Many of the second-generation gay men I interviewed spoke about the "culture shock" they experienced when starting college. Most hailed from neighborhoods and schools where people of color comprised the majority of the student body. Most were the first in their family to go to college. Among Latinos, having parents who had not gone past high school (or even elementary school) was not uncommon; they were mostly first-generation college students. Among Filipinos, many had parents with college degrees, but from universities in the Philippines. As education scholar Tracy Buenavista argues, these "1.5-generation" college students share commonalities with those who are first generation, including their unfamiliarity with the college application process and college-going culture in the United States.[12]

Both the Filipino and Latino men I interviewed said stepping onto a college campus—even ones that were racially diverse—felt like walking into a sea of Whiteness. Sociologist Erica Morales writes that college campuses with racially diverse populations may still be "traditionally rooted in Whiteness, reflecting White values and norms."[13] For example, at many of the California State University and UC campuses, students of color make up the majority of students; and yet, this diversity is not at all reflected in the faculty and administrators, who tend to be predominantly White. Another example is the classroom curriculum. With the exception of ethnic studies programs, most college majors center the research and writing of White male scholars. By default, college students of color are marginalized within higher education by the Whiteness of its power structure.

This is why student of color spaces mattered for many of the men I interviewed.[14] They noted that their first point of connection with the university came by way of student organizations or programs established to support underrepresented students. Filipinos made their way to the booths of the Filipino American student groups during orientation week and signed up for "big sibling" programs in which they'd be mentored by Filipino American juniors and seniors. This being Southern California, the campuses they attended had organizations catering to specific interests—Filipino American fraternities and sororities, preprofessional societies, traditional and hip-hop dance troupes, and activist groups.[15] Similarly, Latinos spoke about being introduced to such groups in their first year. Several were active members of MEChA, the Movimiento Estudiantil Chicano de Aztlán, which focuses on political mobilization, racial justice, and the educational empowerment of Chicano and Latino students. Others joined Latino fraternities and other brotherhood organizations. Many said their point of entry into the Latino community in college came by way of summer bridge and educational outreach programs for students of color who were the first in their families to attend college.[16] More informally, Filipinos and Latinos said that they gravitated to the Brown students and other students of color they met in their classes, dorms, dining halls, and other social spots on campus—an affinity they didn't instinctually feel with the White gay students and White gay spaces at school.

While the men agreed that student of color organizations and spaces were important, they acknowledged that they weren't always welcoming of all members of the ethnic community. Within these collectives, there were unwritten rules for who belonged and who did not. Walking into a Filipino club meeting was harder for the Filipinos who grew up in predominantly White neighborhoods, instead of one of the "typical" Filipino communities in Carson, Eagle Rock, or West Covina. Setting foot into a Latinx social event was more intimidating for the Latinxs who couldn't at least understand Spanish or were unfamiliar with musical genres from Mexico and Latin America. Filipinos and Latinos who were of multiracial heritage worried about fitting in because members of the organization might not immediately recognize that they were Filipino or Latino. On paper, student of color spaces celebrated inclusivity; however, for those whose stories didn't align with other members of the group, these spaces could also feel cliquey and uninviting.

For some, being gay was another factor that affected their sense of belonging within student of color organizations. This was especially true among those who attended college during the mid-1990s through the mid-aughts—a period some described as "less accepting" of gay people. According to the men who were in college at this time, student of color spaces weren't necessarily a safe haven for LGBTQ people of color.

The late historian Dawn Mabalon was a prominent member of the UCLA Filipino American student and alumni community in the 1990s. In 1995, she published an article in the *Daily Bruin* about the homophobic climate of student of color spaces on campus. At the time, Mabalon was working for the Filipino American retention center—which was located next to the retention centers for African American, Chicano/Latino, Native American, and Southeast Asian undergraduates—when she overheard a conversation between two men of color. "You know, when I see two men kissing each other, I just feel like throwing up," one of the men said. The other man nodded in agreement. "It's like, it's just not right, not natural. It makes me sick," he added. When Mabalon heard the exchange, she felt embarrassed and ashamed. "What if queer students who utilized the services of our retention projects had been within earshot?" she wrote. "I would surely never come back to a non-queer-friendly program. Additionally, the comments seemed to refuse to acknowledge the existence of queers of color, and [implied] that the only gay, lesbian, and bisexual people are the White ones in West Hollywood."[17]

Mabalon called out her Filipino American peers for their unwillingness to consider the intersectional identities of some of their community members: "Some Pilipinos even take personal offense at the mere existence of their queer brothers and sisters, as if coming out of the closet and identifying themselves as gays, lesbians, and bisexuals would somehow signal a break from the Pilipino community, as if they are saying, 'I am now gay, and no longer Pilipino.' Nothing could be further from the truth."[18]

Unfortunately, some Filipino Americans who were in college around this time felt it was difficult to embrace both their racial and sexual identities within student of color organizations for all the reasons Mabalon cited. The summer before Aldo Quijano moved to Southern California to attend Cal Poly Pomona, he connected with Filipino Americans at the campus through MySpace, a social networking site popular in the early 2000s. One of the first people he met on the site was Joey, who happened to be one of the leaders of Barkada, the Filipino American student organization (*barkada* is the Tagalog word for "friendship"). When Aldo arrived on campus, Joey invited him to attend Barkada meetings and social events. For the first few weeks of their friendship, Aldo assumed that Joey was straight. "I didn't know he was gay," Aldo explained. "I didn't know anyone else was gay in that organization."

It wasn't until Joey invited Aldo to a hangout at his apartment that he learned that he—and a few other members of Barkada—were gay. "I went to the party at his apartment and noticed that it was all guys," Aldo said. "I was like, Where are the girls?" When the guys at the party started dancing and flirting with each other, Aldo put two and two together. The party at Joey's apartment was the first time Aldo had ever met gay people who were also Filipino. After that night, Aldo began spending more time with Joey and the other Filipinos he met. They would trek to West Hollywood every Friday to attend GAMeboi, a weekly club event catering to Asian American gay men. On Saturdays and Sundays, they would be at Ozz, a club in Orange County geared toward queer men and women of color.

Through his friendship with Joey, Aldo became more comfortable with his own sexuality. He noticed, however, that when they were in the presence of other members of Barkada, Joey and the other gay Filipinos kept a tight lip about their weekend treks to the gay clubs. Although Aldo never heard anyone in Barkada say anything outright homophobic, their collective silence let him know that in that space it wasn't necessarily okay to be openly gay. He and other gay members felt they had to keep their gay lives a secret in order to maintain their social standing within the group. Within the Filipino American community, Aldo, Joey, and other gay members felt compelled to maintain what sociologist Marcus Hunter has described as "up-down identities," a "conceptualization of self . . . best captured by connecting the two identities with the word *then*."[19] Because Barkada wasn't a space where intersectional identities were understood, they saw themselves as Filipino-*then*-gay, privileging their ethnic identity over their sexuality.

Interrupting Heteronormativity

There were a handful of men I interviewed from that era who decided they weren't willing to hide their sexuality from other members of their ethnic communities on campus. Arvin Salonga was one of these men. He matriculated at UCLA a few short years after Mabalon's article in the *Daily Bruin* was published. After only a few days on campus, he joined Samahang Pilipino, the Filipino American student organization (*samahang* is the Tagalog word for "togetherness"). Even though Arvin felt the need to escape his tightknit Filipino family in Carson, he wanted to be part of the Filipino American community at UCLA. He was drawn to the political consciousness he observed among Samahang members. During his high school years in Carson, he had been part of the Filipino club, but joked that it "had nothing to do with Filipino issues [and] had nothing to do with Filipino history." While he did have the opportunity to learn and perform Filipino traditional dances, Arvin felt it was mostly a "social club" whose members "wore Tommy Hilfiger and Nautica" and talked endlessly about "[Honda] Accords and [Acura] Integras."

Samahang was a different kind of Filipino organization. Like his high school club, the members of Samahang performed traditional cultural dances, but they also learned about Filipino American history, from the immigrant farmworkers who arrived in the early twentieth century to the veterans who fought in World War II to the nurses and other professionals who migrated to the United States after 1965. They enrolled in Filipino American studies and Tagalog language classes together, ran outreach programs for local high schools with large Filipino American populations, and organized community dialogues about the challenges that Filipino American students face in college.[20]

One topic that wasn't addressed, however, was sexuality. "When I joined Samahang, I didn't feel there was a space to talk about my sexuality," Arvin said. "I didn't feel comfortable coming out." As much as he appreciated the social consciousness of the group, most of the members were heterosexual, and they weren't cognizant, let alone outspoken, about LGBTQ issues. Arvin recalled the time Samahang held a community dialogue about gender during his sophomore year. The dialogue moderator asked members to go into separate rooms based on gender to discuss the distinct issues Filipino men and women faced in their families, among friends, and in society (this was long before "nonbinary" became part of the everyday vernacular of college students).

Arvin suddenly felt anxious. "I didn't feel comfortable going into the guy-only space because I didn't identify as straight," he said. Evident in his comment was the implicit association between masculinity and heterosexuality. None of the Filipino men in Samahang had ever been hostile toward Arvin, but they embodied the hypermasculine archetypes he had encountered back in Carson—their bravado, love for basketball, hip-hop attire, and zeal in chasing women. When the other men were speaking about the unique experience of being a Filipino American man, their narratives didn't resonate with him.

For as long as he could remember, Arvin gravitated toward women as friends. He was unapologetically effeminate, and his closest connections were with women. And so, he opted to move to the room where the women of Samahang were convening, assuming they would welcome him. "You're still not a girl," one of the Filipinas said. "You're still afforded male privilege." Arvin understood her resistance and acknowledged her claim. Still, he felt hurt. "I do get male privileges because they assume me to be a man, until I open my mouth, and they realize I'm gay. I felt like she invalidated my experiences and feelings. I was crying about it. I totally felt alienated because I wasn't feeling part of my group [the men], and they [the women] weren't having me in theirs." While he acknowledged the existence of male privilege, he had hoped that someone in Samahang would understand how his queerness made his life more difficult than those of other Filipino men. Ultimately, Arvin's experience illustrated how the lack of queer consciousness within student of color organizations can adversely affect LGBTQ members.

The community dialogue was a watershed moment for Arvin. "I realized I needed to own and be comfortable about who I was," he said. After the event, he approached the leaders of Samahang and explained how hurt he felt after that day. To his surprise, they welcomed his critiques. "That's when everything changed, and I started challenging people about gender and sexuality," he said. The organization's leadership created a new officer position that focused specifically on LGBTQ issues and tapped Arvin for the role. "For my third year, I was the gender and sexuality coordinator. They decided that I could be a successful example of a queer leader for the first- and second-year students who were coming in."

Beyond his new leadership position, Arvin found other ways to interrupt the heteronormative atmosphere of Samahang. He started doing drag on the weekends and adopted Alesandra as his drag name. From 2004 to 2005, a decade before I began writing this book, I would see Arvin dressed as Alesandra at a club in West Hollywood at a time when I wasn't yet secure in my own queerness. I was transfixed by Arvin's unapologetic transgression of Filipino American masculine gender norms, an act of resistance against gay people who attempted to "pass" as straight or assimilate into straight worlds. Having grown up in a community much like Carson, I knew the pressures Filipino American men felt to adhere to the rules of masculinity. And here was Arvin, without uttering a single word, sending a clear message: screw masculinity.

Arvin admitted though that embracing his queerness came at a cost. "I don't identify as close to being Filipino as I once did," he said. "I feel like the identity that really defines my experience is that of being gay."

"Why is that the case?" I asked.

"Maybe it has to do with the struggles that I experience in large part because of the fact that I'm gay. What I'm not afforded in this society. Literally all my struggles. Me coming out. Me dealing with my sexuality. Gay rights. Struggling to value myself as opposed to devaluing myself because we are a minority in this heteronormative, heterosexual society. Outside of UCLA, I didn't really think about what it means to be Filipino. If I was discriminated against, I would assume first that it's because I'm gay rather than if I was a person of color. I can play butch or play straight, but I don't. I choose not to."

Echoing Hunter's research on "up-down identities," Arvin once saw himself as someone who was Filipino-*then*-gay. But after some challenging moments with the Filipino American student organization at UCLA, he experienced an identity shift—he began seeing himself as gay- *then*-Filipino.[21] These were the days before "intersectionality" became part of the lexicon. Despite elevating the queer consciousness of Samahang, Arvin felt a dissonance between his Filipinoness and queerness, instead of seeing these identities as interconnected.

Like Arvin, Omar played a role in interrupting the heteronormative climate of the student organizations he joined. In the winter term of his freshman year, he pledged a Latino fraternity. Omar came to know about the fraternity while participating in a summer bridge program for first-generation college students; several of the brothers served as mentors. Being more than a hundred miles from home, he wanted to be part of "a family that understood my culture," especially because his campus was "hella White." At first, Omar was drawn to the fraternity because it was a Latino brotherhood organization, but his interest piqued when he learned that several of the brothers "played on the same team" as him.

"Turns out four or five out of the twenty [members] were gay," he said.

"How did you know?" I asked.

"They were open about it. I mean, they wouldn't bring it up at meetings, but they were open about it."

For the first time in his life, Omar had friends who were both Latino and gay. Still, he didn't feel like he could talk about his sexuality with the same level of openness that his straight brothers did. There were a few brothers in his organization who were afraid of being perceived as "the gay fraternity"—not just at UC Santa Barbara but also within the larger network of Latino Greek organizations beyond the campus. By his sophomore year, though, Omar grew tired of catering to the comfort of his straight brothers.

"I got drunk one day, and I sent an email to national [the listserv that included brothers from every chapter of the fraternity]," Omar said.

"I was like, 'I'm gay, just so you know—this is my coming out thing. I'm sick of everyone talking shit about us saying that UCSB was the gay chapter. *I* am, but *we're* not."

I asked Omar if he regretted sending out that drunken email. He didn't. "I got nothing but positive feedback," he said. "I'm sure there were haters, but they weren't going to say anything. It was a big relief after that. I was able to be myself." Not only was Omar no longer afraid to talk about being gay; he also came to embrace the sex positivity of his gay fraternity brothers. He no longer wanted to play respectability politics.

"You know, a lot of the gay bros were whores—like, fucking sluts," he said, proudly. "At the same time, a lot of the gay bros were into organizing and were socially conscious." As Omar pointed out, the gay members of his fraternity were the same ones leading initiatives and programs aimed at uplifting the Latinx community, including educational outreach programs to immigration reform protests to labor rights rallies. He felt that if he and other gay Latinos were advocating for Latinx causes, then they should have the right to be fully themselves at all times.

Embracing Intersectionality on Campus

My conversations with second-generation gay men who attended college in the late 2000s and early 2010s revealed a shift in campus climate for LGBTQ college students of color: they were emerging as a visible force on their respective campuses.[22] Their visibility had come not by way of LGBTQ centers and organizations, however; they had carved out their agency through their leadership within student of color organizations and progressive social movements on campus. As compared with the older cohort of men I interviewed, this younger cohort (those born in the late 1980s and early 1990s) felt they didn't have to choose between their racial and sexual identities.

From the moment they entered college, and sometimes even before then, these men were exposed to queer students of color who unapologetically embraced both their racial and sexual identities. Edwin Perez

(b. 1987), a Salvadoran American media strategist, mentioned that he was unable to find a community at his university's Pride Center because they weren't his "kind of people." He cultivated connections with other students of color on campus. He began participating in social justice organizing campaigns in his first year at UC Berkeley. There he connected with queer POC leaders. Some were gay children of immigrants like him; others were undocumented and queer (also known as "undocuqueer"). "I met a lot of the Salvadoran activists who were part of USEU [the Unión Salvadoreña de Estudiantes Universitarios], and a lot of them were queer," Edwin recalled. "A lot of people in POC spaces happened to be gay." For the first time in his life, he had queer role models of color who provided the emotional support he needed to come out as queer himself.

Fernando Serrano had a similar experience with the Mexican American activist organizations at UCLA. In the spring before his freshman year, he attended Raza Admit Weekend, a MEChA-sponsored recruitment event for Latinx high school seniors who were admitted to UCLA (it has since been renamed Latinx Admit Weekend). As one of the few Latinxs from his high school to be admitted to a four-year university, he was thrilled at the opportunity to connect with other Latinxs who were in college, especially ones who were politically engaged and community oriented. He was pleasantly surprised to learn that many of the leaders in MEChA were gay—and out. "There were a lot of queer men in MEChA," he recalled. "Only one or two [of the leaders] were straight, I think."

In high school, Fernando had known just one other gay student, but at Raza Admit Weekend, it felt like there were more queer Latinxs than he could count. Beyond MEChA, these queer leaders were involved in a variety of other student-led initiatives, including student government and educational outreach programs. "A lot of the people in student government were queer people of color too," he said. "UCLA is, like, ran by queers, so it's a very comfortable space."

The queer leaders of MEChA were the first students to welcome Fernando when he arrived on campus. "From my first day at school at UCLA, I knew a lot of people already," he remembered. For most of his life, his sexuality had hindered his ability to connect with people—in his schools, in his family, in his neighborhood. But at UCLA, it was his identity as a queer Latino that facilitated his sense of belonging on campus. "Something I learned was that the older queer men, they take care of each other," he explained. "If you know that there is someone who is queer, or who might be queer—one of the younger ones—you talk to him, and you take him under your wing. They [the older queer men] have been my mentors."

Through their involvements with MEChA and other activist organizations on campus, Latino interviewees who attended UCLA in the early 2000s learned about student organizations and friendship groups that were specifically queer and Latino. This was how Bernardo became involved with La Familia, an LGBTQ Latinx organization on campus. When I interviewed Bernardo, he was serving as an officer for La Familia—or LaFa, for short. During our conversation, he reflected on the positive impact of meeting queer Latino role models, even if they were just a year or two older than he was.

During his first year of college, Bernardo began attending weekly film screenings sponsored by LaFa. The first film they screened was *La Mission*, starring Jeremy Ray Valdez and Benjamin Bratt. The film depicts the story of Jes (played by Valdez), a Latino teenager growing up in the Mission District of San Francisco who is coming into his queer sexuality. Jes is being raised by Che (played by Bratt), a single father and a formerly incarcerated ex-gang member trying to turn his life around. Che reacts violently when he learns of Jes's relationship with another young man, a White high school student from a more affluent part of San Francisco. Given the experience Bernardo had with his own father, the film resonated deeply. It was the first time he had seen a queer story line depicted by a Latino cast.

For Bernardo, LaFa was a space unlike both MEChA and the LGBTQ center on campus. In LaFa meetings, the experience of being both queer *and* Latino was central in every program, in every conversation. Back in high school, there had been only one classmate who was openly gay, a White boy who always acted like he was above Bernardo. But in LaFa, Bernardo met others who could commiserate about what it was like being gay *and* a child of immigrants *and* a person of color *and* a first-generation college student. "I think in a lot of organizations, people just want to socialize, but in LaFa, they would tell us histories of being queer, they'd talk about the New York ballroom scene, which was predominantly queer minorities," he said. Through LaFa, Bernardo attended conferences that focused on queer Latinx issues and connected with queer Latinxs at other universities; he met queer Latinxs who were pursuing master's and doctoral degrees. Bernardo said he not only felt a sense of community but also felt part of a larger history of queer people of color.

LaFa was also a place where he could talk openly about queer sexuality and race. Bernardo recalled how awkward he felt in his freshman year dorm when the conversations with his (mostly straight) dormmates turned to sex. In contrast, at LaFa gatherings he could ask questions about queer sex without feeling ashamed. "I learned about the whole top-bottom dichotomy," he said. "Many of the [other gay men] identified as bottoms, and so they empowered the term. There's a perception that tops are automatically more masculine, but I met a feminine-presenting friend who talked about being a top." Bernardo also appreciated that, beyond sex, he could also commiserate about dating and hookups—topics young gay men rarely get the chance to talk about openly during junior high and high school. LaFa was also a space where he felt comfortable venting to other members about his racialized encounters with White queers. "They knew what it was like to feel excluded but also feel exoticized in White gay spaces," he said. "Like when they [White gay men] go up to you and say stupid shit like, 'Oh talk to me in Spanish, Papi.'" The other members of LaFa understood the struggle.

Filipino Americans also spoke about the influence of LGBTQ students of color who mentored them in college. When I first interviewed Franklin, he was only a sophomore but had already established himself as one of the most visible student of color leaders on campus. He worked as an intern for student government and organized for the federal Development, Relief, and Education for Alien Minors (DREAM) Act, which proposed to make undocumented students across the country eligible for in-state tuition.[23] In less than a year's time, he became the third Filipino American—and the first openly gay man—to be elected student body president of his campus.

I asked Franklin what drove him to become so involved with politics on campus. "The mentors I first had when I got to UCLA were queer activists, and I think they played a big role in me figuring things out," he said. "My mentors were also undocumented and queer, so that was a big part of it too. I'm not undocumented, but I think I saw a lot of my story in them. . . . Before my sister and I went to college, my mom actually thought she wouldn't be able to afford it. She didn't know anything about financial aid." Franklin acknowledged, of course, that as a citizen by birth he enjoyed many protections that his undocumented peers did not. Still, he knew the challenge of navigating institutions that weren't designed with him in mind; this shared struggle cemented their connection.

With the mentorship of undocuqueer upperclassmen, Franklin became a student organizer. He visited classrooms to speak about undocumented student issues. He participated in phone banks to call legislators to support the DREAM Act. He teamed up with other UC students to fight tuition increases, which disproportionately harmed undocumented and low-income students of color. The folks leading the charge on these movements unapologetically embraced all of their intersecting identities—queer, Latino, and undocumented—and emboldened Franklin to do the same. The more he participated in these movements, the more he saw his queerness as inseparable from his identity as a Filipino American and a person of color.

Beyond student government, Franklin was also a part of Samahang. The organization had evolved on queer issues in the decade since Arvin expressed his grievances; Samahang felt like a space where gay members could embrace both their Filipinoness and queerness in equal measure. "When I was in Samahang, I became part of a mentorship line of queer Filipinos," Franklin said. He named the Filipino Americans who were part of this queer genealogy, and spoke lovingly about the queer Filipino American men who, despite having already graduated, took him under their wing and mentored him. He proudly shared the accomplishments of these queer Filipino alumni, from the pursuit of graduate school to their work on presidential election campaigns.

With queerness came community, the opposite of what Franklin experienced before his college years. "Camaraderie was about acceptance and love," he said of the queer people of color at UCLA. "But in a way, too, it was about working on behalf of a larger cause." For Franklin, the definition of success wasn't just about earning a degree; it also meant doing all he could to dismantle systems of oppression that adversely affected immigrants, people of color, and queer people.

What about Queer Studies?

Out of all the men I interviewed, Ryan Respicio (b. 1991), a Filipino American college student, was the only one who had ever taken a queer studies class.

Once.

Given that many of the men went to college to explore their sexuality, I wondered why so few had embraced the opportunity. From my conversation with Ryan, it was clear that taking a queer studies class was a positive experience.

When we spoke, Ryan was a third-year student at UC Irvine, where he was majoring in psychology and minoring in education. He couldn't recall a single time in his psychology classes when LGBTQ issues were even mentioned. But for his minor, he was excited about one of the course offerings: LGBT Experiences in Education.

Like some of the gay men I interviewed, Ryan had participated in discussions about LGBTQ issues within student organizations, but he'd wanted the opportunity to learn about LGBTQ history and communities in an actual classroom. In the course, he read historical accounts of the gay liberation movement, as well as social science research on LGBTQ students. "It made me feel at peace to learn how [the gay rights movement] came about," he said. Ryan also appreciated being in a classroom where the majority of students openly identified as gay. "I really liked learning about other people's experiences because it made me feel okay with mine."

What impacted Ryan most, however, was seeing how invested his straight classmates were in class discussions. "To hear a straight, White fraternity boy talking about intersectionality, talking about how they feel about hate crimes—just to see it—it was my way of seeing that people outside of the community really do care [and] were taking the time to learn," he said. "I have no problem with those people who say, 'I love gay people,' but I think it takes more than that to be an ally." It also struck Ryan that there were nonqueer folks enrolled in the class even though it wasn't a general education requirement; they were taking the class out of genuine interest, not just to check off a box for graduation. "I took it as a requirement [for the minor], but there were others who signed up for that class out of their own free will," he explained. "I feel, like, for those people who took the time to really understand someone in this community—that really spoke magnitudes to me."

Social scientists have documented the positive impact of a queer studies curriculum across every level of education. Education scholar Danné Davis has found that incorporating queer literature in classes "provides schoolchildren *and* teachers the opportunity to favorably see people and characters who are queer and in normative situations."[24] For high school and college students, LGBTQ studies helps students of all sexual identities disrupt heteronormative understandings of history, sexual health, family formation, and a variety of other topics.[25] Incorporating LGBTQ content into the curriculum positively impacts professional development. A study conducted by psychologist Markus Bidell found that psychology graduate students who took an LGBTQ studies course saw a marked improvement in their counseling abilities and self-efficacy (their confidence in their ability to complete a particular task).[26]

And yet, only one of the men I interviewed had taken a queer studies class. Why?

Some of the men felt that taking queer studies classes was less of a priority compared to their "real" classes. Arvin explained that while queer studies was an example of "relevant education" in that "you were learning about yourself," he felt pressured to focus his energies on "something practical." "Whenever I talk to my family, I *always* say I'm an economics major," he said. "Econ is dry, and econ is boring. It didn't interest me, and it didn't speak to me. I hated it. But there's a pressure to fulfill my parents' desires because I know how hard it was for them to emigrate." Taking queer studies was a "luxury" he couldn't afford.

Others said they couldn't fit in queer studies because they were too busy with the demands of their majors. With the exception of ethnic studies and gender studies, queer studies courses weren't built into the prescribed curriculum for most majors. For those majoring in science, technology, engineering, and mathematics, topics like queer sexuality, race, and gender were rarely discussed. Even among those majoring in the social sciences, in which social inequality is a central theme, few could remember course offerings that focused on LGBTQ experiences. Ryan himself admitted that he might not have taken the LGBTQ education course had it not been required for his major; his admission suggests that there is merit to incentivizing students to take at least one queer studies course, as a general education requirement.

In his essay "Integrating the American Mind," Henry Louis Gates, professor of African American Studies at Harvard University, writes, "Intellectuals . . . can be defined as experts in legitimation. And the academy, today, is an institution of legitimation—establishing what counts as knowledge, what counts as culture."[27] The absence of LGBTQ studies courses within majors reinforces the belief that queer history, queer people, and queer communities aren't worth studying. It also sends the message that academic experts on LGBTQ issues aren't worth hiring as professors. The men I interviewed may have been less inclined to take LGBTQ studies because everything about their education has conditioned them to believe that queer experiences don't count as knowledge.

Fortunately, some of the men carved out opportunities to engage LGBTQ issues even if a course wasn't explicitly about sexuality. Franklin was able to do this when he enrolled in a Chicano studies course and was assigned to a section taught by a queer Latino graduate student. "I loved my TA [teaching assistant], Guillermo," he said. "He was the best teacher I ever had at UCLA. And it's in part because he always affirmed my queer identity. Guillermo was a huge part of what made my classroom experience. It was like me realizing there was a teacher who knew my ideas and the communities that I cared about—that these things I cared about can be supported in the classroom."

Franklin appreciated that Guillermo, himself a queer son of immigrants, didn't hesitate to share his own life experiences, both in and beyond the classroom—something the professors outside his ethnic studies courses rarely did. Part of what drove him to take the Chicano studies course in the first place was his frustration with his own major, sociology. Franklin had chosen sociology as a major so he could study the topics that drove his campus activism—immigration, race, educational inequality, and LGBTQ issues. He quickly became disillusioned because of the disconnect between the academic study of social inequality and the work he was doing "on the ground." "I hated it," he said of his major. "My sociology faculty weren't the most vocal about the issues happening on campus." Franklin's critique highlighted an ongoing debate within the field of sociology. There have been prominent sociologists, mostly straight White men, who have argued that activism taints the quality of sociological work. Feminist and antiracist sociologists have fought against such an assertion and maintain that the field has a responsibility to speak out on these issues beyond the academy.[28]

In contrast to his sociology courses, Franklin appreciated how queerness, curriculum, and community were interconnected in Guillermo's classroom. Beyond teaching the history of social movements, Guillermo spoke often about his own political commitments beyond the ivory tower. "He would say in class, 'Yes, I am attending this rally for LGBT rights,'" Franklin recalled. "His class really made me want to go to class because it was directly tied to who I was and what I was doing. That made me feel empowered outside of class." Although this course wasn't specifically focused on queer issues, Guillermo's willingness to weave in queer content made all the difference for Franklin's experience both inside and outside the class.

Octavio Lara (b. 1983), a Mexican American graduate student, never enrolled in an LGBTQ studies class at California State University–Northridge. LGBTQ studies classes "weren't in my area," he explained. "My degree was in something else, and I didn't want to waste my [course] units." This was a common sentiment among first-generation college students, who, in an effort to be economical, felt they needed to take only the classes required to graduate and nothing extra. Still, Octavio wanted to learn more about queer issues, especially after an Asian American studies professor encouraged him to use his class projects to explore his identity as a gay Latino. (As part of the general education requirements in Octavio's school, all students were required to take at least one ethnic studies course.). "After that Asian American studies class, everything I did revolved around queer identity, people of color, specifically gay men, specifically Latinos," Octavio said. He started doing research outside of class on everything from LGBTQ mental health issues to queer social movements in Mexico. At the time, his parents weren't accepting of his sexuality, and he believed that gathering research would help change their tune. Unfortunately, it did little to sway them. "They would always bring up the Bible or talk about the rates of HIV, or the dangers of being gay, the levels of unhappiness, the lack of being able to stay in a stable relationship," he recalled. "And I'd try to explain those are mental health issues that the community is dealing with *because* of the history of oppression." I understood Octavio's approach; it was one I'd attempted myself in the early days of coming out to my own family. And like Octavio, I found that the approach failed. And I asked myself, Why would academic knowledge resonate with people it has historically excluded?

Octavio was hurt, but not deterred. As a mass communications major, one of his senior project assignments was to produce a documentary. He decided to focus it on gay Latino men in Los Angeles.

"What made you want to do that?" I asked.

"Wanting to tell my story. Wanting to help other people that were going through the same thing with their families. Wanting to see that story on camera," he answered.

Octavio remembers seeing only White gay characters on television and movies when he was growing up. This was years before queer POC were able to film their own stories and instantly upload them to the internet for millions of people to see, years before films about queer POC were just a mouse click away. Octavio realized in college that he wanted to see himself, his story, on-screen. He also wanted to show people beyond the LGBTQ community that gay Latinos weren't a monolith. The documentary featured three individuals with vastly different life experiences from distinct neighborhood contexts—an undocumented immigrant from Mexico living in Downtown LA, a Salvadoran American college graduate living in Silver Lake, and a Mexican American living in a low-income community in South Los Angeles.

Once Octavio completed his documentary, he held screenings at gay establishments and film festivals in Los Angeles. Local queer media outlets covered these screenings, and Octavio found that the film resonated with a variety of people, not just queer Latinos: "White people who see it are, like, 'We have never seen this story told,'" he said. This was true even among White audiences in Los Angeles, a city where one in every two residents is Latino. The film earned Octavio admission into a prestigious master of fine arts program. Years after he graduated, Octavio was invited to screen his film in Mexico City for an international film festival. In college, he had read about a 1901 raid where police arrested forty-one men dressed in women's clothing, and now here he was, a century later, screening a film that centered gay Latinos.[29] Before he left Mexico City, Octavio commemorated the experience by getting a tattoo of the number 41 on the left side of his chest, on top of his heart.

For most of his life, everything Octavio ever heard about gay people—from his family, from his classmates, from his church—was negative. And with one film, he was able to rewrite the story of a community—*his* community—for audiences in LA and all over the world. This is the kind of transformative art that is possible only when gay artists of color like Octavio are granted opportunities to queer the curriculum and tell stories from the perspective of a queer person of color.

Reimagining Possibilities

For many of the second-generation gay men I interviewed, pursuing higher education presented opportunities to rewrite the stories of who they were and who they were becoming. Whether campus was a short drive or a plane ride away, college felt like a place where they could explore their sexuality without the looming presence of family and old friends. The newfound independence these men experienced in college allowed them to reconfigure their social worlds. They met other gay men of color who, like them, dealt with the unique pressures of growing up in an immigrant family. From these queer POC role models they learned how to embrace being gay in a society that had conditioned them to see queerness as a liability. They also learned to reject the idea that one has to choose between racial and sexual identities. They joined and led student of color organizations and made them into spaces where they could unapologetically center being both Brown and gay.

In her book *Learning to Be Latino*, sociologist Daisy Reyes shows that student organizations allow students of color—often marginalized and underrepresented within higher education—to not only explore their identities but also develop the skills to advocate for themselves and the communities they represent.[30] As the stories of the gay men I interviewed illustrate, these organizations also position them to cultivate the queer consciousness of the members of the group and, in some cases, the campus as a whole. Unlike in previous chapters of their lives, it was their queerness that facilitated a sense of belonging in college—not just with other gay students of color but also to a larger history of queer POC resistance.

The queer-conscious space of Samahang was how Franklin developed the confidence to make a little history himself. After he was elected student body president, one of Franklin's responsibilities was to welcome the incoming freshman class during fall orientation. After all the mentorship he had received from queer activists of color, he felt an obligation to be transparent about who he was. "I had to give a speech for fall convocation for the incoming freshmen," he told me. "I came out in front of the school, actually. It was the most nerve-racking moment of my life. I felt like I was going to pass out."

In front of an audience of six thousand first-year students, Franklin spoke about the sacrifices his mother had made for him to have an education. He spoke about the responsibility to give back to the communities the students were part of. The moment compelled Franklin to ad-lib. "I am standing in front of you as a queer Filipino raised by a single mother," he said. After that line, the crowd erupted into applause. He recalled, "They started clapping, and I'm like, Holy shit! I would have never expected that to happen."

Years later, Franklin would learn the impact of that one line. Two years after he had graduated from UCLA, he went back to visit the campus. While walking through the quad, a random student—who happened to be queer and POC—approached him to tell him how much he had appreciated that speech; he had been one of the six thousand first-year students in the audience that day. "It was really powerful," the student told Franklin. "When I came in, and I saw I had a gay Filipino who was my president, it meant a lot." Seeing a queer person of color elected student body president signaled to this student that UCLA was a place where it was okay to be a person of color who was openly gay.

Franklin often thought of his year as president as one of the most emotionally draining experiences of his life. He worked so hard he lost touch with his friends. The job was so stressful that he even started smoking cigarettes for a while. Hearing that his presidency had an impact on this student helped him reframe that year in his mind. "There was a lot of stuff happening in my life that year," Franklin said. "But I think what kind of helped me through was realizing that I could be a role model for people."

And on that day revisiting the UCLA campus, Franklin finally had proof that he was.

5

Becoming Brown and Gay in LA

Tonight is one of those nights when I am growing, changing quickly, without warning, new shapes and configurations, and I don't know where this all goes.

In that moment, I feel more at home than I ever have, not in San Francisco, not on earth, but in myself. I am on the other side of something and I don't know what it is. I wait to find out.

—Alexander Chee, *How to Write an Autobiographical Novel*

In the early morning of June 12, 2016, a domestic terrorist entered Pulse, a gay nightclub in Orlando, Florida, and opened fire. The gunman was equipped with a semiautomatic rifle and a nine-millimeter semiautomatic pistol he had purchased legally at the St. Lucie Shooting Center about a week earlier.[1] Saturday was Latin night at Pulse, and that evening there were somewhere between two and three hundred clubgoers, mostly queer Latinxs and other people of color.[2] By the end of the attack, forty-nine people were dead, and more than fifty others were physically injured. Among the dead were a recent high school graduate, a sales associate, a military veteran, a choreographer, a theme park employee, an undocumented immigrant, several college students, and a mother of eleven who had twice beaten cancer.[3] The attack occurred less than one year after the US Supreme Court declared gay marriage legal.

Later that day, Rick Scott, the governor of Florida at the time, was quick to opine that radical Islamic terrorists were behind the Pulse shooting; he was part of a chorus of Republicans ready to weaponize the shooter's racial identity to advance their own anti-Muslim agenda.[4] In their first set of news conferences and tweets, Scott and his Republican colleagues described the Pulse shooting as an act of terror against "Americans," conveniently omitting that the attack targeted queer Latinxs and people of color.[5] These "straightwashed" and "Whitewashed" framings of the Pulse shooting minimized the unique devastation felt by LGBTQ Latinxs, both in and beyond Orlando.

For LGBTQ Latinxs, this wasn't just a mass shooting at a nightclub. As journalist Veronica Bayette Flores notes, "The Pulse nightclub shooting robbed the queer Latinx community of a sanctuary."[6] Four days after the attack, poet and writer Rigoberto Gonzalez penned a piece for BuzzFeed explaining why Pulse felt so personal. "Latino gay clubs or Latin nights at any other gay club appealed to my sexuality and to my ethnicity," Gonzalez notes. "Oh, yes, how I cherish the time I have spent in clubs like Pulse in cities like Orlando, where gay Latinos . . . gravitate because we love men and we love our homelands, and that's one of the places our worlds converge."[7] For Flores and Gonzalez, Latin night at a gay club is one of the few spaces where they can just *be*—unapologetically.

The Monday after the Pulse shooting, I attended a vigil at Grand Park in Downtown Los Angeles, where I ran into several of the men I had interviewed for this book. When I said my hellos, many echoed some version of "That could've been us." One of the interviewees I ran into was Enrique Sandoval (b. 1983), a Mexican American artist. The Pulse shooting hit him especially hard. While he had never been to Pulse specifically, he knew what it meant as a cultural and community space. Enrique's queer coming of age was inseparable from the gay Latino scene, and especially Friday nights at Circus Disco, which for decades had been one of Southern California's most prominent Latino gay clubs before it was torn down in 2016.[8] Circus was a massive two-story club with several dance floors: hip-hop and reggaeton might be playing in one room, Beyoncé and Britney Spears in another, and Spanish rock in a third. The crowd comprised mostly Latino gay men, but they were as diverse as the music blasting in the respective rooms.

"Circus is like church," Enrique had told me a few years earlier. "It's where everyone meets up. It's where everyone who is a Latino gay guy at some point comes to see all the people they know. It's that mecca that feels like home." Circus was where Enrique came to embrace being gay after a lifetime of associating it with shame. It was where he first connected with the gay Latino friends who eventually became part of his chosen family. At Circus, he found the social support and acceptance that he lacked in his home life. Unlike many of the other men I interviewed, Enrique didn't attend college, where there were student organizations and cultural centers in which he could explore his sexuality, so Circus became a campus of sorts to him. It was where he became familiarized with gay pop culture. It was in which he learned about local gay Latino organizations. It was where he learned about how HIV/AIDS disproportionately affected Black and Latino gay men. For much of his early adult life, the community at Circus mattered more to him than his blood family and his childhood friends.

Gay men of color, for most of their lives, rarely find themselves in spaces where they can fully embrace both their racial and sexual identities. In their families, they're marginalized for being gay; in their schools and the larger society, they're marginalized for being gay *and* people of color. Gay bars—especially those frequented by other gay people of color—provide opportunities for connection and community. As the anthropologist Martin Manalansan writes, the gay bar "is the most prominent space for socialization and, for many, authentic belonging to the community."[9] Although many of these establishments cater to White gay men, ethnic-themed parties like Latin night provided rare opportunities for queer people of color to express and experience their full humanity—the three or four hours in the week when they can strut and dance and gab and love as fiercely as they desire, where they can stand out without standing out.[10]

Discovering these queer communities of color in LA wasn't always straightforward. The second-generation gay men I interviewed came to learn about places like Circus and other queer POC scenes through meeting other gay men of color, both in person and online, who bro-kered their entrée into these spaces.

T-Parties and Queering "the Hood"

Justin Ruiz (b. 1981), a Mexican American hair stylist who grew up in Echo Park, first started hanging out in West Hollywood (WeHo) when he was a sophomore in high school, more than two decades ago. At age fifteen he and his friends weren't old enough to get into the bars and clubs, so they'd sit outdoors for hours at restaurants and coffee shops along the main strip of gay establishments on Santa Monica Boulevard.

"We would take our asses to West Hollywood just to go, almost like mall rats, but like West Hollywood rats," he recalled, nostalgia radiating from his voice. "You would go be a fucking West Hollywood rat at that one pizza place and literally just eat pizza and hang out and just meet other young gays. That's what a lot of the young gays would do, because you couldn't get into any of the clubs at the time." Justin and his friends were what sociologist Theo Greene calls "vicarious citizens"—they were young gays who felt part of the WeHo community, even if they didn't live there.[11]

The drive from Justin's home to WeHo took more than half an hour, but he made it a point to make the trip at least a few times a week "just to be around the gays." This was the late 1990s, when teenagers were just starting to connect through the internet. Back then he "didn't really do the AOL chat room thing," so making the trek to WeHo was the only reliable way to connect with other gay people his age.[12]

That is, until he met Raymond Martinez (b. 1983). Raymond was a member of Infamous, a Latino party crew in East LA known for throw-ing "T-parties," social functions that catered specifically to gay Latinos. Party crews (both gay and straight) were a staple of LA Latino culture during the 1990s and early 2000s. As artist and writer Virginia Arce ar-gues, Latino party crews were an alternative to gang culture, a space "where familial bonds were established and strengthened." Party crews were also a "resistant cultural practice," a response to the negative ways Latinos were targeted as "illegal" and "criminal"—by teachers in public schools, by conservative politicians, and in Hollywood story lines.[13] Each weekend, party crews would throw backyard parties in predominantly Latino neighborhoods throughout Southern California, in East LA, South LA, Santa Ana, and the Inland Empire. The parties seldom took place in the same location, and they were often broken up by police within hours; nevertheless, Latinos from different regions continued to congregate by the hundreds every weekend.[14]

Justin and Raymond met when they were teenagers, in front of a WeHo pizza parlor, where Raymond was passing out flyers for a T-party. "On this little party flyer, there was a number I had to call to find out where the T-parties were gonna be," Justin explained. "It was like some cholo guy on a voicemail that was like, 'Wassup, party people, the place to be tonight is . . .' and then it told me the address and direction of where the party was that night." One Friday night in 1997, Justin went to see what a T-party was all about. For the next two years he was hooked. "We were at those T-parties every motherfuckin' weekend."

* * *

Besides Justin and Raymond, there were a handful of other men I spoke with who frequented T-parties in the late 1990s and early 2000s. All of them were Latino and born in the early 1980s. They hailed from different parts of LA—from Echo Park to the San Fernando Valley to West LA—but I learned, during the course of my interviews, that some of them knew of each other through the T-party scene.[15] Having never been to a T-party myself, I asked each of them to describe what the scene was like. Regardless of whether they took place in East LA, South LA, or the Inland Empire, the setups of T-parties were remarkably similar.

The parties were "always in the hood" and "right off the freeway," according to Justin. Most of the time they took place in a backyard of a house or in the back lot of an apartment complex, but occasionally they would take place at other sites. One man I interviewed remembered a

T-party that took place in the parking lot of a South LA laundromat. Justin remembered attending a T-party at an auto repair shop in Historic Filipinotown. "It was crazy. I went to one that was at an auto body shop, and it turns out it was the same auto body shop my grandfather owned in the fucking sixties!" he said. "The party was covered up [black tarp surrounded the outer fence], but I mean any cop could see it driving by. Like fucking lights and shit, strobe lights, and all these fucking queens dancing and just lining up outside."

"A lot of teenagers kick it at the mall or go to school dances. What was the appeal of going to T-parties?" I asked Justin.

"Probably the fact that we knew there was going to be lots of other gay boys or men our age," he answered. "It was just the idea of being able to meet other gay kids that weren't at my school. And I feel like it was just the lure of nightlife at that age. I think it was just enticing to me. It was like the closest thing I thought I would get to going to a club or being in a room filled with kids that were just like me."

T-parties pulled crowds of around one to two hundred people. The overwhelming majority of partygoers were Latino teenagers and young adults, with a handful of Black and Asian American queers in attendance. "We never really saw White kids there, that's for damn sure," Justin said. Sometimes there were men who came to the party in drag. "There were a few drag kids, obviously, who wanted to put on a dress and some pumps. The T-parties were like a perfect reason for them to do it since they probably couldn't do it at their high school." At every party, there was a station where beer and "jungle juice" were served. There was always someone selling balloons filled with nitrous oxide (NOS) which partygoers would inhale to experience a momentary euphoria. In the middle of the party, there would be groups of young men dancing to deep house music, each one taking a turn in the center to showcase his moves.

Jesse Madgiral, a Mexican American graphic designer, was fifteen when an older gay cousin took him to his first T-party, in South LA. Most of the men at that first T-party were Latino; many were wearing crisply ironed white T-shirts or plaid long-sleeved flannels, with baggy jeans or Dickies, a brand of workmen's pants popular among Latino youth. The men dressed like the gang members from his high school, but after talking to them, he discovered they weren't gang affiliated. As cultural theorist Richard Rodriguez notes, these young men were "queering the homeboy aesthetic," adopting a style typically associated with Latino male heterosexuality and taking ownership of it. The young men who weren't dressed like "cholos" (Jesse's descriptor) were usually dressed like "rebels"—a style among Latinos that evoked James Dean's look in *Rebel without a Cause*—in white T-shirts, black faux leather jackets, snug-fitting jeans, and with slicked-back hair.[16]

While the young men at the party embodied an aesthetic Jesse was familiar with, he was "mind blown" to see them engaging in same-sex public displays of affection. "You'd see these straight-up gangsters with tatted out heads making out with other guys," he said. "I was like, What the fuck? Like freakin' cholos making out." It was the first time Jesse saw other young men who embodied the Latino masculine aesthetic he'd grown up with being physically affectionate with other men: dancing together, hugging each other, kissing one another. "T-parties were an eye opener," he said. In his high school, he was the only student who was openly gay; at T-parties, the men in attendance looked just like the men he knew in his family and school; they looked like *him*.

For Raymond, joining a party crew provided a community and family he had lost in the aftermath of coming out. In his early teens, he had been part of a Catholic youth ministry at his local parish. One weekend during a retreat, Raymond tearfully revealed to friends in the group that he was gay. They didn't outright reject him, but he felt something change after having shared this secret. Soon he stopped going to meetings and disassociated from his friends in the group. A few weeks after the retreat, Raymond's parents found a shoebox full of letters he had been exchanging with a male friend. "They confronted me about the letters," he said. "I got clumsy and they saw some of my emails. Then they started to eavesdrop on the phone and hear that I was talking all affectionate with a guy." Raymond's parents took him to see a priest and, later, a psychologist—all in an attempt to steer him away from being gay. The psychologist informed his parents that there was nothing wrong with Raymond. "He basically told them that I didn't need help. That being gay was not a mental issue. That the only thing that mattered was that I was happy." On the one level, Raymond felt validated to know that a mental health professional was on his side. On the other hand, he was devastated that his parents sought out conversion therapy in the first place.

When Raymond went to his first T-party, hosted by Infamous, he was enamored with the sense of camaraderie the members had. He found himself crushing on one of the crew's veteran members. "Sammy, the main guy that was throwing all the parties, he was a smart cholo," he said. "He just came off so intelligent, and when he saw me, he was like, 'You are really cute. You are never gonna have to pay here when we have a party, ever again, okay?'" By the next party, Sammy had Raymond on NOS duty. "Here, your job is to sell balloons," he told him. "Two for three dollars." Before Raymond knew it, he was helping each week to plan Infamous's T-parties—scouting for the location, booking a DJ, designing the flyers, and distributing them outside of all-ages clubs like Arena in Hollywood and Ozz in Orange County. Within a few months, Raymond had established himself as one of the most well-known promoters in the T-party scene. He recalled fondly, "This was our world, and it felt good to be recognized at every party I went to."

Ultimately, as these men got older and the option to attend bars and clubs became available, the appeal of T-parties waned. "A friend gave me a fake ID, and then I stopped going to T-parties," Justin explained. "It said I was twenty-six, and I was definitely still seventeen at the time, but I never got turned away. Not once did I get turned away, which is crazy because it said I was from Pennsylvania and it wasn't even my photo. But it worked." Justin's fake ID gave him access to bars and clubs throughout WeHo, Long Beach, Orange County, and the Inland Empire. He began dating a marine ten years his senior. "Bitch, I was fucking *seventeen*, dating this grown-ass man like the bad bitch I was!" he told me. When presented with the options of a brick-and-mortar gay establishment or a T-party likely to be broken up by the cops within hours, Justin and his boyfriend preferred the former.

Jesse said he stopped attending T-parties after an altercation with the police. "The last time I went to a T-party, the cops stopped us and put us up against the wall," he remembered. They cuffed him and his friends and ran his name through a database. After finding that none of them had a record, they let them go. While Jesse escaped the incident unscathed, he feared that another encounter with police might compromise his future. He was a few weeks away from starting college when this incident occurred. "I had just turned eighteen, and I was like, I don't need to go there. I am not going to do this again."

Reimagining Gay Identity Online

T-parties weren't the only spaces in which second-generation gay men could engage with other gay men. Growing up, Alfred Rojas (b. 1984), a Filipino American property manager, had never heard of T-parties when he was younger. Even if he had, he likely wouldn't have gone to one given how strict his parents were. During high school, Alfred's parents expected him to come home immediately after classes let out. In the rare instances he was allowed to hang out with friends, his parents mandated that he be home by sunset. "My mom always wanted me to be kept inside," he recalled. "I was just bored at home a lot of the time."

There was one activity, however, that Alfred's parents seldom monitored. "They never said anything when I was on my computer," he told me. "After school, I'd be online all night. My parents just assumed I was doing homework or studying." It was through the internet—specifically the early iterations of social media—that Alfred started to explore what it meant to be gay.

Since the late 1990s, gay people have harnessed the connective potential of the internet. For gay teenagers, in particular—who often felt boxed out of real-life social worlds in their families, communities, and schools but who didn't yet have the autonomy that adulthood affords—the internet was a lifeline.[17] A 2016 study in the *American Journal of Men's Health* reported that the internet served several important functions in the lives of young gay men.[18] The internet provided access to a range of reading and viewing materials (everything from message boards to articles to pornography) that validated their same-sex attractions. Social media presented opportunities to virtually connect with gay people and gay communities—online encounters that often evolved into real-life ones. These gay connections facilitated by the internet helped young gay men affirm their own identities and find the strength and support to come out to family members and friends.

Internet chat rooms were Alfred's safe space in high school. He came across them accidentally. "At first, I was searching to see if there was a cure [for being gay]," he admitted. "I had questions in my mind—like, Why am I feeling this way?—but at the same time I'd see some videos of people trying to 'cure' [gay people] and it just looked bizarre." Alfred eventually found blogs and message boards, where people anonymously shared their experiences of what it was like to be gay. He found himself reading testimonials from people of different ages, genders, and races living across the country. On those blogs and message boards, Alfred also read about chat rooms. He learned that there were different ones that catered to gay men, gay Asian Americans, and gay youth in Southern California. "When I was young, I'd be in GAM4GAM [a chat room for gay Asian men] every day after school. Now that I think about it, it's just so nostalgic. It's kind of how me and a lot of my friends today first met. At the time, it was how we kept in touch, especially because many of us couldn't really go out clubbing or hang out [in person]. We would just hang out online and eventually became *real* friends."

With his online friends, Alfred was unafraid to ask questions that he would never ask his friends in high school: When did you know you were gay? Have you ever had a crush on a guy? Does anyone in your family know? But what he appreciated most about his online friends was that they talked about these questions alongside "normal" topics.

"I remember people talking about regular stuff like having a project due in school or sharing the same interest in terms of art or being part of band. Stuff I could relate to more because of my age." With each conversation Alfred noticed that he felt less ashamed about being gay. But more important to him was that he felt less alone.

Social media also helped some decipher which of their peers would be accepting of them. Edwin Perez said the anonymity of chat rooms during the "AIM [AOL Instant Messenger] days" helped him become more comfortable with his sexuality during high school. "With AIM you didn't even have to have a picture on your profile," he said. "That was huge for me, especially since I wasn't very outgoing in high school. I needed that [to explore] my gay stuff."

One day, Edwin started chatting with someone named Jay, and as their conversations progressed, they discovered that they attended the same high school. "It just so happened they weren't just from my same high school," Edwin said. "We actually had third period together. We sat across from each other!" For the entire time Edwin had known Jay, he'd never once even suspected that he might be gay. And here they were, on their respective computers, confiding to each other about their struggles with sexuality. They started hanging out in person, mainly outside of school. With Jay, Edwin shared his first kiss and his first sexual experience. When Edwin and Jay were on campus, however, they rarely interacted with each other; neither wanted anyone at school to know they were seeing each other. But without the internet, they would never have had the chance to cultivate a relationship.

Armando Garza also used the internet to explore his gay sexuality, though in his college years. Like Edwin, he had come across a profile of one his classmates, Rafa, on a gay social networking site during his first year at Georgetown University. In this instance, however, it was Rafa's presence on the site that deterred Armando from setting up a profile and posting a picture of himself. He and Rafa were "like, one of the seven Mexicans" at Georgetown, and he worried that Rafa might out him. Because of this, Armando opted to chat only with men who lived in other states. If they happened to live in Southern California, where he had grown up, he made sure to only send a photo of himself once he determined that the person had no connections with his high school classmates or family members. "I was still scared to put a picture up," Armando said. "I didn't want people to know I'm gay. I thought, What if my parents see it?"

One of Armando's first romantic relationships was with a man he met online. "There was one guy in New Mexico, and we were having, like, a *relationship*," he said. "We would chat, we would have a lot of fun camming. He wanted me to go visit him in New Mexico during spring break because he was falling in love with me, and I was kinda falling in love with him." Armando ultimately got cold feet and didn't end up making the trip. Plus, as a broke college student surviving on financial aid, he didn't have the funds to travel. Soon after, their chats grew more sporadic and the relationship fizzled out. A few months later, however, when Armando was back in LA for the summer, he connected with Hugo, a Mexican American man he'd been chatting with online. Armando originally met Hugo in a chat room for Latino queer men that was housed on a gay social network site. It turned out that Hugo lived not too far from where Armando had grown up in El Monte. When Armando flew back to LA from the East Coast, Hugo picked him up at the airport, and they went to a local diner for breakfast. I don't know how this works, he remembered thinking while in the car. He immediately thought of the sexual escapades Rafa would boast about at school (though he never let on that he was eavesdropping): "I remember Rafa saying that he would meet guys online, and they would meet up for coffee, and then go to the car and have sex." Rafa's stories were the only narratives Armando had to draw on when it came to navigating queer dating in real life. And so, after breakfast, Armando didn't object when his date suggested they go for a walk in a nearby park.

"Here I was, this awkward virgin nineteen-year-old kid," Armando recounted. "He was like, 'There's this park nearby. You wanna go there?' We ended up behind this bushy area, and we started making out, and

I was like, 'This is my first time ever kissing a guy.' And the first time I kissed him, I had this weird moment. I felt like a puzzle piece was missing and I never knew, and then all of a sudden I found the piece that fit. I was like, Oh my God, I *am* gay. Next thing you know, he unzipped my pants and started sucking me off, and I was like, Wow, wow, wow! That was my first time getting a blow job, and then I came in his mouth, and it was like, Wow. I'm gay. I'm *super* gay, and I love it!"

For both Edwin and Armando, the internet provided a safe avenue for developing meaningful connections with other gay people—relationships that, at the moment, didn't seem possible within the heteronormative constraints of their real lives (this was the early 2000s, a time when people's online and in-person lives weren't entirely enmeshed).[19] In both of their stories, the pursuit of gay friendships and relationships were negotiated with the potential costs of being outed among their existing social circles. Whereas their heterosexual peers had free reign to cultivate romantic connections in almost every context they entered—in their neighborhoods, in their schools, at the mall, at a bar, at a coffee shop—they had to go to great lengths to seek out queer connections online while hiding their desires in public.

Armando's story, in particular, shows how race shaped the way the gay men I interviewed navigated these online connections. On the one hand, Armando limited his presence on gay social networking sites because he didn't want to be outed to the handful of Latinos at his predominantly White university. On the other hand, most of his first online encounters were with Latino men and in Latino chat rooms because that was whom Armando felt most comfortable interacting with. Several of the second-generation gay men noted that the first queer connections they made online were with gay men of the same ethnic and racial background.

Through social media, the men I interviewed were exposed to the heterogeneity of gender expression within the gay community, including among gay people of color. Like most people, Arnel Manalo (b. 1984), a Filipino American mortgage broker, assumed there was a correlation between gender expression and sexual identity—he assumed that all gay

men were effeminate. After graduating from high school, Arnel got a
job at Express, a clothing store chain, and many of his new coworkers
fit what he thought of as a gay stereotype. They wore deeply cut V-neck
shirts and tight-fitting jeans. (This was the early 2000s, before skinny
jeans became mainstream.) They kept their hair long. They spoke as
loudly with their hands as they did with their voices. They were everything young men, especially young men of color, weren't supposed to
be, Arnel thought at first. "They were queeny," he said. "I couldn't relate
to them." In contrast, the young men Arnel had grown up with adhered
to the masculine aesthetic prescribed by hip-hop culture: baggy jeans,
sports jerseys, oversized hoodies, mint-condition sneakers. They cut
their hair once—sometimes twice—a week so that their fades always
looked fresh. They played basketball, they learned to pop and break-
dance, or they spun vinyl records. Part of the reason Arnel hadn't enter-
tained the idea that he might be gay was because his way of presenting
himself aligned with the latter.

Still, Arnel insisted he had no issue befriending his gay coworkers,
most of whom were Filipino American and Mexican American. He admitted he would've been afraid to do so back in high school. There was
one openly gay person in his grade, and anyone seen interacting with
him was considered "gay by association," which Arnel always thought
was stupid. "I'm always cool with people," he said. "You should never
judge a book by its cover. I respect individuality, and I respect people for
who they are." Nevertheless, Arnel's openness toward his gay peers had
its limits. "If they tried to flirt with me, I would freak out," he admitted.
Beneath the freak-out, however, Arnel began questioning his own sexuality. He found himself enjoying the same-sex attention from coworkers,
but he was afraid to respond. What if someone from high school were to
walk into the store and see him?

Then, one day, he overheard some of his coworkers talking about
a new social networking site called Downelink. Arnel walked over to
them and showed a polite interest; deep down, he realized he was genuinely curious. "One of my coworkers was complaining about a guy he

met on Downelink," he recalled. "I asked about the website, and he said it was like MySpace, but for gay people. I asked him if only gay people can have [an account]. He said, 'No. If you are friends with gay people, you can have one too.' Later after work, I logged on, I set up a picture." I asked Arnel whether he was afraid of his picture being on a gay social networking site. He said he wasn't. There was a setting on the Downelink profile where users indicated their sexual orientation, and it included an option for users who were not gay or queer. "On my profile, I put that I was a *stag*, which is basically the male version of a fag hag," he explained.

Soon after logging in, however, Arnel realized he was not, in fact, a stag.

"I went through Downelink and looked at people's profiles here and there," he said. "There were different types of gay guys. Yeah, there were guys like my Express coworkers. But then there were guys from the Bay Area who looked urban." By "urban," Arnel meant they followed the scripts of masculinity that most young men of color from his neighborhood adhered to. They wore baggy jeans, hoodies, jerseys, Air Jordan sneakers, Timberland boots, baseball caps with straight brims, and blinged-out earrings. Some dressed like hip-hop artists. Others "looked like cholos." None of them, as Arnel put it, "looked gay."

Indeed, social media was the first place where many of the men I interviewed began to disentangle the link between gender expression and sexuality. For the most part, they'd grown up conditioned to see a strict correlation between the two: that is, feminine equals gay and masculine equals straight. But in the salon of social media sites, they came across profile after profile of gay men of color who embodied the masculine ideal type they were familiar with in their neighborhoods and schools; rarely would they see gay men of color who presented masculine on television, in movies, or in person.

When Arnel and others encountered gay men who presented masculine on social media, they tended to rate them as more attractive, and at times lauded them for being able to "pass" as straight (Arnel and others at times would use "straight-acting" as a synonym for "attractive," which was problematic because proximity to heterosexuality became their ba-rometer for attractiveness).[20] This was the case even among those who embraced being effeminate. "You wouldn't even think he was gay if you saw him," one of my interviewees said about a man he once dated. (It's worth noting that while many idealized an aesthetic associated with het-erosexual masculinity, they were critical and outright hostile toward gay men who *actually* attempted to pass as heterosexual.)[21]

Arnel didn't say it outright, but his attraction to other men—and his willingness to date them—was clearly predicated on their ability to "pass."[22] Recounting the first time he met up with someone from Downelink in person, he said, "I started messaging people, and I hit up this guy Randy, who I thought was cute." Randy was Mexican American; Arnel was initially afraid to hit up anyone who was Filipino because, in his words, "all Filipinos know each other, and word could get around." In his profile picture, Randy "looked masculine." He had a shaved head. He had tattoos. They hung out one evening after Arnel got out of work.

"Randy was the first guy I kissed, the first guy I went on a date with."

"What did that feel like?" I asked.

"It was a *huge* sigh of relief. It was like, you know what, I *am* gay! It wasn't like, I'm curious. It was like, *I am gay.*"

"Were you worried [about this self-revelation]?"

"No. I wasn't worried. I actually felt like this was exactly where I needed to be. The whole time before that I felt like I was carrying a heavy burden. After [kissing Randy] I literally felt lighter."

Given his exuberance, I assumed Arnel would have wanted to pursue something more serious, but as it turned out, there *was* something he worried about. "We went out again, and then I was iffy. Because of his demeanor. I realized he was like my friends from Express. So I was like, this guy is cool, but I never thought he could be a boyfriend, though. He wore shoes that were pretty girly looking." Beyond Randy's cloth-ing choices, Arnel said, "His feminine side was coming out more." At first Arnel chalked this up to "just who I'm attracted to." In later conversations, Arnel explained why he felt apprehensive about Randy's effeminateness.

When he first started dating, Arnel preferred men who could "pass" because he worried about being outed. If someone saw them on a date, they could easily be read as friends. On some level, Arnel also felt that whom he dated was a reflection of his own masculinity. He already had a sense that masculine-presenting men preferred masculine-presenting men. Plus, he was thinking in the long term. If ever he were to come out to his mother, he thought, it would lighten the blow to know he was dating someone who "acted like a guy and not a girl." What social media provided was a marketplace full of men, including men of color, that Arnel felt would be "suitable" to bring home to the family, to bring home to Mom. To this day, Arnel's perception of a man's masculinity factors into his assessment of who he will hook up with or date seriously.[23] Several other men I spoke with expressed orientations toward dating that echoed Arnel's.

Beyond being a space for connecting and hooking up with other gay men, social media was also the point of entry into gay organizations and social functions. Through social media posts and pages on Facebook and Instagram, some of the Latino interviewees discovered organizations like Bienestar and The Wall Las Memorias, which were established to support LGBTQ Latinos.[24] A few of the Filipino interviewees were part of Barangay, an organization that focused on increasing awareness of LGBTQ issues in the broader Filipino American community.[25] It was through the friends they made online that men knew which clubs and bars to go to if they wanted to run into other gay men of color. In a region as large and racially diverse as the Greater Los Angeles Area, there were a number of bars and clubs that the men could frequent where the majority of patrons were gay men of color.[26]

Some men expressed hesitation about being openly gay on social media, especially on platforms like Facebook, where heterosexual family members regularly engaged with each other. Nick de la Cruz (b. 1986), a Filipino American retail manager, had close to a hundred gay friends on Facebook, but remembered worrying when family members—both in the Philippines and the United States—started setting up accounts and sending him friend requests. Before he was out to his family, he would decline requests from his aunts, uncles, cousins, and even his own sister. Nick was apprehensive about what social media researchers call a "context collapse"—the convergence of his immigrant family life and his gay life on Facebook.[27] "I wouldn't want my mom to find out about me [being gay] from other people in the family," he explained. "I think it would devastate her to know that I didn't tell her but yet I was advertising [my sexuality] on Facebook."

Other men saw it differently: social media was their avenue to be openly gay in front of their entire social network without the burden of having to come out to individual friends and family members. This is what social media experts term a "context collusion."[28] As one of the men said, "I would post news stories of gay issues or about marriage equality on my Facebook page, or I'd post pictures of me and my gay friends out in West Hollywood. I think people got the point and could read between the lines." More often than not, such posts were followed by an avalanche of likes and supportive comments. Friends and family members (and even strangers) would write messages of support: "I got your back!" "We love you no matter what!" "So proud of you!" Another interviewee recounted the response he received when he posted a photo of himself and his first boyfriend on Instagram. The anxiety he felt before posting it gave way to relief when he saw the comments: "You two are so adorable!" "So happy for you guys." Some of the messages were from former classmates and family members he hadn't spoken to in years. What surprised him most were the likes and comments from straight male friends and relatives who earlier in his life had made homophobic remarks to him directly or in his presence.

Of course, not all context collapses are intentional. Some of the men spoke about what social media researchers describe as a "context collision," the unintentional meeting of their different social circles.[29] The story mentioned in an earlier chapter about Manny Roldan was an example of a context collision. His high school classmates—unaware that he was gay—came across the photo of him and his boyfriend kissing on Instagram, and without his knowledge, began circulating the image among each other. He spoke about the devastating consequences when "that shit went fucking viral." His classmates gossiped about him behind his back. The teachers never once intervened. He stopped attending class and fell into a depression. And his relationship ultimately fell apart. Manny's classmates weaponized his social media post—an act of courage in itself—for public humiliation, not public support. What should've been a celebration of first love became fodder for a very public takedown at his school.

In some cases, a context collision unexpectedly led to the discovery of allies within one's family. Franklin Flores recounted the humorous story of how he learned his aunt was supportive of his being gay: "I just changed my profile picture for fun, and one of my friends were like, "So are you *bae* now?" His aunt, an immigrant from the Philippines unfamiliar with millennial jargon, misinterpreted the term of affection for something malicious. "She thought they called me *gay*!" he recalled. "And she was like, 'Franklin, you're still my favorite nephew! I will support you, whatever makes you happy.'" At that time, he was Facebook friends with his aunt, but not his mother; he didn't want her to see LGBTQ-specific content—photos of gay friends, gay news stories, other friends' comments—that would out him before he was ready. His aunt's public support on his page, however, helped him realize that, when he decided to come out to his mom, he would have an ally of his mom's generation in the family.

For the second-generation gay men I interviewed, the internet was a necessary outlet for exploring gay identity and building friendships and community with other gay people. It was through these online connections that many of the men found their way into the different gay social scenes throughout Southern California.

A Darker Shade of Gay

Gay Latinx and POC bars and clubs, lovingly dubbed "the scene," provided second-generation gay men a space where they unlearned the rules of masculinity and leaned into their sexual attraction to men who also shared their upbringing and racial background. Many learned about the scene through friends on social media. Whenever the men spoke about the scene (always singular), they were referencing the circuit of social functions that catered specifically to gay men of color. In sociological terms, a "scene" refers to a social space where attendees congregate based on a common lifestyle, cultural taste, hobby, or identity.[30] Major metropolitan areas like LA house a diversity of music scenes, art scenes, food scenes, and—of course—the gay nightlife scene. Scenes matter because they provide a sense of belonging and community, an antidote to the anonymity one feels when living in a city of millions. The scene referenced by the gay men I interviewed included bars and clubs where gay men of color congregated.

There were a number of bars, clubs, and parties that these second-generation gay men could frequent on any given night of the week. There were establishments that—as evidenced by their flyers, music selection, drag queen performers, and go-go dancers—catered specifically to gay men of color. There were Mexican bars that played *banda* and *ranchera* music and drew a predominantly immigrant crowd.[31] There were gay clubs that played a mix of hip-hop, pop, and reggaeton and drew mostly Black and Brown gay men.[32] At the Faultline in Silver Lake, there was once a monthly party that catered to queer Latinos who loved Depeche Mode and Morrissey.

Most of the Latino men I interviewed told me that their first forays into gay LA nightlife happened at establishments where the majority of patrons were gay people of color. Many of the venues were located outside WeHo, miles away from the strip of bars along Santa Monica Boulevard. Beyond Arena, Circus Disco, and Club Tempo located just east of WeHo, there were Alibi East in Pomona, Chico's in Montebello, Club

Cobra in North Hollywood, Executive Suites in Long Beach, and Ozz in Buena Park. Jaime Avila, a Mexican American bank employee, said he felt most comfortable at Latino gay clubs. "At first, it was definitely like, I wanted to see Latinos," he said. "I wanted to see my kind. I started doing the Long Beach thing, and [Executive Suites] used to have this Latino night on Thursdays. And then I made it out to Circus, and for a good year, I was at Circus, like, every Friday night. Circus was a godsend." Jaime appreciated being in gay spaces where the people, culture, and music reflected the Latino communities he had grown up in. He appreciated the fact that he could walk into places like Circus or Executive Suites and hear patrons speaking both English and Spanish, seamlessly switching between the two, just like he'd heard growing up.

Armando echoed Jaime's sentiments, and he added that in these clubs, he could revel in the diversity of the Latino gay community. "Circus is super Latino—you get the gay Latino cholos, gay Latino hipsters, and there are the immigrant Latinos that only speak Spanish," he said. "Unlike West Hollywood, Circus is the mecca of Latinos. You have such an immense diversity. Those clubs are where I feel more comfortable. Like I'm at home." He started frequenting Circus when he came home for summers during his college years, and then more so once he moved back permanently. For Armando, Circus offered a refreshing change of scenery from the predominantly White gay scene of Washington, DC, where Latinos and other men of color were tokenized, fetishized, or made to feel invisible.

Filipino American interviewees spoke of a different club that served as a hub for Asian American gay men: a Friday night weekly party, GAMeboi, hosted at Rage in WeHo, a two-story eighteen-and-over club on the corner of Santa Monica and San Vicente Boulevards.[33] GAMeboi's name was an homage to the online chat rooms for "GAMs," or gay Asian males, popular in the 1990s. (Despite the party's name, a smaller, but visible segment of the patrons were Asian American women.) Like Circus, the rooms were demarcated by styles of music: the first floor played pop songs by Britney Spears or Katy Perry, as well as K-pop; the second floor played mostly hip-hop. When Arnel started going to gay clubs, Rage was the only club in WeHo he went to for years because that was where he felt most comfortable. "At Rage, it was perfect because it was a group of people that, in a sense, were like me," he told me. "I was like, Oh shit, this is the type of crowd that I want to be surrounded with. I didn't even know there was a Micky's or an Abbey [two popular WeHo bars within blocks of Rage]. All I knew is that if we were driving to WeHo, then we'd be at Rage. That's it."

Friday nights at Rage were one of the few times when Filipino American gay men would find themselves in a majority gay Asian American crowd. Danny Tolentino (b. 1985), a Filipino American medical technician, recounted his nervous excitement when he first went to GAMeboi. He had been invited by another Filipino American he had met online whose friends were regulars. Danny was stunned to see hundreds Asian American gay men congregated in a single space. "They took me to Rage, and as soon as I walked in, my heart dropped," he said, smiling. "I was overwhelmed by everything that was going on. I kinda just froze in place. I'd never seen so many gays in one building, let alone a building of gay Filipinos and Asians."

What struck Danny the most was the diversity he saw, even within a crowd that was predominantly Asian American and gay. "The crowd was mixed," he recalled. "There was a bunch of different types. There's different shapes and sizes. There were guys who were very feminine or very boyish." By "boyish" he meant men that resembled his brother. "My brother was a gangster. Some of them looked like the type of guys my brother would hang out with. I remember telling my friends, 'Oh my God, I would have never thought some of these people are gay.' I kept asking them, 'Is *that* guy gay? Is he *really* gay? Are you *sure* we're in a gay club?' And they'd be like, 'Um yeah, we're in a gay club.'"

Danny's reaction revealed how little exposure he'd had to the diversity of gay communities, especially in terms of gender expression. "It made me realize I had no image of gay people whatsoever besides ones who were very feminine." As he was speaking, I couldn't help but notice the difference in his tone when referring to gay men who were "boy-ish" versus those who were "feminine." Although Danny never outright disparaged the men who were effeminate, he was clearly enamored with those who presented as masculine. GAMeboi may have offered him the chance to meet men with different gender expressions, but his tone signaled the existence of a hierarchy—one in which masculine-presenting men were considered more desirable.[34]

Even so, it was within clubs like these that second-generation gay men witnessed for the first time that femininity among men could be celebrated, not disparaged. Justin, fake ID in hand, became a regular at Ozz, a gay club in Orange County. Ozz hosted a Hip-Hop Night every Sunday that drew young gay men and women of color. Justin's favorite part of the evening was the drag show.

"I used to go to Ozz religiously, like, every Sunday," he recalled. "The line would literally go around the block. There was this notorious drag show hosted by Raja, who you might know was one of the girls who won *RuPaul's Drag Race*. That Sunday night was *her* drag show. And I remember it was so funny, because everyone would be dancing, and then all of a sudden you would hear someone on the mic, and then everyone would just stop dancing and sit on the floor. It was the weirdest thing, because it would be a full club vibe and then they would be like, 'Show's starting!' And then everyone would just drop to the floor and sit down to watch this drag performance. There wasn't even a proper stage. It was just right there on the dance floor. It was almost like everyone was sitting like kids in kindergarten waiting for story time, but by these drag queens."

In other social settings outside of the gay club, the men were more accustomed to seeing people, especially other men, admonish such gender transgressions. Within the context of a gay club, however, it was the men who perfected an amplified performance of femininity who were being celebrated (it's worth noting that the point of drag is not to pass as a woman; one should be perceived as a drag queen). That such celebrations took place in a space dominated by queer patrons of color mattered too, given the way masculinity among men of color was policed in other arenas of their lives. "It was crazy because everywhere else, people would be like, 'Look at this freak in a dress'—it'd be looked down upon," Justin said. "But at Ozz it was definitely cool. They'd be lip-syncing, like, Mariah [Carey] or Janet [Jackson]. It was so entertaining to watch."

And with those four words—"so entertaining to watch"—I was reminded that the embracing of femininity, even within the context of a queer space, was still spectacle. There were other men who spoke about the joy they felt watching drag performances, but it at times felt like they preferred to appreciate drag and drag queens from a distance. Of course, there were some who admitted they could never do drag because of the elaborate skill and craft involved, but there were a few men who, upon my asking if they would ever do drag, responded quickly and defensively—"Oh, I would never do drag," one interviewee said—as if the admission of the desire to embody femininity would detract from their own sense of masculinity.

Nevertheless, Latino and Asian American clubs like Circus, Ozz, and Rage expanded the boundaries for what men, and especially men of color, could do and how they could be. In their childhood and adolescent years, these second-generation gay men held rigid ideas of how young Filipino and Latino men were supposed to act. They felt a pressure to adhere to certain norms of masculinity in how they walked, talked, dressed, and loved. But the moment they stepped into a gay club, they realized they could break the rules that, for most of their lives, had hindered their ability to be fully themselves.

Racism in the Gayborhood

One afternoon in the fall of 2016, one of my former students Esmir peeked his head through the doorway of my campus office and excitedly shared some news. The previous week, a friend had dragged him to an eighteen-and-over party at one of the WeHo clubs—his first foray into a club of any kind. Esmir considered himself "shy" and "not like a club person," but was surprised at how much he enjoyed the lights, loud music, and steamy atmosphere of the overcrowded dance floor.

"I love West Hollywood!" he exclaimed. "It's the first time I went, and everyone's just so expressive. Everyone's just there to express themselves. I like how you feel very liberated when you get there. I saw this one guy who looked pretty chill and laid back, and then suddenly he's dancing with this random guy and making out and he's, like, very free and expressive. I just like how he came in all tensed up and nervous, and then he basically blossomed like a flower."

Esmir saw himself in this man and, watching him throughout the night, caught a glimpse of where he himself hoped to be one day. "I'm always tense," he told me. "I just want to let my guard down like that. I liked the feeling of being there. I desperately want that freedom in my life." I commended Esmir for stepping out of his comfort zone, and assured him that there were many young gay people in and beyond WeHo who knew exactly how he was feeling.

As Esmir was about to leave my office, he mentioned he would be heading to WeHo again that weekend. A few years shy of twenty-one years old, Esmir and his friend were planning to sneak into the Ivy Lounge (a pseudonym), one of the trendiest bars in WeHo.[35] I told him to be safe and wished him well.

Esmir's visit transported me back a decade and a half to my early twenties, the honeymoon days of my own WeHo clubbing experiences. I was happy for him. But the moment Esmir mentioned the Ivy Lounge, a cynicism crept in. This was the same bar that, for years, had contracted my friend AJ as a graphic designer.

In August 2016, AJ and I would meet a few times a week at a coffee shop to get work done. One summer afternoon, AJ and I were at a Starbucks in Eagle Rock, trudging along on our respective projects. In the middle of our work session, he flipped open his laptop to show me the flyer he had designed for the Ivy Lounge's annual Labor Day Weekend party. "Check it out!" AJ exclaimed.

Filling the screen were eight shirtless men, their arms around each other's shoulders, their smiles as bright as their oiled torsos. "Look! I even managed to sneak in a Black guy!" AJ said. The second person from the right was Black, his skin barely a hue darker than the manufactured tans of the seven White men in the image. AJ turned his laptop around and continued fiddling with the flyer. I inched my chair closer to him and saw that he was trimming the barely visible love handles off one of the White models.

"What if you were to put a Latino and an Asian guy on it?" I asked.

"Yeah, right—I wish. They'd send it back." AJ reminded me that in a city full of aspiring graphic designers, a freelancer's longevity was predicated on the ability to adhere to the client's "preferred aesthetic." He added, "I remember when I was doing the flyer for MLK Weekend, Rob [the events manager] jokingly warned me not to make the flyer *too Black*." But AJ knew that Rob wasn't joking. The flyer he made for the Martin Luther King Weekend party was similar to the Labor Day one, except that he had managed to sneak in a second Black model—a small act of resistance in AJ's eyes. The day the nation commemorated a slain civil rights leader was, for these clubs, little more than an opportunity to lure gay men to party harder on Sunday evening. Ivy Lounge was hardly the only WeHo bar that was guilty of this.

Esmir was still in my office when this memory flashed in my mind. I kept smiling, not wanting to diminish his romanticized version of WeHo. But I wondered if and when Esmir—whose race and body type didn't resemble the men on AJ's flyer—would eventually have to reckon with the fact that WeHo nightlife, for all its talk of inclusivity, was not created with him in mind.

From a bird's-eye view, bar hoppers and partygoers in WeHo—albeit predominantly cisgender gay men—are a diverse group. On any given night, there are men of different racial backgrounds, gender expressions, body types, and ages. There are Latin nights and hip-hop nights that attract gay patrons of color who might not otherwise spend their evenings in WeHo. As compared to most gay neighborhoods around the country, the evening social scene along Santa Monica Boulevard is among the most racially diverse.

And yet, the notion that WeHo was "super White" and "not for us" came up time and again in my conversations with second-generation gay men. The statistics support this characterization: a whopping 90 percent of residents in the city are White, and most belong to the upper middle class. A one-bedroom apartment in WeHo costs close to $3,000 per month to rent—twice as much as rentals in the predominantly POC neighborhoods in LA where most of the men I interviewed lived.[36] When reflecting on their times in WeHo, some men spoke about racist incidents they'd experienced. Arnel angrily recounted a time he overheard a pair of drunk White men whisper, "Who invited people from China?" when he and his group of friends ambled by them in an overcrowded bar. Edwin shared that while he himself had never had an "outright racist" experience, he once remembered a friend phoning him upset about an encounter he'd had at one of the clubs. "My friend, he's Latino, and he said that he rejected this White guy, and he [drunkenly] called him a beaner," Edwin said. Still, both Arnel and Edwin acknowledged that WeHo was one of the few public places where they could freely embrace being gay without worry. It was why they both continued to frequent the boulevard. Nonetheless, such incidents reminded them that racism can happen everywhere, including a place that was established precisely as a response to discrimination.

While the men I interviewed maintained that incidents of overt racism were few and far between, several mentioned that subtle forms of discrimination were commonplace. For example, some felt that bouncers and bartenders at certain bars and clubs showed favor to White patrons by letting them cut in line, serving them drinks more quickly, or being more outwardly affectionate toward them. Sal Gonzalez (b. 1989), a Mexican American urban planner, felt that staff at the Abbey, one of the most popular bars in WeHo, gave preferential treatment toward its White clientele. One Saturday night, when the bar was at peak capacity, he and a group of friends—all Mexican American—tried to order drinks at one of the crowded bars. "We were waiting for, like, twenty-five minutes for a drink, I kid you not," he said. "All the while, random White people would go up to the bar and get their drinks right away. That place is shady."

When Edwin first moved back to LA from Berkeley in 2009, he was a regular at the Abbey on Sunday nights. The resident DJ played hip-hop, which drew large crowds of Black gay men to WeHo. From Edwin's perspective, Sundays were one of Abbey's most vibrant, well-attended nights, thanks to the Black men and other men of color who patronized the bar. But he remembered how, out of nowhere, the Abbey ended its Sunday hip-hop night and replaced it with karaoke. "I haven't seen discrimination outright at the Abbey, but you can sense it when they suddenly changed up the music on Sundays," he said. "I would hear more hip-hop, and it was mostly Black people on Sundays. And now it's virtually nonexistent. That was a big surprise, because that night was so popular. It was really bizarre." After they changed the music, he noticed Sundays no longer drew large crowds of Black and Brown gay men. In fact, it didn't draw large crowds at all. To Edwin, it was almost as if the Abbey would rather have an empty bar than become the watering hole for gay men of a darker hue.

Some of the men shared similar grievances about other WeHo bars. Nick de la Cruz told me about the "power-tripping" bouncer who wouldn't let him into Fiesta Cantina. One night, Nick and his friends made plans to hit the bars on Santa Monica Boulevard and decided to make a pitstop at Fiesta Cantina to take advantage of their two-for-one drink specials and "hella strong" cocktails. After waiting in line for fifteen minutes, the bouncer informed them they wouldn't be allowed in because they were violating the bar's dress code.

"You can't wear that hat in the bar," the bouncer said, sternly.

"But those guys inside are wearing hats," Nick said, pointing to several other men on the patio wearing baseball caps.

"You can wear hats, but just not ones that say 'LA' on them."

"Well, can we just take our hats off?"

"No, you can't bring them in at all."

Nick relented. Rather than have his entire group of friends wait in line again, he offered to take their hats to the car, much to the chagrin of one friend, who had worn a hat just so he wouldn't have to spend a half hour styling his hair.

Nick's story didn't surprise me, because I, too, had been subjected to this rule on more than one occasion when I wore an LA Dodgers cap. Of course, I couldn't help but notice how this rule was inconsistently enforced; the petty side of me considered ratting certain patrons out to the bouncer (though, of course, I wouldn't). I was fully aware of the racist connotations of such a dress code (man of color + LA Dodger cap = gang-affiliated), but on a night out with friends, this was hardly a battle worth picking. There was one subsequent incident, however, that prompted me to reframe what had happened.

One Saturday afternoon, I was with my former roommate and his girlfriend enjoying brunch and drinks on the patio of the bar. On the opposite end of the patio, I spotted a tall, twentysomething White man wearing a trucker hat. As he socialized with his friends, I noticed the design on the hat: a rainbow Confederate flag. Apparently, sporting a hat with a Confederate flag was considered acceptable, but wearing an LA Dodgers cap was not. I contemplated confronting him—in retrospect, I wish I'd had the courage to do so—but the man was clearly intoxicated and the bravado with which he carried himself suggested he wouldn't take such an altercation lightly. Even if he weren't drunk though, I wondered if I would have engaged, knowing how violently resistant White men can get when called out on their racism.[37]

On the surface, what happened to Sal, Edwin, Nick, and me could be dismissed as harmless. Having to wait a few extra minutes for a drink or having to put something back in the car seem like minor inconveniences that shouldn't ruin a good evening. But as psychologists have shown, such "racial microaggressions" are everyday occurrences in the lives of people of color—in their schools, neighborhoods, workplaces, and public interactions.[38] Racial microaggressions include "brief and commonplace daily verbal, behavioral, or environmental indignities, whether intentional or unintentional, that communicate hostile, derogatory, or negative racial slights and insults toward people of color."[39] Part of the difficulty of addressing racial microaggressions—and racism, overall—is that White people instinctually gaslight people of color and try to convince them that they are overreacting. To such stories, they might counter: "Maybe the bartender was just busy that night" or "The bouncer was just doing his job." Ultimately though, these incidents must be situated in the larger pattern of people of color being excluded from bars and clubs under the guise of dress code violations. While many of the men I interviewed continue to frequent WeHo, there were also those who avoid it altogether because of stories like these. Experiencing racial microaggressions while witnessing the preferential treatment of White gay men felt like death by a thousand cuts.[40]

Conversations about race and belonging in WeHo often segued into conversations about race and desirability. Several men spoke about, as one interviewee put it, the "WeHo aesthetic," which canonized White gay men with slender or athletic builds as the gold standard of attractiveness.[41] For Phil Rosario, the WeHo aesthetic negatively impacted his sense of self-worth, especially in his first few years of partying there. When Phil first moved to Southern California from the Bay Area, his best friend Melissa offered to take him barhopping. He was excited, as he had long craved the opportunity to meet other gay people his age. But within minutes of strolling along Santa Monica Boulevard, Phil found himself feeling self-conscious about his physical appearance. "In WeHo, all you see are all these pretty people," he told me. "Honestly, I had really bad self-esteem, and I was really fat."

"What's fat?" I asked. Years before interviewing him, I'd seen Phil in WeHo several times and he'd always been slim in my eyes.

"I was probably, like, 185 or 186 at my biggest."

"Which is a regular guy's weight," I interjected.

"Yeah, but I'm, like, five-foot-nine," he asserted. "I was a big guy. West Hollywood has all these guys that are really hot."

Phil hadn't specifically mentioned how race played into what he considered to be "hot," but there were things he said that suggested that race was part of the equation. At one point in our conversation, he mentioned a mutual friend we had, and almost as a reflex said, "He's pretty hot for an Asian guy." That he attached that qualifier—"for an Asian guy"—signaled to me that he'd somehow internalized the idea that Asianness was antithetical to attractiveness.

The gay content that Phil consumed also factored into his schema of desirability. Years before he moved to Southern California, when he was still grappling with his sexuality, he would watch gay television shows and read gay magazines—always late at night, long after his parents had gone to sleep. "I didn't know how to be gay, so I'd watch *Queer as Folk* or read gay books or read gay magazines I would pick up from the Castro," he said. "I was trying to teach myself how to act gay." It struck me that most of the gay reference points Phil spoke of centered on the experiences of White gay men. *Queer as Folk* was a show about four White gay men frequenting a White gay club and navigating relationships with their White partners, families, and friends. A 2015 *HuffPost* article described the show as "progressive for its time," but also "a bit problematic and over the top—and very white."[42] The selection of magazines Phil read, including the *Advocate* (one of the longest-running LGBTQ publications in the country), overwhelmingly featured White gay men. In his book *Geisha of a Different Kind*, sociologist C. Winter Han writes, "Asian men, and other men of color, rarely appear as subjects of a story" and "are virtually nonexistent within the pages of [gay] magazines."[43] In the same way, Phil could never see himself on-screen or in print, he had difficulty imagining how someone like him could fit into a WeHo landscape where Whiteness and muscles reigned supreme.[44]

Several of the Latino gay men I interviewed added how the WeHo aesthetic made them aware of their racial and socioeconomic marginalization in the so-called gayborhood. They associated the Whiteness of WeHo with class privilege and a superficial obsession with physical appearance. Several said they hated going to establishments in WeHo because of this fact. "I don't like going to the Abbey," said Rolando Muñoz (b. 1982), a Mexican American clothing designer. "It's nothing but a fucking train of attractive people there. I see it as kind of rich. I think it's more White. I don't think I have the body for the Abbey, or the look—slim, slender, twink. Kind of more, like, beautiful guys. These are guys that want to be perfect and have a perfect life, and it seems really fake to me. I'd rather go to a gay dive bar." Octavio Lara echoed this sentiment: "I do feel otherized. I don't have the same references in pop culture. I don't go to WeHo. I've avoided it. WeHo is very into looks, into body, materialism, looking good. It feels like everyone is shit talking. I think sometimes when I am in a mostly White area, I do still have a hint of feeling like I'm being judged. I do feel like people would look down on me just because of my skin color."

Fortunately for the men who felt othered in WeHo, there were a plethora of establishments beyond Santa Monica Boulevard where they could cultivate connection and community. Rolando, Octavio, and others (Filipinos included) found a home at Latinx and other POC gay clubs and events in the Greater Los Angeles Area—in East Hollywood, Long Beach, the San Fernando Valley, the San Gabriel Valley, and, later, Downtown LA (in 2015, two gay bars, Precinct and Redline, opened and draw racially diverse crowds from around the city). This is not a new story. As Lillian Faderman and Stuart Timmons point out in their book *Gay L.A.*, a satellite of Black and Latinx establishments emerged outside of WeHo precisely because gay people of color felt marginalized, invisibilized, or fetishized in the gayborhood. In a region as rich as the greater LA region, there are countless gay people of color who don't need WeHo to be and become who they are. "I wasn't trying to be at any of the White clubs [in West Hollywood]," said Danny Maravilla (b. 1978), a Mexican American magazine editor. "I don't pay attention to those guys. They're invisible to me."

Community Matters

For much of their childhood and adolescent years, the gay men I interviewed struggled with coming to terms with their sexuality. For the most part, their families, friends, classmates, and teachers offered little help in this department. The isolation they felt drove them to find connection, and later community, with other gay people who could relate to their experiences. The queer camaraderie they found at T-parties, online spaces, or at the club were a source of oxygen for these men, long suffocated by the pressures of having to exist within heteronormative environments. Discovering these spaces allowed them the chance to redefine and expand the boundaries for what it meant not just to be gay, but to be a gay man of color and son of immigrants. The conversations we had about these experiences elicited excitement and nostalgia for so many of my interviewees.

"It was kind of amazing for me to go down memory lane because I haven't thought about this shit in a long time," Justin said at the end of our conversation. Now in his late thirties, Justin is no longer a regular in any scene; he's pivoted his focus to his career and relationship. He joked that he's now "retired" from going out, but he acknowledged that the friendships he built at T-parties and gay clubs were so formative of who he is today. There were a number of second-generation gay men who echoed his sentiments.

Many admitted they romanticized gay spaces when first encountering them. Whether they were brick-and-mortar or virtual, gay spaces allowed the men to feel freer than in most other contexts of their lives. These were sites where they could test out and experiment different versions of themselves, a contrast to the way they policed their behavior in their families and schools. Still, as liberating as that may have felt, these spaces weren't immune to the structural inequality that pervaded the larger society.[45] The men were keenly aware of how their belonging and desirability hinged on their race, gender expression, perceived class status, and body type.[46] There were many second-generation gay men who felt they didn't fit the archetype of the "ideal" gay man within queer spaces, both virtual and in person. This queer POC representation within these spaces matters tremendously; queer people of color, like the gay sons of immigrants I interviewed, help rewrite the story of what LGBTQ community is and can become.

6

Not That Gay

I . . . decorated myself to the point of absurdity. In all aspects of my life, I did
what I could to prove my merit. . . . Merit, it stood to reason, would prove my
worthiness. Excellence, like armor, would make me bulletproof.
—Matt Ortile, *The Groom Will Keep His Name*

There came a point when compartmentalizing gay life and immigrant
family life became too difficult for Nate Sarmiento (b. 1985), a Filipino
American nursing student. When he was eighteen, dipping his toes in
the Los Angeles gay scene felt like enough—a few hours here and there
chatting with other men online, one or two nights out at a gay club, sporadic hookups with men he'd never see twice. In his words, he'd go out
and get his "fix" and then come home to his family. When at home, he
never talked about this other part of his life.

By the time Nate was twenty-one, straddling these two worlds felt impossible. At the time, he was working any minimum-wage job he could
get just so he could afford to go out. Five to six times a week, he rotated
among gay bars and clubs in Long Beach, Orange County, and West
Hollywood. "I needed to pay my bills and go shopping," he explained.
"All I'm thinking about is my gas, my apartment rent, and money to be
able to go out, and to buy clothes for going out."

The friends Nate had once referred to as his club friends—because
initially he would only see them after ten o'clock at night—evolved into
real friends whom he would hang out with any chance he could, day or
night. He had fallen in love with one of these friends. They would all
go on road trips together to Las Vegas, San Diego, and San Francisco,
where they would connect with other gay men of color they'd met, either

in WeHo or through social media. "Social life and having a boyfriend—that was my priority," Nate told me.

The financial and time demands of keeping up his gay social life—or, rather, his *life*—took a toll on his family relationships. Whenever Nate went out, he wouldn't tell his parents or even his siblings where he was going. When it came to his friends, he'd only invite them over if the rest of his family was out. Nate hardly spent time at home, opting to sleep over at his boyfriend's or friends' homes most days of the week. If ever he and his family were home at the same time, he'd usually be in his room chatting with friends on the phone or online. Occasionally his mother would try to engage him, inquiring about his life or his friends, but he kept his answers curt. "Who are you laughing on the phone with?" his mother would ask, and his answer was always the same: "Just a friend." Nate couldn't pinpoint the exact moment when gay life became real life; a world he felt he was just dabbling in became his world. His gay friends weren't just people to go out with; they became his chosen family.[1] His boyfriend wasn't just a hookup; he was someone to imagine a future with.

Even as Nate was cultivating queer community, he still felt the pressure to partake in Sarmiento family gatherings, which happened at least once or twice a month. Family functions were stressful for Nate given how nosy his aunts and uncles were. Within minutes of showing up to a family party, the interrogation—and judgment—began: "Where is your girlfriend?" "Oh. Why don't you have a girlfriend?" "When are you going to get married?" "When are you going to give your parents grandchildren?" Nate hated making up excuses, but what he hated more was seeing his mother put on the spot by the gossipy relatives he knew she didn't care much for.

Nate stopped going to family parties. Eventually, he stopped hanging out with his own family.

"So your parents wouldn't see you at all?" I asked. "Like, ever?"

"Hardly ever," Nate said. "And that lasted more than five years."

"So you'd avoid them even on Christmas and Thanksgiving?"

"Yeah, I would just go out. I'd always be in West Hollywood or something with our friends. They wouldn't be with their families either."

"How'd that feel, not being with your family on holidays?

"I don't know. I was kinda detached. It sounds pretty bad, but I was detached, and after a while, I just didn't really care. Most of the time, I was working or out with my friends."

When Nate was in his early twenties, his mother would nudge him to attend family gatherings, or to at least spend holidays with the immediate family. He always made up some excuse—usually that he had to work. But one Christmas, Nate acquiesced to her wishes that he join the family for a gathering at his uncle's house in Mission Viejo, sixty miles away from WeHo, where his friends and boyfriend were hanging out.

Time away from the family had not made the heart grow fonder; if anything, it made everything more awkward. Relatives not only interrogated Nate about his love life but also guilt-tripped him for not showing up all those years. "I remember crying in the bathroom and feeling like, Why did I come? I should have just stayed with my friends," Nate told me. Crying in his uncle's bathroom, with his family celebrating just outside the door, was the tipping point. He decided it was time to tell his family that he was gay.

But how? In the past he had heard his parents disparage gay people as immoral. He had witnessed his brothers and their friends clown on each other for being "fags." He had listened to sermons at church about "traditional marriage" between "one man and one woman." How would he be able to let his family in on who he really was?

Coming Out in an Immigrant Family

Coming out is not a onetime act of confession, a singular event; it is a catalyst for the immigrant family to engage more openly about LGBTQ issues. Still, all of the second-generation gay men I interviewed said they were afraid to come out to members of their family, and especially to their parents. They spent years imagining worst-case scenarios: Will my parents see me as a disappointment? Will they kick me out of the house? Will they disown me? Will they continue to love me? These were the kinds of questions that floated in their minds the moment they considered they might be gay. Many said they had lived with these worries since they were young children. They were made to believe that being gay was immoral and wrong, and that living as an openly gay man was an impossibility. But by forging connections with other gay people and embedding themselves in gay social circles, they started to reimagine what was possible not only for themselves but also for their families.

Most of the gay men I interviewed described coming out as a daunting decision, one that forced a collision between the value systems of the gay community and the immigrant family and its community. For example, within the gay community, there is an ethos that one should be out and proud about one's sexuality; however, in the context of the immigrant family and community, where being gay is associated with stigma and shame, some men said their parents encouraged them to keep mum about their sexuality to "save face" with other relatives. Being gay felt incompatible with the conservative teachings of the church, homophobic attitudes among members of their family and community (both in the United States and the home country), and the immigrant dreams their parents had for their American-born children.

A few days after the 2016 Pulse shooting, journalist Matt Thompson penned an essay in the *Atlantic* that captured the conflict that gay children of immigrants feel with their families. Thompson writes,

> My own parents were the very last people in my life I was out to, years after I'd been out to friends and colleagues. I didn't know how they'd react to the fact of my sexuality, and among my friends, there was often impatience with that uncertainty. *If they're good parents*, these friends would say, *they will love you without conditions and without hesitation.*

But this reaction was rare among those of us who grew up, like me, knowing that our parents left their homes and settled here mainly in pursuit of visions of what their children's lives would be. They had imagined their sons as men with wives, and their daughters as women with husbands, and cultivated these visions throughout our adolescence and beyond. Some of our parents had tended to these visions so zealously that they missed all the signs that these weren't, in fact, the people we'd become. When we came out, they were forced both to reckon with these people they no longer recognized and mourn the visions of us they had nurtured all those years.[2]

Thompson's sentiments were echoed by many of the men I interviewed, including Franklin Flores. "I was worried [my] being gay would ruin my parents' immigrant dreams," Franklin confessed. In his eyes, the sacrifices his immigrant parents made to come to this country mattered more than the sacrifices he endured as a gay man of color. Franklin and several others expressed concern about the "grief" their parents would experience when learning their son was gay, often minimizing their own pain in the process. With each man that uttered such a remark, it became clear how adhering to heteronormative concepts of family ended up hurting both gay sons and their immigrant parents.

Despite the potential fallout, these second-generation gay men felt they *had* to come out to family. The need to come out—that is, explicitly uttering the words, "I'm gay"—is something that distinguishes gay sons of immigrants from gay immigrants, research suggests. As compared to their US-born counterparts, researchers have found that immigrant gay men are more likely to treat their queer sexuality as an open secret. For example, in his book *Tacit Subjects*, gender studies scholar Carlos Ulises Decena found that the Latino immigrant gay men in his study would introduce romantic partners to their heterosexual family members, but they tended to refer to them by their names or as their "friends" (as opposed to explicitly referring to them as boyfriends or partners).

In other words, their sexuality was, as Decena describes, "tacit knowledge" within the family.[3] When I asked my interviewees whether they would be okay with their sexuality being "tacit knowledge" among their relatives, nearly all of them asserted that coming out was essential to cultivating genuine relationships with family. "I need to tell my parents more about my life," said Omar Reynaga. "I don't want them to pass on without them really knowing me."

As the United States and other countries become more progressive on LGBTQ issues, coming out may become the pathway for Asian Americans and Latinxs regardless of where they were born. According to data from the Social Justice Sexuality Project at the City University of New York, nine out of every ten Asian Americans and Latinxs are out to at least some members of their families. These findings were based on the largest national survey of LGBTQ people of color to date, and it included both immigrant and US-born Americans.[4]

Still, as the narratives of these second-generation gay men will reveal, the process of coming out was more complicated than uttering the words "I'm gay." Their stories of coming out illustrate how concerns over masculinity and respectability shaped *how* they disclosed their sexuality to family.

Reinforcing Respectability

Jordan Estigoy (b. 1986), a Filipino American working in real estate, was in his early twenties when he decided to come out to his family. He was most afraid to tell his mother, the person in his family he felt closest to. "I felt like I didn't want to disappoint her," he explained. "I was scared. The one thing I didn't want was to make her cry. That'd be the worst."

I asked Jordan about the thoughts running through his mind. He worried that his mother would see him as a gay stereotype.

"What were you thinking her impression of gay people was?" I asked.

"Glitter and unicorn and fairies and wings. Being gay in the Philippines is like you are a girl, basically."

Back in his early twenties, that wasn't at all the image Jordan wanted his family, and especially his mother, to associate him with (although now that he was in his thirties, he admitted he was much more comfortable embracing traits that were considered effeminate). Jordan decided he needed to "set the stage" for his coming out by gradually complicating his family's perception of gay people. To accomplish this, he turned to one of the few television shows at the time that centered a gay story line: *Will & Grace*. The NBC comedy, which first ran on primetime television from 1998 to 2006, chronicled the misadventures of a gay lawyer, Will Truman, his straight best friend, Grace Adler, and their two over-the-top companions, Jack McFarland, a perpetually unemployed gay actor, and Karen Walker, a straight alcoholic socialite. Conveniently, *Will & Grace* aired right after *Friends*, which Jordan's family had already started watching together every Thursday evening.

"It was kind of like testing the waters," Jordan said. "Taking them to a one-foot-deep pool of being gay. I had my mom watch *Will & Grace*, and there was a point when it became a tradition for the whole family to watch it."

"Why did you do that?" I asked.

"Because obviously the characters are gay, but you give them two perspectives of gay. There's Will, and then you have Jack."

Jordan hoped that Will and Jack's polar opposite personalities would complicate his family's perception of gay people. Will was the accomplished attorney zealously chasing a long-term relationship. He embodied respectability politics, and at different moments in the series, revealed an aversion to being (seen as) effeminate. Meanwhile, Jack was unapologetically flamboyant, and for much of the series, boasted about his sexual conquests. Unlike Will, he didn't mind being the stereotype. While Jack was often presented as the jokester, it was he who ushered Will safely out of the closet.

As his family became more invested in the show, Jordan mustered up the courage to feel out their potential responses to his own sexuality. "They loved the show," he said. "Even my older brother, who is an alpha male, loved it. And so, I came to the point where I was comfortable, and I asked my mom, 'What if I was like Will?' She looked at me and said she didn't know what I was talking about. Then I asked, 'What if I were like Jack?' She said, 'Oh my God, I would slap you.'"

"Did you tell her then?" I asked.

"No, I didn't tell her."

Jordan took note of his mother's divergent responses to Will and Jack. His mother's measured reaction to Will and her visceral reaction to Jack sent a message: being a gay man with an established career and stable relationship was better than being a stereotype. It was then that Jordan decided to present himself as being more like Will and as different from Jack as possible.

There is an episode in the first season of *Will & Grace* that centers on Will's antipathy for Jack's unapologetic effeminateness. The episode begins with Will and Jack at the gym. Sometime during their workout, Jack ends up flirting with a (presumably straight) client of Will's, much to Will's chagrin. Later, Will complains to Grace: "Sometimes he's just such a fag." Will rationalizes his hurtful remarks by boasting that he is not the type of gay man who "wear[s] my sexuality like a sash and tiara, like Jack does."[5] This was precisely what Jordan was doing in his conversation with his mother. He was distancing himself from gay stereotypes to bolster his own standing as a "respectable" gay man, one who could "pass" in the company of straight people.

Jordan's need to be the respectable gay in his family's eyes emerged in other ways. Before he came out to his mother, he began introducing his friends to her, but wouldn't mention that they were gay. He said he wanted her to get to know them independent of their sexuality. "I thought if I involve[d] her more, she would feel comfortable to accept the fact that I'm gay," he said. "So I would bring more of my gay friends around." I pressed Jordan and asked if he extended the invitation to *all* his gay friends, including those who were more "like Jack."

"Actually, to be honest, I would have to make sure that they weren't acting too gay or anything," he said.

"Why?" I asked.

"Only because like, out of respect of the home, you know? And plus, if they were too rowdy or too crazy or talked about all this [sexual] stuff, it's always in the back of my head that [my family's] gonna be really uncomfortable. So that's why I didn't bring them to the house." Jordan's remark about "respect" was repeated by several gay men I interviewed. For them, maintaining respect seemed to entail a willingness to throw effeminate gay men under the proverbial bus to garner acceptance. If they were to have any shot at being openly gay, they had to ensure family members that they were not *that* gay.

With *Will & Grace* and his gay friends, Jordan was setting the stage for his coming out. On some level his efforts helped to complicate and expand his family's understanding of who gay people were. That they were more than a caricature to be laughed at. His family had few cultural references and personal connections to gay people, and so Jordan manufactured them.

Ultimately, Jordan's efforts fell short of transformative. In demarcating which of his friends were "acceptable" to bring home, he was privileging a version of gayness that adhered to heteronormative sensibilities. He wasn't the only one who felt self-conscious about the gay friends that would meet the family. Several of the men acknowledged that they were less inclined to introduce their relatives to gay friends whose gender expression challenged masculine gender norms. For some, this was an attempt to stave off speculation by their parents or other relatives about their own sexualities. Jordan insisted that he was merely trying to complicate his family's narrow views on gay men; he wanted them to see gay men as more than "guys who acted like girls." His remarks exemplified an irony in the coming out stories of these men: gay sons of immigrants may have been victimized by masculinity, but in their attempts to maintain rapport and support from family, they were willing to denigrate other gay men in the process. In this respect, they were complicit in maintaining a logic of masculinity that devalued effeminacy.

This was evident when Jordan shared his coming out story. "I told my mom while she was driving, which was a bad idea," he said. "I was really worried, so I brought up *Will & Grace*. I told her, 'Don't worry, mom, I'm like Will.'" Jordan then began listing the gay friends his mother had met. "I told my mom, 'You know Jay, Javi, and Peter?' She was like, 'Oh, did you tell them [that you were gay] too?' I then told her that they were all gay, and she was shocked! She was like, 'Really?' All she knew of gay people were White gay guys, drugs, parties, and AIDS."

"Where did she get her impressions?" I asked.

"Media, obviously. She thought I was going to be a big girl with the big hair and dress up. Little did she know. I told her I haven't changed. I'm still the same person. I told her that she did a really good job in raising her son, that I'm going to school. I told her I really want her to be there when I get married."

What Jordan wanted was for his mother to see him as a respectable gay man. On the one hand, he was able to move his mother's understanding of gay people beyond stereotypes. On the other hand, by valorizing and aligning himself with gay men who presented as masculine and embodied a certain type of middle-class success, he was reinforcing the idea that there were "good" and "bad" ways to be gay. Even if his mother's impressions of him (and other gay men like him) remained positive, his approach to coming out did nothing to change her impression of gay men who were effeminate or living with HIV or cared little for respectability politics.

Historically, coming out wasn't just about confession. Nor was it about assimilating with the straight world. Coming out was meant to be transgressive. In his book *One-Dimensional Queer*, Roderick Ferguson reminds us that coming out was part of the radical politics of gender-transgressing queer activists of color like Marsha P. Johnson and Sylvia Rivera during the late 1960s and 1970s.[6] As people of color who transgressed gender norms and engaged in sex work, neither Johnson nor Rivera was positioned to benefit from the assimilative strategies of White cisgender gay men. Ferguson writes, "In a social and political context in which activists experimented with the radical possibilities of differences of race, gender, class, and sexuality . . . coming out was part of that radical experiment." In other words, the empowerment of queer people of color was about recognizing and declaring their differences, not insisting on their sameness.

When the gay men I interviewed shared their coming out stories, I found myself wondering: Whose feelings counted more? Those of the gay son or those of the straight immigrant parents? What was once considered an act of collective defiance felt more like an act of confession drenched in apology, I observed. In an op-ed for the *New York Times*, the writer Meredith Talusan describes how when transgender people come out to family, there is a tendency to "[absorb] their loved ones' grief" and to "[provide] solace to people who mourned as though they died."[7] While Talusan's piece focuses on transgender experiences of coming out, I recognized the same sentiment at play in Jordan's story.

After Jordan came out to his mother, the next person he told was his older brother. "When I told my brother, he first blamed himself," he said. "He thought about all the gay comments that he said towards me because I was very flamboyant as a kid. He thought that because of the teasing throughout my life, that's what brought me to be gay. So, I explained to him that wasn't it. He said he would be careful making all those gay comments, and I told him, 'Why? It's not like you are derogatory towards me.'"

In any heteronormative environment, including one's family, the well-being of straight people often takes precedence. In Jordan's case, heteronormativity conditioned him to prioritize the emotional needs of his straight family members above his own. In focusing his attention on his brother's comfort, he missed an opportunity to transform how his family thought—not just about him being gay but about queerness overall. The therapists I know would argue that Jordan couldn't be blamed entirely—he did what he needed to do to survive. Still, I had to acknowledge that in that moment, Jordan could've done more. He could've corrected his brother's inclination for homophobic behavior instead of offering complicity. Maybe I recognized what Jordan was doing because of the way I've fallen short in standing up for *all* LGBTQ people. In reflecting on his story and parts of my own, I see how, in the name of masculinity, second-generation gay men are capable of marginalizing others, just as we've been marginalized ourselves.

The Trauma of Being Outed

Not all of the gay men I interviewed had the opportunity to set the stage for their coming out like Jordan. There were a handful who were outed to their families without their consent. Diego Zamora (b. 1980), a Mexican American nonprofit program manager, grew up in a household where homophobic remarks were commonplace. Diego was one of the men whose father went on a tirade after seeing a gay character on television. "If I ever found out my son was like that, I would beat him," Diego recalled his father screaming. "I would kill him. If I didn't kill him, I would disown him."

The church community his family belonged to reinforced the homophobic beliefs of his father. I asked Diego about the kinds of messages he heard about gay people. "Everything from homosexuality is a sin to all homosexuals molest kids," he answered. "Not so much directly from the church, but from the churchgoers." Diego knew the influence this church had had, because his father would regurgitate some of the same fallacies at home; he would warn him about "gay men touching little boys."

Throughout middle school, Diego also struggled with body image, which compounded the struggles he already had with his sexuality. He'd long known he wasn't like the other boys in his class, who picked on him for being "too sensitive." With the stress he was facing at home and at school, Diego gained seventy pounds in the span of a year. The bullying worsened. Diego found refuge with one classmate, Cesar, who he sensed shared his same struggles. "He was the first boy I fell in love with," Diego told me. Unfortunately, their friendship was put to a halt by

Cesar's mother, who sensed a bourgeoning flirtation between the two. She confronted Diego and forbade him from seeing her son.

"His mom was like, 'My son is not like that, and I know what you are feeling. I have a lot of friends that are like that, but please leave my son alone,'" Diego recalled.

"She confronted you?" I asked.

"Yeah. And I was heartbroken. I never advanced any feelings toward him, but she just shattered it. Put a stop to it before I could even say anything."

Cesar's mother outed Diego to her son in a time when Diego had barely come to terms with his own sexuality.

This experience in middle school scarred Diego, but it didn't deter him from wanting to explore his sexuality. When he entered high school, at a campus with more than five thousand students, it was much easier to fly under the radar. He befriended a group of Goth kids and met other young men who were queer or questioning; all of them sported gender-transgressing fashion choices—makeup, long hair, leather boots, fishnet shirts—that invited inquiries about their sexuality. Diego felt comfortable, even emboldened, around these new friends, who were unafraid to sport mascara or nail polish and who didn't care whether others saw them as gay.

In Diego's sophomore year, a high school counselor, who happened to be a gay man, launched an official club for him and his group of friends. "It was kind of a little gay-straight alliance," Diego explained. Their meetings had no agenda; they mostly just hung out in a classroom together during lunch. But it became a space where the gay students were able to open up to each other about their experiences—same-sex crushes, volatile relationships with parents—and give each other support with coming out.

A few months after the group launched, a classmate of Diego's who attended the same church caught wind of his involvement. Things took a turn for the worse. "Midway through tenth grade, I was outed to my dad by this lady from church," Diego said. "Her daughter went to the same high school as me, and she told her mom I was going to this group with gay people, and that I am hanging out with the wrong people. She told her mom to tell my dad. She told my dad, 'It's embarrassing that he is holding hands with guys at school. What are people going to say?'"

Diego was totally unaware that his classmate had divulged this information. He arrived home one afternoon and was greeted by his father's wrath.

"Is it true?" he remembered his father screaming. "I already told you how I feel about it if you are like that. I don't want you here. You're dead to me."

"What was your response?" I asked.

"At that point, it was anger. I was like, 'Why do you hate me so much for this? It's not something I can control. What she is saying is none of her business, and she is just a stupid bitch.' It got pretty violent at one point. He wouldn't hit me too much, but he shoved me. He threw me around and things like that."

After this violent confrontation with his father, Diego's options were limited. He came from a low-income household that struggled to make ends meet. Most of his friends were in the same socioeconomic situation and couldn't take him in for more than a day or two. Not too long after he came out, his father kicked him out of the house, and he had no choice but to drop out of school and find a job. In the book *Coming Out to the Streets*, sociologist Brandon Robinson notes how the repercussions of coming out are felt harder by gay youth of color who are from a low-income background because they are more likely to lack economic and social safety nets.[8] This is precisely what happened with Diego. Given his age and lack of experience, the only job he could find was for a company in Northern California selling magazines door to door. With no savings, he moved to the Bay Area, and for several months he lived in an extended-stay hotel with his coworkers, many of whom were queer kids who "had no relationship with their parents and were already homeless." When they weren't working, they spent their free time drinking and commiserating about how much they hated their parents. Some were so enraged they fantasized about killing their parents.

Despite the harm his father inflicted on him, Diego didn't feel the same way. "I didn't have that type of anger," he told me. "I didn't have that much resentment. Yes, I had been disappointed. Yes, I had sadness, but it wasn't to the point that I was angry and hated my parents." After a few months of living in the Bay Area, he returned to Southern California to try to resolve the tension with his father. Unfortunately, his father didn't rise to the occasion. "Obviously, it wasn't enough time for my dad to process, and so he started hitting me again."

It was difficult for me to accept that Diego had no antipathy toward his father, especially given how violent their relationship became. Whether he was angry in that moment, I couldn't know for sure; what was clear was that even through the violence, Diego held on to the hope that his father would come around. His father eventually came to accept him—many years later—which perhaps explains why he never focused on his anger toward him during our interview. But before that shift would happen, the volatility of their relationship drove him into a depression.

One afternoon, after a particularly hostile confrontation with his father, Diego waited for his family to leave the house. He went searching for his father's gun. When he found it, he sat on the floor with the gun on his lap. "I knew I wasn't going to do anything," he admitted. "Just the thought of having the gun there knowing I could end it, it was running through my head." Minutes later, his older sister came home to find Diego, gun in hand. He started sobbing. For the first time in his life, someone in his household listened to him and comforted him.

Although he had the support of one person in the household, the tension between Diego and his parents didn't wane. After he and his father kept butting heads, he had hoped his mother would protect him from his father, but instead she was complicit. "My mom is very passive," he explained. "She tried to be a mediator, but she wasn't very successful at it. She was like, 'You know your dad. He's not going to change.' And that's pretty much it." Even if she was more accepting of his sexuality than his father, it pained Diego that his mother didn't have his back when he needed her most.

One last violent encounter would be the straw that broke the camel's back. Diego was in the living room watching *Queer as Folk*. His father happened to pass through the living room during a sex scene between Brian (the sexually adventurous main character) and a random man in a gay bathhouse.

"What the fuck are you watching?" his father screamed. "You are not going to be doing that kind of stuff in my house. I hope you don't feel comfortable doing that. I hate the person that you are. I'm ashamed."

Even after hearing some of the most hurtful words a parent could utter, Diego responded with compassion. "It got so heated, and I finally told my dad, 'I don't care how much you hate me or the person that I am. I will always love you, and I will always be here with open arms for when you're ready to love me. And when you're ready to love me, you can come around. But if not, then, oh well.'"

For the second time in two years, Diego moved out. He had barely turned eighteen. This time he was able to move in with two queer women he had known from the support group in high school. For the next few years, communication between Diego and his parents was sporadic. Despite the heartbreak of being driven away, he kept empathizing with his parents. "I think in their own world, they were just trying to figure things out," he said.

It would be six years before Diego and his father would make peace with each other. By the time he was twenty-four, Diego had held several jobs—as a flight attendant, property manager, and sales associate—so he could support himself. Without a college education, there were challenges securing work, but he hustled hard enough to support himself. I asked Diego if it was his economic stability that allowed him to reconcile with his father. It wasn't. He suspected it had more to do with his father's confrontation with his own mortality.

"Now my father is the most sensitive man you will ever meet," he said. After several years of radio silence, Diego was surprised by his father's repeated requests for forgiveness. "I don't know what specifically made him turn like that. I don't know if he had an epiphany or maybe like a life-or-death experience. He was getting his regular checkups, and the doctor started talking to him about prostate cancer and things like that. So I think all of that was going on, and he was like, 'Oh my gosh, I am mortal. I can die anytime soon. Either I am here for my kids or I am not.'"

Diego forgave his father, as well as his mother. Although they are on good terms now, he couldn't help but imagine that things never had to unfold the way they did. He wished they could've been better.

Coming Out as Collective Effort

A number of the gay men I interviewed elicited the help of siblings when coming out to their parents. Marco Aguirre (b. 1986), a Filipino American engineer, first came out to his older sister Melissa when he was in college. One weekend, during his senior year of college at San Diego State University, Melissa and her boyfriend had taken a weekend trip from LA to visit him. Marco suggested they meet in Hillcrest, the gay neighborhood in San Diego, at a brunch spot that had a "mixed crowd" of both queer and straight young people. Marco invited Damon, the man he was dating at the time but whom he had never mentioned to his sister as anything more than a friend.

Marco worried about how his sister might react. They had both grown up in a "very Catholic" Filipino family, and although he never remembered her saying anything homophobic growing up, nothing signaled that she would be an ally to him either. When he arrived at the restaurant with Damon, he wondered whether to introduce him to his sister as his friend or as his boyfriend. He ultimately decided to forgo the euphemism.

"Melissa, this is my boyfriend, Damon," he said. He hadn't anticipated how nervous he'd be to add that extra syllable in front of "friend." He scanned his sister's face for a hint of a negative reaction, but it never came. "How awesome. Nice to meet you, Damon," Melissa said. Over omelets and mimosas, they caught up about the usual topics: school, mutual friends back home in LA, family drama. But for most of their meal, they talked about Marco's emotional journey with his sexuality. He told her about knowing he was different around age five; his first boy crush, at age ten; and his first boy kiss, at age sixteen.

"Why didn't you tell me before?" Melissa asked.

"I just didn't want you to look at me differently. Plus, I didn't want mom and dad to find out."

"You're my brother. I'll love you regardless, you know." Marco was mildly annoyed that she didn't seem to get why he hadn't told her sooner. Ultimately though, he was happy to have her on his side for when he would tell their parents.

That moment would come a few months later, during Marco's spring break visit to LA. Ever since he had started college, Marco rarely visited home, even during the summers when he didn't have classes. He rarely called his parents, either. The distance that grew between them over the years made this rare visit an especially tense one.

"I don't know why you're always so rude to your dad and me," his mother told him. "You aren't being open with us." Marco wondered whether his mother was hinting at something. She began questioning him about his choice of roommates—why he opted to live with three women. His father interjected, "In high school, I had a lot of friends who were girls and people started to say I was gay." The three of them were in the kitchen. Marco could barely stand to look at them. He felt like they were pressing him to come out.

"Oh my God! I'm guessing you already know that I'm gay," he said, enraged that he was backed into a corner. Their immediate response enraged him further.

"Are you sure?" his mother asked, oblivious to the distress her son was experiencing. "Have you tried having sex with a girl?"

"No!" Marco screamed back. This was the first time in his life either of his parents had brought up sex in conversation.

"You should try it," his mother insisted. Marco was at a loss for how to respond. His parents continued to probe despite his obvious discomfort. His mother brought up a gay man she knew in his forties and how he didn't have a family.

"I just don't want you to be alone like him. And I want you to have a family," she said.

"I *can* have a family. With a husband!"

"No, not like *that*!"

Marco's mother couldn't help but make his coming out about herself. "Was it me? Was it something I did? Was it because your dad wasn't here a lot because of work? Was it because I babied you too much?" All the while, his father stood by, silent.

Marco realized there was no amount of reasoning he could offer to quell their concerns. He excused himself from the kitchen, and he packed up his belongings so he could drive back to San Diego early the next day.

The months following were awkward between Marco and his parents. They tried reaching out to him by phone, but Marco kept the conversations short. "I talked to them, but just about school, or random things," he said. "We never talked about anything personal like relationships. It was more sane that way."

Enter Melissa. In the aftermath of coming out, it was Melissa who fielded many of the questions and concerns their parents had about Marco's sexuality. When their parents insisted that Marco was going through a phase, Melissa assured them he was not. When they tried to argue that Marco could "try being straight" with one of his female friends, Melissa pointed out how ludicrous their proposal was. When their mother expressed worry that Marco would be alone for the rest of his life, Melissa explained that same-sex couples were more than capable of having healthy relationships, even ones more stable than heterosexual ones. She explained that Marco could choose to have children if he wanted to, either through adoption or surrogacy. When they responded by saying that "wasn't normal," Melissa scolded them: "Stop being so closed-minded and messed up. That's your son."

Marco couldn't necessarily measure the impact of his sister's interventions. In the year after he came out to his parents, there wasn't a marked improvement in their relationship. Still, Marco felt relieved that his sister was advocating on his behalf behind the scenes, doing her best to shepherd their parents to a place where they would accept him (and his relationship) in the same way they would with their heterosexual children, nephews, and nieces.

While most of the men I interviewed said their siblings were supportive of them, there were a handful of men with siblings who were not. One of the most painful stories I heard was from Chris Mojica. When he came out to his older sister in his senior year of high school, she basically condemned him.

"I don't know if I'd be okay with you being gay or not," she said to him. "I just need to have a dream where God tells me if it's right or wrong."

"Are you fucking serious right now?" he said. "You're being, like, magical. You want a dream that will tell you if you should love your brother or not?"

"If God tells me that it's wrong, it's wrong."

"You're stupid. I mean, you're so smart, but religion is making you so stupid. Like, blind. *So* not logical. Out of touch with the real world."

"My friend says even the Bible says it's wrong."

"Show me." Chris knew her ability to cite actual Bible passages was nonexistent.

"Well, it was her interpretation."

"Well, I'll just wait for you to have your dream with God then."

What pained Chris most was that he had seen himself as his sister's biggest advocate. Growing up, he was always the more social of the two. If ever he overheard classmates or cousins "talk shit" about her, he would immediately come to her defense. And in a moment when the reverse was happening, she wouldn't reciprocate. "My friends are questioning me because they've been seeing your pictures," she said, referring to photos of Chris with other men who were rumored to be gay. "They wanted to know if you're gay. I'm really embarrassed." It was clear to Chris that she was more concerned about the opinions of her friends than his well-being. It felt like a betrayal.

Other men described their siblings as merely tolerant of their sexuality. When Ivan Ybáñez (b. 1991), a Mexican American college student, came out to his parents, they insisted that he was going through a phase. The tension between Ivan and his parents took a toll on him; he found it difficult to focus on school. A few weeks after he came out to his parents, his older brother offered him a place to stay, but under certain conditions. "Right now, I live with my brother and his wife, and they said they don't have a problem with me being gay," Ivan told me. "But the fact is they said they didn't want their kids to be exposed to *that* right now because they want them to grow up 'normal' and know what normal is. So they don't want to hear, see, or talk about anything that's gay." Even though Ivan described his brother and his wife as "accepting," such remarks show how their acceptance came with conditions. He had little choice but to hide the gay aspects of his life—his gay friends, his romantic partners, his gay books and magazines—when in the presence of his brother's family, which he knew was something none of his straight relatives ever had to do. He said he did it "out of respect" for his brother's family, but in truth, his living situation depended on it.

* * *

Nearly every man I interviewed described the experience of coming out to family as distressful. Psychologist Kevin Nadal notes that professional counseling and therapy can be beneficial to LGBTQ people of color because it can provide a space for them to safely process their experiences with homophobia, both within and beyond their families.[9] Unfortunately, only a few of my respondents had gone to therapy and, sadly, the reason some of them began seeing a therapist was because their parents were hoping they could be converted. Fortunately, the mental health professionals that these men encountered were not conversion therapists; they were ones who affirmed that it was perfectly okay to be gay.

Dario Garcia (b. 1981), the Mexican American clinical social worker introduced in chapter 2, told me this was how he first came into therapy. When he was fifteen, he wanted to gauge how his family might react if he were to come out. He started wearing a rainbow bracelet, and when his mother asked what it symbolized, he told her it represented the gay community. "I was kind of test driving to see how she would react, and she didn't say much, but a week later, [my parents] confronted me," he said. His parents sat Dario, his twin brother, and his older sister in the living room for a family meeting, which Dario found unusual. "You know minorities. We don't have family meetings," he quipped.

During the meeting, his parents vehemently expressed their disappointment. Dario's father insisted that his sexuality was a phase that would pass; he expressed worry that Dario would soon be "thinking like a girl" and "dressing like a girl." Like many other parents, his reflex concern was his son's gender expression, whether he'd still look and act like how he believed young men should. Dario maintained that he wasn't going to be like a girl at all, that he "just liked guys" (it was commonplace for second-generation gay men to assert their maleness and masculinity rather than challenge the problematic notion that it wasn't okay for men to be effeminate). His mother brought up religion. "This is not right," she told Dario in front of the family. "This is a sin." Dario found it laughable that she was suddenly religious; it had been at least a few years since either of his parents had set foot in a Catholic church.

The reaction of his siblings surprised him. Dario had assumed that his brother would react negatively, but he ended up being the most supportive. "No matter what, no matter who you like, you're my brother, and I love you," his brother told him. His sister, on the other hand, sided with his parents during the meeting. "My sister had the same stance as my mom," Dario said. "I had pictured that she would be more open-minded because she was in college. Soon after that though, my sister and my mom advocated that I see a psychologist." Their intention was not for Dario to receive the mental health support he needed; their aim was for him to go through conversion therapy, the now discredited form of therapy that aims to "change" the sexual orientation or gender expression of LGBTQ people.[10]

Dario was in such despair after the family meeting that he acquiesced to their demand for him to see a therapist, even if their motivations were ill placed. When they entered the therapist's office, he was a ball of nerves. "It was nerve-racking," he said. "When we were in the waiting area, he was looking over at us a lot. *Why was he looking at us so much?*" Dario didn't understand it at the time, but what he now realized, given his own training as a psychotherapist, was that he was being evaluated to see if his mental state was sound. After briefly observing them, the therapist invited him into his office.

"Tell me why you're here today," the therapist asked his mother.

"My son is gay, and I don't want him to be gay," she said.

With those words, Dario's heart sunk. "I *haaaaaated* her," he told me. "I didn't *hate* her, but I just really disliked what she said at the time. I really felt no love in that moment."

The therapist didn't immediately respond to Dario's mother. He proceeded with a set of questions that, in retrospect, Dario recognized as a mental status exam.

"Do you see anything that's not there?" he asked Dario.

"No."

"Do you hear any voices?"

"No."

"Do you sleep well?"

"Yes."

"Are you having bad dreams?"

"No."

"Did you have any traumatic experiences?"

"No."

"Did someone hurt you?"

"No."

"Did someone die?"

"No."

"Okay."

The therapist turned toward Dario's mother.

"I see that your son is quite normal," he told her.

He turned to Dario for one last question.

"Do you like the same sex?" he asked.

"Yes," Dario responded.

The therapist shifted his gaze back to Dario's mother.

"There's nothing we can really do about that," he told her. "If this is how he feels, then we support him, and we will continue to support him."

I asked Dario how his mother reacted to the psychologist's conclusion.

"She was livid," he said. "She just kind of turned red, and she was just very upset. And I was thinking to myself, *Thank God!*"

Dario was relieved that the therapist he happened to encounter was one who affirmed LGBTQ identity. When he encountered this therapist in the mid-1990s, conversion therapy had yet to be publicly discredited as a pseudoscience by the American Psychological Association. According to the Williams Institute at the UCLA School of Law, there are over 700,000 LGBTQ Americans who have experienced conversion therapy, which researchers have found increases the likelihood of depression, anxiety, and self-harm.[11] This encounter with a therapist could've easily taken a bad turn for Dario.

Looking back, Dario suspected that the therapist he saw might have been gay himself; he realized there were moments the therapist tried to signal this to him. His relationship with his parents and older sister didn't improve much after meeting with the therapist; their beliefs didn't soften until many years later, when Dario was finished with college and in graduate school to pursue a master's in social work. But in that moment, when he was still a teenager, it helped Dario tremendously to hear an authority figure validate and normalize his sexuality. It was what inspired him to become a mental health professional as an adult.

Repairing Relationships

By the time the second-generation gay men I interviewed came out to their families, they had had both time and support to process their understanding of their sexuality; for their parents, however, the processing of their sons' sexuality began with the moment of disclosure. Ulises Arias (b. 1993), a Mexican American college student, described coming out to his mother as a "bumpy" process. Like many of the other men, he was the one who pushed his parent to talk more openly about his sexuality when he came out to her; often, the parents of the men I interviewed preferred to stay silent about their son's sexuality.

Ulises first told his mother when he was a junior in high school, where she happened to work as a librarian. During that year, he had been romantically involved with one of the other queer students in his grade whom he had met while attending a gay-straight alliance meeting. Seeing as how his mother worked at his school, he didn't want her to find out about his relationship from someone other than him. A few weeks before the school year ended, he decided to come out to his mother because the boy he was dating had asked him to prom.

"She knows everything about me, so I couldn't hide that from her," he said. "After going shopping for my prom stuff and buying me everything, I can't lie to her and tell her that I'm going with some girl after she spent three hundred dollars on me."

"How did she react?" I asked.

"She told me she knew. She could see it in my eyes. She said she had heard things in school."

Ulises's mother suspected, but she let him tell her when he was ready. He was grateful, too, that his mother offered to learn more about LGBTQ issues on her own. She offered to join PFLAG, an organization and support group for parents and friends of queer children. Even though she was among the more accepting of parents, there were moments when her discomfort about Ulises's sexuality popped up. When Ulises referred to the boy in his class as his "boyfriend," she lashed out, much to his surprise. "No lo llames tu novio!" she said. "Don't call him your boyfriend! It's weird."

Although his mother's remarks hurt him, Ulises felt he had to be patient with her. "I realized it takes time for everybody," he said. "If it took me time to accept that I was queer, then it was going to take her time to accept that she has a child that is queer."

Other men spoke about how their attempts to be transparent with their parents were brutally rebuffed. A few years after his mother took him to therapy, Dario made several efforts to gain her acceptance, including being more open with her about his dating life. His efforts backfired. "If I straight up told her that I'm seeing someone, she would straight out put up a wall," Dario said. "She would say, 'No, you can't go out with him. No, you can't do this or that.' She would set limitations, and so I would just say, 'I'm going out with a friend.'" After a while, Dario stopped seeking his mother's approval. Even so, he realized that he needed to forgive his mother, his father, and his sister, even if they hadn't offered their acceptance of him.

I asked Dario how he was able to have so much empathy for his family, even though they had hurt him. He explained that trying to see the parallels between his experience being gay and his parents' experience as immigrants helped him forgive them. "I think the battle that I have as a gay man is like the same battle immigrants go through in the United States. It's equivalent in the way you have to come out, deal with identity, deal with society, deal with yourself, find yourself, and leave your parents in some way." Dario likened his parents' journey to understand his sexuality to their journey migrating to the United States. While that didn't necessarily repair the rift in their relationship, it was the framing he needed to hold on to in order to reconcile how he was treated by them.

NOT THAT GAY | 161

For Nate, the interviewee whose story opened this chapter, the epiphany that kick-started the reconciliation process came not from him but from his father. For more than five years after having come out, Nate had avoided his family. But suddenly, shortly after his father had major heart surgery, there was a shift in their relationship. "He had a pacemaker put in, and then that's when he became more open with me," Nate said. "I guess it took him being near death to get more involved in my life. He started asking me questions, everything from my personal life to my work life." His father's medical condition also prompted his mother to be more affectionate in ways she had not been in years. "I don't remember what day it was, but out of the blue, I remember my mom telling me that no matter who I like or who I love, she was going to love me for who I was." Nate was genuinely surprised. He lamented though that it took a near-death experience for them to come around. Ultimately, he was thrilled that he now had the chance to share all of himself with his parents. He introduced them to the man he'd been dating for the past five years. They welcomed him to family gatherings and treated him like a son. And when Nate decided it was time to move in with his boyfriend, his parents were supportive. "I think it's time for you to grow up and move out and see what life has out there for you," his mother told him.

Acceptance from parents doesn't always manifest in their words. For some, it came in more subtle forms. Danny Maravilla, a Mexican American magazine editor, said he and his parents never had an explicit conversation about his sexuality after he came out to them in his early twenties. In the months after he came out, however, he began bringing his boyfriend Will to family get-togethers. He debated whether he would introduce Will to his family as "just a friend" or as his partner, and he decided on the latter. "I brought my boyfriend Will around to parties and would say, 'This is my partner,' and I noticed [my family members] didn't care. It wasn't an issue." If ever he attended family events alone, his uncles and aunts—all of whom were born in Mexico and had migrated to the United States as adults—would ask, "Where's Will?" It was a simple question, but for Danny, it meant everything to be welcomed by family he had never expected to be accepting.

There was one troubling pattern that emerged from these stories of second-generation gay men reconciling with their parents: it was often predicated on their ability to be seen as respectable, not in their willingness to reckon with queerphobia. There was this notion of, "I can be accepted by my parents if I just show them that I'm the right kind of gay man"—that is, a gay man with the "right" level of education (i.e., a college degree), the "right" job (i.e., a middle-class occupation), and the "right" boyfriend (i.e., one who presents as masculine). Dario captured this sentiment when he told me the story of how his mother came to accept him.

"I think my mom saw that I was gonna graduate [from college] and she thought, 'Whoa, my son broke the stereotype, and he's actually thriving,'" he said. "I broke that image of the typical gay guy who gets STDs [sexually transmitted diseases], and it changed her perception of me. It allowed her to be more open about my sexuality. After that, I actually started talking about the guys I was dating."

The reality remains, however: gay children shouldn't have to *earn* their parents' love and acceptance. And yet, as Dario's remarks illustrate, the second-generation gay men I interviewed often believed that familial love and acceptance was contingent on their willingness to assimilate into a particular vision that their parents had for them. Accumulating accomplishments may have complicated their parents' perception of them as gay men, but it also highlighted how these men felt they had to prove their worthiness in ways their heterosexual siblings would never have to.

7

Beyond Acceptance

When you can't find someone to follow, you have to find a way to lead by example.

—Roxane Gay, *Bad Feminist*

I'd known Joe was a keeper, but something he did five months into our courtship sealed the deal. It was a sunny September afternoon in 2013. We were window shopping, hands held, at Downtown Disney in Anaheim, California, the promenade of shops and eateries next to Disneyland. At one point, while standing in front of a confectionary watching the workers transform candies into cartoon characters, Joe embraced me from behind. Not sweetly necessarily, but more in that "I just saved you from stepping in dog shit" kind of way.

"What are you doing?" I asked, craning my head toward him. Joe motioned his eyes toward the people to our right. A thirtysomething White man was with his two young boys, a baby in his arms and a toddler standing by his side. I looked back at Joe, confused.

"Look!" he mouthed.

I looked again and saw that the White man's palm was shielding his baby's face, which was odd considering that we were all standing in the shade. He bent down to his toddler and whisper-shouted several times, "Cover your eyes." The boy placed his hands over his eyes like a game of peekaboo.

I recognized the White man's tone. It was the same tone that the gay men I spoke with described their fathers using if ever they were caught paying mind to anything remotely queer.

That's when I realized what this father was protecting his children from.

Us.

Suddenly, Joe and I were playing a game of chicken at the Happiest Place on Earth. The man kept looking in our direction, visibly bothered by our unwillingness to untether. Joe doubled down with a kiss to my neck; his pettiness made me smile. Moments later, the father whisked his children away in a huff.

"But that's the minority anxiety, right?" asks the queer Latinx writer Carmen Maria Machado in her memoir, *In the Dream House*. "That if you're not careful, someone will see you—or people who share your identity—doing something human and use it against you."[1] It certainly felt like this father at Disneyland was using our humanity against us, and as much as I tried to fight it, the anxiety stayed with me long after he'd left our presence.

I had to remember: queer people of color publicly embracing our humanity—our joy—makes an impact. I saw it during my interview with Manny Roldan. We were at an outdoor café in Westwood Village, a few blocks from the UCLA campus. Manny was telling me the story of the social media post of him and his boyfriend kissing that "went fucking viral," the one that led to him being outed both in his high school and at home. He was telling me how the arguments with his parents were so volatile he ended up punching a mirror with his bare hand. As Manny was recounting this story, I saw his gaze shift to something behind me. I turned around and saw two Latino men, both around Manny's age, walking hand in hand. "You see that a lot around here," Manny said. "It's pretty cool." I saw how the tension in Manny's face softened as the couple strolled by our table. A story of hopelessness interrupted by two people who exemplified new possibilities.

I couldn't help but wonder how different Manny's high school experience would've been had the sight of two young men holding hands been as mundane as it was in that moment. If the idea of two young men falling in love was an everyday occurrence, then surely the post of Manny and his boyfriend kissing wouldn't have gone viral. How different would the lives of the second-generation gay men profiled in this book have been had they had access to different models for how gay men of color could be? Instead, their existence and agency were limited by frameworks of masculinity and race that constrained their possibilities. As the chapters in this book have revealed, the survival of these second-generation gay men took the form of suppression, assimilation, and overachievement. And, too often, their acceptance was predicated on a willingness to throw effeminate gay men or transgender women under the bus.

Admittedly, what some of these young men accomplished in their pursuit to prove their worthiness was remarkable. Many of the men I interviewed were the first in their families to graduate from college. They were financially supporting the parents who had reprimanded them for being gay. They became student leaders, filmmakers, artists, and activists. Nonetheless, as Machado reminds us, "It's not being radical to point out that people on the fringe have to be better than people in the mainstream, that they have twice as much to prove."[2] These men shouldn't have had to labor for worthiness in the first place.

For many of the men I interviewed, familial and societal acceptance was the goal. Having spent much of their lives feeling marginalized, stigmatized, scrutinized, and harangued for their sexuality, many expressed relief about the times they were accepted and supported by their mothers, fathers, siblings, aunts, uncles, cousins, classmates, and friends—even if acceptance and support wasn't extended to the larger LGBTQ collective. "It's less about coming out and more about letting people in," writes Jose Antonio Vargas in his memoir *Dear America: Notes of an Undocumented Citizen*. "I learned that you come out to let people in. The reality is that the closet doesn't only hide you from strangers, the closet also hides you from people you love."[3]

I myself have felt this relief. When I came out to my parents, in my early twenties, they weren't shy about sharing that they had had other dreams for me—to marry a nice girl and have children. It took us years to recalibrate our relationship. But then I started dating Joe, and I witnessed their change of heart in the most ordinary of moments. The times my mom went outlet shopping and bought Joe whatever she bought for me but in a different color. The times my dad would ask Joe to burn him a CD of his favorite songs from yesteryear because I was too impatient to play tech support. The times my mom would share secret family recipes and cooking tips with Joe in the kitchen where I grew up. Whenever I catch one of these interactions, I remember that the journey to these ordinary moments was long and hard fought. It was clear from my interviews that many second-generation gay men felt the same way.

The fact that these gay men had to work for such small joys made it easy to forget that acceptance, especially from family, should never be contingent on their willingness to labor. And yet, so many of them understood this burden as a given. In many respects, their willingness to contort themselves for acceptance was congruent with the narrative of the hardworking immigrant: Work hard for the American dream, don't make a fuss, and you will be rewarded. Too often, though, the men I spoke with were content to bask in what felt like the hard-earned victory of social acceptance, without further interrogating the systems that facilitated their marginalization in the first place. I've been guilty of this myself. On a structural level, assimilation reinforces the status quo. And if there's anything we've learned from the disruptive queens of Stonewall, it's that real cultural, institutional, and political transformation doesn't come by way of assimilation.

Fortunately, there were second-generation gay men who saw the need to move beyond individual acceptance. Through acts small and large they not only rewrote the paradigm for whom second-generation gay men could be but also understood the need to fight against and dismantle systems of oppression more broadly. Franklin Flores, the Filipino American college graduate whose story opened this book, was one of these men. In high school, Franklin wore his academic accomplishments like a cape, a cover to draw attention away from his emerging queer sexuality. Such an approach, while advantageous to Franklin, did little to benefit other gay students beyond him. Plus, it was a strategy that depended on being racialized as one of the Asian American "model minority" students at his predominantly Black and Latinx high school.

In college, Franklin's sexuality became the catalyst for engaging in student-led movements for social change. In embracing his identity as a gay Filipino American, he was able to find community with a coalition of undocuqueer activists fighting for immigration reform—an issue that affected a broad range of LGBTQ people of color, but one that was neglected in mainstream conversations about LGBTQ rights. Franklin was not undocumented, but he learned to see the connections between undocumented immigrant rights and LGBTQ rights—from the way the law worked to suppress their communities to social movement campaigns to fight systemic oppression. It was through working with undocuqueer activists and other LGBTQ students of color that Franklin ultimately gained the social support to become the first openly gay and third Filipino American student body president of his university. Through his work and visibility as president, Franklin helped transform his campus not only into a place where LGBTQ students felt they could belong but also a place where they could *lead*.

I opened this book by sharing Franklin's story, about his plan to come out to his mother once he received a graduate school acceptance from Harvard. Months after our last conversation, Franklin received several acceptance letters from top programs across the country. But in the process of applying, he realized that his tendency to chase academic goals had been an avoidance tactic. "I've spent too many days never being present in the moment," he said. "I made it routine to uproot my life in search of a new start any time that I faced conflict or uncertainty. Applying to grad school was a distraction from the present-day conflicts that may have been in the back of my mind." At the top of this list was not being out to his mother. When Franklin eventually told her in the spring of 2017, the urge to pursue graduate school dissipated. "I decided not to go back to school and instead focus on cultivating habits and relationships that would make me feel alive." Two years later, Franklin would make his way to Harvard, but on his own terms—not because he needed to fulfill a preordained immigrant family dream.

Armando Garza, the Mexican American city planner and Georgetown University graduate, was another second-generation gay man who redefined success in ways that went beyond earning a college degree, getting a good job, and receiving validation from family and other heteronormative institutions. Harnessing his connections with other LGBTQ Latinxs and his passion and training as a writer, Armando began writing plays about the diverse experiences within this collective. It was important for him to showcase the heterogeneity of the queer Latinx community and feature stories of queer Latinxs of different genders, gender expressions, generations, ages, regional origins, and legal statuses. His plays chronicled not only the struggles that LGBTQ Latinxs faced but also the joy, humor, and resilience threaded throughout their everyday lives.

One of Armando's plays premiered in a local playhouse in East LA in 2012, and the show sold out every night. I managed to secure a ticket on the final weekend of the play's run. I found myself in tears more than a few times, sometimes because I was laughing so hard my belly ached, other times because the play had me reliving some of the most difficult moments of my own queer coming of age. What Armando told me, years later when I interviewed him, was that his brothers were in the audience that weekend too, including the one who had tormented him for years when they were children.

"All my brothers went to the play," he said. "We're in such a better place now as adults than we were as kids." On some level, having his brothers watch the play made it easier to convey the emotional turmoil he felt as a gay kid growing up in a Latino immigrant family. There was no conversation where his brother reckoned with how they treated him as a child; nevertheless, Armando felt a conversation wasn't necessary. "Even though they don't talk about it, they can see the turmoil."

Armando opted not to invite his parents to watch the play. "I was still living at home for various reasons, and there was still some uneasiness about me being gay and me being their son. I felt we still had to do more work in our relationship before exposing them to a public space where I'm so [openly] gay." Years later, however, when Armando wrote a sequel, his mother was in the audience. For Armando, it was a full circle moment to see the woman he saw as his best friend, the person who inspired him to become a storyteller in the first place, in the audience applauding a work of art that centered his identity as a gay Latino man. The beauty of that moment wasn't just in his family's willingness to attend; it was in their willingness—and the willingness of Latinxs from the surrounding city—to listen and learn about the beautiful, messy stories of people who, for so long, have been relegated to the margins of the community.

After speaking with Franklin, Armando, and others, I got to reflecting on what constitutes "success" for second-generation gay men. There are some agreed-upon metrics of success within my field of sociology: earning a college degree, securing a middle-class profession and moving into a middle-class neighborhood, and ultimately surpassing the socioeconomic standing of the immigrant generation. Stories like Franklin's and Armando's showed me, however, that the way gay children of immigrants conceptualize success transcends these measures. They had graduated with the prestigious degrees, obtained the right jobs, and were living the American dream. But in the end, their individual success wasn't enough; they felt compelled to do their part in dismantling the systems of oppression—racism, sexism, and homophobia—that for much of their lives hindered their ability to be fully themselves. For them, the concept of success was predicated on their ability to achieve justice for the marginalized communities with which they identified.

* * *

I embarked on writing this book because of a disconnect I witnessed between my academic training in sociology and my everyday life as a queer Filipino American son of immigrants. In my pursuit to become a sociological expert on immigration, it was my queerness and membership within queer communities of color that equipped me with a lens through which to see: existing narratives on immigrants were incomplete. For much of my life, I'd seen my sexuality as an impediment—to my sense of belonging within my family and community, to my academic and career pathways, to my ability to imagine a future for myself. But in my years as a PhD student, and now as a college professor, I've come to see my sexuality as a unique intellectual asset that, along with my racial identity, allows me to better understand the mechanisms underlying structural inequality in this country—within schools, neighborhoods, politics, media, cultural institutions, and more.

In my opening chapter, I shared a question posed by the scholar Imani Perry that drove much of the writing of this book: "How do you become in a world bent on you not being, and not becoming?" What I came to realize, as the writing of this book progressed, was that second-generation gay men's ability to exist—as well as their ability to write themselves into existence—depended on their willingness to situate their stories as tragedy or triumph. Their inclination was to speak of gayness and queerness as either limiting or liberating, with little else in between. The professional worlds of academia and publishing are often unable to conceptualize the experiences of marginalized people beyond these tropes. The problem is, situating the experiences of marginalized people and communities within such a limited framework erases the full spectrum of their humanity.

As I was putting the final touches on this book, I happened upon a podcast conversation between Ocean Vuong and Bryan Washington, two writers whose lives and intellectual perspectives were shaped by the intersection of immigration, race, and queerness.[4] Vuong was born in Ho Chi Minh City, Vietnam; early in his childhood, he migrated to Hartford, Connecticut, where he spent most of his childhood and adolescent years. Washington, who traces his roots to Jamaica and the American South, was born in Kentucky but grew up mostly in Black and Latinx communities in Houston, Texas. Vuong and Washington spoke candidly about how they approach writing queer stories—how each understands his own queer story.

"I often talk about this notion of what I think is radical okay-ness, which is where I hope queer narrative can move forward towards," Vuong tells Washington. "Which is not hyperbolic triumph or travesty, but a radical new realization of being okay."[5] Hearing this forced me to reckon with the ways that my field, sociology, incentivizes a certain kind of storytelling—one that rewards researchers when they amplify the most painful moments of marginalized people's existence. This is apparent, too, in the way academia incentivizes marginalized scholars—the people often best positioned to conduct research on marginalized communities—to advance a version of their story that emphasizes trauma in order to win prestigious fellowships and research grants aimed at mitigating their marginalization. To put it another way, queer people of color, unlike White people, aren't allowed to be just okay if they want to succeed, and it is for this reason that Vuong considers being okay a radical act.

Echoing José Esteban Muñoz's conceptualization of queerness as "a longing that propels us forward" and "that thing that lets us feel that this world is not enough, that indeed something is missing," Vuong adds that queerness saved his life.[6] "Often we see queerness as deprivation, but when I look at my life, I saw that queerness demanded an alternative innovation from me," he says. "I had to make alternative routes. It made me curious. It made me ask, '[Is this] not enough for me?' because there's nothing here for me." Immediately, I thought of the parallels between Vuong's assessment and the creativity and choreography with which the gay men in this book navigated their own lives. How in the absence of models, they forged their own pathways, and when they honed this skill set, they passed along this knowledge to others who faced similar hurdles.

Washington, in turn, spoke about the evolution of his queerness from a mechanism of constraint to a key to new possibilities. "Those initial steps that you take [coming out], you can feel like a pariah," he told Vuong. "You can feel deeply ostracized for the fact of being yourself. But that shift, for me, seeing that many things can be true simultaneously, that my queerness wasn't an impediment—it opened me up to the world outside of the world that I couldn't even have imagined. I did not even know what I didn't know. That felt and feels like such a gift."

The conversation between Vuong and Washington, along with the stories of second-generation gay men in this book, stand as a reminder: the very thing that was once weaponized to dismiss your humanity, con-strain your agency, and obstruct your opportunities can—if embraced and harnessed—become the very thing that sets you free.

ACKNOWLEDGMENTS

Thank you, first and foremost, to the second-generation gay men who offered their stories for this book, and in the process, relived—and honored—some of the most emotionally challenging moments of their lives. Although I can't thank you all by name or include all your stories, know that each conversation was so necessary to the development of this book. I hope I've done your stories justice.

Thank you to my editor at NYU Press, Ilene Kalish, for shepherding me through the writing of this book. I almost gave up on writing it altogether, but your enthusiasm reignited my passion. To the anonymous reviewers and copy editors, thank you so much for your feedback and confidence in this work. I am grateful to Steven Pahel, who shared an iconic photograph of Los Angeles on Unsplash that now graces the cover of this book. Thanks also to Neda Maghbouleh for reminding me that I had to see this book to the end, even before I'd even finished a chapter. Jenny Gavacs and Marcela Maxfield, I'm thankful to you both for your insights in the early development of this book. Thank you to my former students who assisted me as the book progressed—especially Armand Rene Gutierrez, Audrey Aday, José Cuchilla, Archibaldo Silva, and Alejandro Zermeño.

I'm so grateful to the community of writers, scholars, and friends who have supported me through the highs and lows of writing a book. Thank you to my two main writing crews, the Bruin Book Club—OiYan Poon, Janelle Wong, and Ellen Wu—and my Voices of Our Nations Arts (VONA) Foundation writing family—Cynthia Greenlee, Joyce Chen, and Ruby Murray—for never failing to push me intellectually and creatively. Cynthia, I'm forever indebted to you for seeing the writer in me that I couldn't yet see in myself. I wouldn't be the writer I am today without you.

Claire Schwartz, thank you for teaching me how to make sentences as beautiful as the sociology. You read every single word of this book and offered the most lovingly rigorous feedback. Sylvia Zamora, my ride-or-die, your friendship and companionship since we were in graduate school has meant everything. Daniel Soodjinda, thank you for being my best friend and brother both in the CSU and in life. Forrest Stuart and Jonathan Rosa, thank you for your willingness to hold my hand through some of my most vulnerable moments. Laura Goode, I'm so grateful for your unapologetic kindness and realness. Badia Ahad, Ryan Blocker, Theo Greene, Dana McGarr, Kevin Nadal, Mindi Thompson, Tanya Golash Boza, Irene Vega, Nancy Wang Yuen, and Shannon Gleeson, thank you for your encouragement, support, and friendship throughout the writing of this book. C. J. Pascoe and Mignon Moore, your work and mentorship were the catalyst I needed to embark on this project in the first place.

Thank you to the brilliant writing teachers who have pushed me in my craft, especially Kiese Laymon, Meredith Talusan, Edgar Gomez, Kavita Das, Jaquira Díaz, Kima Jones, Nadia Owusu, Imani Perry, and Gabrielle Bellot. Thank you to the writers I've had the privilege to be in workshop with at Tin House, VONA, Jack Jones Literary Arts, and Catapult—I am a better writer, artist, and person because of each of you. A special thanks to Dayna Cobarrubias for being the first person to help me believe I could be part of these amazing literary communities. Thank you, Roxane Gay, for being the catalyst to my creative nonfiction writing dreams and reminding me that stories of gay children of immigrants matter, even as the publishing industry tried to tell me otherwise. To my agent Amanda Orozco at Transatlantic Agency, thank you for seeing the possibilities in my writing and for pushing me write the books that *I* want to write.

This book benefited from the many organizations—and people within them—who have supported me along the way. I'm thankful to my colleagues in the Department of Sociology and the Office of the Provost at Cal Poly Pomona, especially Anjana Narayan, Erica Morales, Mary Yu

Danico, Amy Dao, Brianne Davila, Leticia Keenan, Alex Morales, and Faye Wachs. Thank you to the Ford Foundation and my mentor Karthick Ramakrishan for supporting me with a postdoctoral fellowship. To Jean Caiani, Felicia Gustin, and Amalia Mesa at SpeakOut, thank you for curating opportunities for me to share my work with the widest audience possible. Thank you to Ashley Westerman for opening doors for me to share my work on NPR. I am grateful to Robin Mohapatra, Mason Colman, Kerry Ann Rockquemore, as well as the team and faculty colleagues at the National Center for Faculty Development and Diversity for empowering me to take risks with my career that I'd normally be too scared to take. Thank you to the many departments, cultural centers, and student groups at universities and organizations across the country who've invited me to share my work; the insights and feedback I received during these trips have helped me become a better scholar and writer. Thank you to the *Chronicle of Higher Education*, Colorlines, *GQ*, *Gravy*, the *Hear to Slay* podcast, *Inside Higher Ed*, KCET, *Life & Thyme*, the *Los Angeles Times's Asian Enough* podcast, NPR, *Catapult*, and *Latino USA* for offering me opportunities to tell stories for audiences beyond academia.

I owe the greatest debt to the people in my life who have kept me grounded, through the good, bad, and ugly. Neil Panchmatia, thank you for helping me see life—past, present, and future—with a new lens. Thank you to my friends in academia who've become my family beyond it, especially my family from the UCLA Department of Sociology. Thank you to the many queer friends who've become part of my chosen family. Thank you to the Ocampo and Crisostomo families for always reminding me what matters most in life. Andrew Rodriguez, thank you for your unwavering support of my writing and of me as a human being. Joseph Cipriano, you've been by my side through the triumphs—but, more important—the trials and tribulations. Still, what I cherish most are the mundane, everyday joys I get to share with you. Thank you to Schmidt, the emotional anchor of our family, who's been by our side making us laugh even when the world was crumbling around us. Finally, my deepest gratitude goes to my mom and dad, who came to this country imagining big things for their only kid. Thank you for supporting me throughout my entire life, whether it's through a random "I love you" text or preparing the most incredible Filipino breakfast every time I'm home on weekends. I feel so lucky.

APPENDIX

The Research Process

One of the main goals of *Brown and Gay in LA* is to bridge scholarly and public conversations around race, immigration, and LGBTQ issues. From academia to media to policy making, these issues have been three of the most talked-about political matters of our time, and yet, it is not often we hear stories from individuals and communities for whom these three issues intersect. As the sociologist Salvador Vidal-Ortiz notes in his co-edited collection *Queer Brown Voices*, academic research related to people of color, immigrants, and LGBTQ people has remained siloed, and this divide is often reflected within race-based and LGBTQ organizations as well. As Vidal-Ortiz writes, "Organizations bolster a racial politics that generally . . . eras[es] Latinas/os (and Asians and Pacific Islanders, Native Americans, and multiracial LGBT people) from the process, while a heteronormative Latina/o mainstream agenda also ignores LGBT populations."[1]

Within sociological studies on race, immigration, and sexuality, LGBTQ children of immigrants are often invisibilized. Within the subfields of immigration and race, sociologists too often presume the heterosexuality of their respondents when developing their studies (it is worth pointing out that beyond sociology, among humanities and interdisciplinary scholars, there is the field of queer migration studies).[2] Sociological research on sexualities, in turn, has focused on the experiences of White gay people, especially cisgender White men. If race is mentioned, the diverse experiences of Black, Latinx, and Asian American gay people are conflated, even though racial experiences vary within and across groups.

My research on second-generation gay men draws inspiration from Black feminist thought. My thinking underlying this study has been influenced by the writings and conversations of Barbara Smith, the Combahee River Collective, Audre Lorde, Kimberlé Crenshaw, Patricia Hill Collins, bell hooks, Imani Perry, Keeanga-Yamahtta Taylor, Brittney Cooper, Tressie McMillan Cottom, among others.[3] These thinkers have advanced the theoretical framework of intersectionality, the idea that multiple systems of oppression—including racism, sexism, and homophobia— converge and function simultaneously to affect the everyday lives and opportunities of Black women and other people with multiple marginalized identities. Of course, intersectionality isn't merely about amplifying forgotten stories of people who exist in the margins of the margins. As their work has shown, centering the experiences of such individuals helps reveal the mechanisms behind structural and interactional inequality. As this book aims to show, centering the narratives of second-generation gay men sheds light on how race, gender, and heteronormativity interact simultaneously within families, schools, and other social institutions.

For this book, I interviewed sixty-three second-generation gay men who were living in Los Angeles (see table A.1 for an overview of the sample). The interviews took place between 2012 and 2016. At the time of the interviews, the men were between the ages of eighteen and thirty-six, with an average age of twenty-six. The sample included twenty-nine Filipino Americans, twenty-nine Mexican Americans, and five Latinos who traced their roots to Central America and South America. Nearly all the interviewees were second generation, meaning they were born in the United States and had at least one parent (usually both) who was born in a different country. Four of the interviewees were born outside the United States but arrived in the United States as infants or children. Like previous sociological studies, I include them as part of the second generation because the bulk of their childhood and adolescent socialization occurred in the United States.[4]

I interviewed second-generation Filipinos and Latinos so that I could understand how sexuality shaped the coming-of-age experi-

TABLE A.1. Interview Sample, Second-Generation Gay Men

Mean Age	26.2	
Ethnicity		
Filipino	46%	(29)
Mexican	46%	(29)
Other Latino	8%	(5)
Educational background		
High School / GED	13%	(8)
Bachelor's degree (or in progress)	71%	(45)
Graduate degree (or in progress)	16%	(10)
Socioeconomic background		
Low income / working class	40%	(25)
Middle class	51%	(32)
Upper middle class	9%	(6)
Mean socioeconomic status* (Filipino)	2.6	
Mean socioeconomic status (Mexican)	3.1	

Notes: $N = 63$. *Socioeconomic status was self-reported on a scale of 1 to 5 (1 = low income; 2 = working class; 3 = middle class; 4 = upper middle class; 5 = upper class).

ences of gay men across different ethnic communities. Filipinos and Latinos share a number of experiences, including their shared history of Spanish colonialism, the close connections of their ethnic culture to Catholicism, the transnational relationships of immigrants and their children, high levels of familial obligation, and the complicated intergenerational dynamics in households and neighborhoods.[5] At the same time, they differ with respect to the immigration pathways of their parents, socioeconomic status, and racialization.[6] Filipino immigrants are more likely to be college educated and work in the professional ranks upon arriving in the United States. Latino immigrants, in turn, arrive with comparatively lower levels of formal education and work in employment sectors with more limited opportunity structures. To be clear, however, this is not a comparative study, as I am not engaging in a comparative analysis of Filipino and Latino gay men's experiences; rather, I draw on Natalia Molina's concept of relational racialization to underscore that communities of color are often racialized vis-à-vis each other.

The Greater Los Angeles Area was an ideal setting to recruit second-generation gay men of color. Los Angeles has been a primary destination city for immigrants, including Filipinos, Mexicans, and other Latinos. In Los Angeles County, there are over 400,000 Fillipino Americans, 3.7 million Mexican Americans, and 800,000 Central Americans, according to the 2019 American Community Survey.[7] Given that LGBTQ children of immigrants make up a small subset of second-generation Filipinos and Latinos, it was optimal to recruit interviewees in a region where the population of their respective ethnic communities was large. Additionally, Greater LA houses a plethora of ethnic-specific and racially diverse gay public spaces, events, and organizations from which I could recruit interviewees. Given that sexuality and immigration researchers have had difficulties accessing and building rapport with LGBTQ communities of color, it was beneficial to have a variety of venues from which to recruit second-generation gay men.[8]

I used a variety of recruitment approaches to find people to interview. I recruited my first set of interviewees from gay bars and nightclubs throughout Greater LA. These men constituted about one-third of my sample. Before my first interview was ever conducted, I had been a frequent patron of the LA gay scene for close to a decade. I had frequented Asian American, Latino, and other predominantly POC events at bars and clubs in West Hollywood, East Hollywood, Long Beach, Orange County, Pomona, and the Inland Empire. I also met a few interviewees by attending Pride events in West Hollywood and Long Beach. By the time I decided to pursue the research for this book, I was acquainted with many second-generation Filipino and Latino gay men. I asked my personal contacts if they could connect me with friends and acquaintances who were sons of immigrants. Through email, text message, social media direct message, or in-person meetings I was able to connect with their referrals to set up interviews.

Of course, I did not want to solely interview second-generation gay men who were embedded within the circuit of LA gay nightlife. In the age of smartphones, there were many interviewees who were not as inclined (or were unable) to frequent gay bars and clubs, especially if they were not yet twenty-one years old. To reach a broader network of second-generation gay men, my research assistant at the time connected me with gay Filipinos and Latinos who were part of student organizations at local universities. Just over a third of the interviewees were recruited through this effort.

The final subset of interviewees came by way of snowball sampling. Each time I interviewed a respondent, I asked if he knew any other second-generation gay men who might be interested in being part of my study. To ensure that I did not oversample from one network hub, I limited interview referrals to two per person. There were a few interviewees who were put in contact with me by someone who had attended a talk or lecture at a university, but I opted not to follow up with people who might have been privy to preliminary findings for this research. If the connection was made during a lecture that was unrelated to the study, however, I made efforts to secure an interview. Once I interviewed the men, many of them added me on their various social media platforms, including Facebook and Instagram. This allowed me to ask follow-up questions when necessary and to maintain friendly communication over the years.

All the interviewees were living in Los Angeles County at the time of our conversation, and the majority were raised in LA and the surrounding cities and suburbs, including the Inland Empire, Orange County, the San Gabriel Valley, the San Fernando Valley, and the South Bay. The neighborhood origins of the interviewees were diverse, both in terms of race and socioeconomic status. Some were from low-income Latinx communities in East LA, South LA, and the San Fernando Valley. Others were from multiethnic, mixed income suburbs in Northeast Los Angeles, the San Gabriel Valley, and West Los Angeles. Only four interviewees grew up in upper-middle-class, predominantly White, communities. Nine of the men had relocated to Los Angeles after high school to attend college and/or move to a new city to freely explore their sexuality. Of the men who grew up outside Southern California, two were from the San

Francisco Bay area, two were from the Central Valley, three were from San Diego, and two were from outside California.

The interviews took place at a location of the interviewee's choosing, such as a local coffee shop, a bookstore, a college campus, an outdoor patio, a café, or a sit-down restaurant. None of the interviews took place at an interviewee's home, which made sense given the anticipated sensitivity of the topics discussed. Interviews lasted anywhere from one hour to over three and a half hours. During my initial outreach, I let interviewees know that I was "writing a book about what it was like growing up gay in an immigrant family." Most of the interviewees expressed excitement to "finally" have the chance to talk about this topic, and for many, my interview was their first opportunity to talk so openly about their experience. Even though the premise of the interview centered on sexuality, I did not lead with that topic. The first ten to thirty minutes of each interview was spent drinking coffee or sharing a small meal to break the ice. For all but ten of my interviews, I recorded conversations using a digital recording device; the remaining men preferred that I interview them without a recording device and instead take notes. As a gay Filipino American, I anticipated that there were few opportunities for the men to talk about immigration, race, masculinity, and LGBTQ issues all at once, so I wanted to ensure that they felt as comfortable as possible when sharing their stories with me.

In the first half hour of the "real" part of the interview, I focused on topics that, on the surface, were seemingly unrelated to sexuality. My first set of questions focused on their early childhood experiences: what it was like growing up in an immigrant family, in their neighborhood, and in their schools. I asked them to describe the racial makeup, socio-economic climate, and social interactions as vividly as possible.

Once I got the sense that an interviewee was open to talking about sexuality, I pivoted with the questions, "When did you first realize that you might be gay?" or "When did you know that you were *different*?" Even when using the euphemism, the interviewees knew I was referring to sexuality. It was at this point that they began narrating their childhood and adolescent experiences from the viewpoint of being gay (and relat-edly, masculinity). They spoke about childhood moments, as early as age four, when they realized that they had violated some rule—stated or unstated—about boyhood or masculinity. Often this meant recounting a time when a parent, older relatives, or friend (usually someone male) scolded or punished them for behaving or speaking "like a girl," or more vaguely, in a way that boys weren't "supposed" to. Although interviewees were a decade or two removed from these events, their emotions ran heavy (as did mine). I let interviewees know that if they needed to pause or take a break, they should not hesitate to do so. Few took me up on the invitation, and most were readily able to compose themselves; I realized later that most of these men had much practice suppressing their emo-tional reaction to trauma and violence. Later I asked interviewees about their experience being gay (or rumored to be gay) in school, from their elementary school years through college.

The latter half of the interview focused on how interviewees came into their gay identity, gay social scenes (both in-person and virtual), and gay communities. I asked them about their explorations of gay top-ics and gay connections on the internet and social media, about their first gay friends and romantic involvements, and about their first time attending a gay event, whether it was a gay bar or an LGBTQ student organization on campus. Throughout these conversations, interviewees peppered in discussions of race, class, gender expression, body type, and physical appearance. Whenever they did so, I probed them to more deeply understand the ways they connected these aspects of their social identity to their sexual identity.

While I had a standard set of questions entering each conversation, some of my early interviews yielded themes that I had not anticipated when designing my interview guide. Drawing on Mario Luis Small's "se-quential interviewing" approach, I took note of new themes that emerged in my early interviews and used those insights to develop questions for subsequent conversations.[9] For example, when one of my early inter-viewees spoke at length about the covert forms of racial discrimination in West Hollywood bars (i.e., a venue changing the music selection on a given night to deter Black and Latinx patrons), I made sure to probe subsequent interviewees about the ways the race of patrons might affect barhopping experiences in the gayborhood.

Once the interviews were complete, I asked interviewees to fill out a short two-page survey. On the form were questions about their neighborhood origin, school, occupation, religion, ethnic and racial identities, sexual identity, and parents' education and occupation. I also included questions about previous relationships, experiences with discrimination, and approximate ages when they came out to different people in their lives.

Each of the recorded interviews was transcribed, and for the interviews that were not recorded, I wrote up a summary to reconstruct the conversation as accurately as memory would allow. Once I had my interviews transcribed, I coded for analytic themes that are typically highlighted in studies of the immigrant second generation, including family dynamics, intergenerational conflict, friendship choices, interactions with classmates and teachers, sense of belonging within the ethnic community, and experiences with racism and discrimination. Given my focus on gay sons of immigrants, I also coded for themes related to gender socialization and sexuality, including masculinity, gender expectations, gender expression, negotiation of gay identity and community, decisions to disclose sexual identity, and sexuality as a source of social connection.

Of course, not every interview touched on these themes, but my hope is that the collective experiences of my interviewees paint a mosaic that helps readers better understand the impact of race, immigration, gender, and sexuality on second-generation gay men and, to a certain extent, other LGBTQ people of color.

NOTES

A NOTE ON LANGUAGE

1 Reyes 2018; Salinas and Lozano 2017.

2 Buenavista 2007; Pimentel 2013. Pimentel interviews the scholar Theo Gonzalvez, who explains that Filipino American college students opted to identify as Pilipino as "an act of defiance and a choice."

3 Ocampo 2016.

4 For a more in-depth discussion of the development of the term *Filipinx*, see the excellent essay by Barrett, Hanna, and Palomar (2021).

5 For examples of books that employ the term *Brown*, see Hamad 2020; and Phillips 2016.

6 Muñoz 2020, 3. Muñoz's work is very much informed by the Chicano-led Brown movements of the 1960s. He writes, "My use of 'brown' is certainly an homage to the history of brown power in this country that was borne out of insurrectionist student movements. I do not mean brown in the way media pundits pronounce the browning of America in relation to national electoral politics. I am reaching back and invoking the sense of brown that was the Chicano walkouts of 1968, brown as in brown berets." Filipino Americans have historically been associated with the term *Brown* and aligned themselves with it. Upon being colonized by the United States, President William McKinley referred to Filipinos as "little brown brothers." *Brown* has not only been a pejorative, however. Filipino writers, academics, and activists have (re)claimed Brownness to signal their colonial experience vis-à-vis Spain and the United States, and to distinguish themselves from East Asians. *Brown* is a commonplace descriptor for everyday Filipino Americans as well. For examples of books that showcase Filipinos' use of the term, see David 2013 and Jamero 2006.

7 As Jenn M. Jackson notes, "Capitalizing the 'w' is only a performative act for white people." Jenn M. Jackson (@JennMJacksonPhD), Twitter, August 2, 2020, https://twitter.com/JennMJacksonPhD/status/1289887251179200512?s=20.

8 Craven 2020.

9 Ewing 2020.

10 Cheves 2019. Taking a cue from sociologist Jason Orne's interview with Cheves, I also use the terms *queer* and *queerness* as shorthand when describing "any non-cisgender, non-heterosexual identity, relationship, behavior, or desire."

11 Vidal-Ortiz 2015.

12 Solnit 2018, 3.

13 Grady 2020. Grady cites the anthropologist Jonathan Rosa, who asserts that "when well-meaning white progressives adopt terms like 'BIPOC' [Black, Indigenous, and people of color] indiscriminately, they end up erasing [historical and structural] differences. They can also end up projecting US-centric ideas of race into racial conversations in other countries, where groups are constructed differently."

PREFACE

1 Lopez 2017.

2 Groom 2016.

3 *Kababayan Weekly* 2016.

4 Santora 2016.

5 Rubin et al. 2016.

6 Brown 2018, 81. Brown asks, "Why do we insist on dress-rehearsing tragedy in moments of deep joy?" She argues that we do so because joy is "the most vulnerable emotion we feel." I would add the experience of dress-rehearsing tragedy is structured by race, class, and gender. For queer people of color who have experienced marginalization in multiple contexts, including the spaces designated to keep them safe, dress-rehearsing isn't necessarily an irrational thing to do given that tragedy is more likely to strike this demographic. Additionally, queer people of color don't have always have access to age peers and elders who look like them that are experiencing joy.

7 Meadow 2018; Robertson 2019. Both Meadow and Robertson, respectively, conducted studies of younger millennials and Gen Zers who came of age at a time when LGBTQ youth were embracing queer and transgender identity as children and teenagers—*with* support from parents and family.

8 Cross and Hillier 2021.

9 Lee and Eaglin 2021. As of February 2021, Bretman Rock, a Filipino American beauty influencer from Hawaii, has amassed 3.8 million followers on Facebook, 5.6 million followers on Twitter, 8.8 million followers on TikTok, and a whopping 15.4 million followers on Instagram. His social media influence has landed him lucrative advertisement deals and a reality television show on MTV.

10 Dry 2020; Lambe 2020. Laverne Cox won a Daytime Emmy Award as executive producer for *Laverne Cox Presents: The T Word*, and Rain Valdez received an Emmy nomination for her role in *Razor Tongue*. *Pose*, a drama series about transgender women of color of the New York ball scene during the AIDS epidemic, has garnered a series nomination and acting nominations and wins for Black queer actor Billy Porter. The transgender women of color who star in *Pose* were shut out of the acting nominations until star Mj Rodriguez was nominated for an Outstanding Lead Actress Emmy in 2021.

11 Ferguson 2019.

12 Terriquez 2015.

13 Carruthers 2018; D. Green 2019. Green's wonderful essay on *Medium* discusses how the legacy of Black queer activists and creators of the 1960s and 1970s is evident in the political and intellectual discourse of Black Lives Matter cofounders Alicia Garza, Patrisse Khan-Cullors, and Opal Tometi.

14 Shoichet 2020; Centers for Disease Control and Prevention 2020. According to a report from National Nurses United (2020: 5), about a third of the nurses who have died from COVID-19 are Filipino, a devastating pattern that gets overlooked when data on Asian Americans is not disaggregated. The Centers for Disease Control and Prevention keep track of the racial disparities in COVID death rates. Their site reports that African Americans, Latinxs, and Native Americans are over three times more likely to be hospitalized for COVID-19 and over two times more likely to die from the virus.

15 Valencia 2020.

16 Jaboukie Young-White (@jaboukie), Twitter, April 14, 2020. https://twitter.com /jaboukie/status/1250209087100510209.

CHAPTER 1. THE GAY SECOND GENERATION

1 Peay and Kmack 2019.

2 Peay and Kmack 2019.

3 Passell and Cohn 2008; Portes and Zhou 1993.

4 Faderman and Timmons 2006, 231–32.

5 Faderman and Timmons 2006, 282.

6 Faderman and Timmons 2006. According to the *Los Angeles Times* Mapping L.A. project, over 80 percent of West Hollywood residents are White. See *Los Angeles Times*, n.d.

7 From about 2004 to 2007, \Rage nightclub\ (which shut its doors in 2020 due to the pandemic) hosted a Latin Night on Wednesdays and GAMeboi on Fridays. \Here Lounge\ (which was purchased by \the Abbey\ in 2016 and renamed \the Chapel\) hosted \Metrosexual, a weekly party\ on Wednesdays catering to Black men (though Latinx gay men would also frequent the event). Metrosexual was featured on the debut episode of the short-lived but popular \Logo television\ series *Noah's Arc*, which featured the story of four Black gay men living in Los Angeles. The acronym AOL refers to "America Online," one of the first and internet service providers; it was most popular during the 1990s and early 2000s.

8 Dinco 2017; Faderman and Timmons 2006.

9 Ellis and Almgren 2009; Portes and Rumbaut 2001; Rumbaut and Portes 2001; Zhou and Xiong 2005.

10 For examples, see Eng and Hom 1998; and Hames-García and Martinez 2011.

11 Ethnic digital media outlets like Remezcla and LGBTQ outlets like Them have produced excellent reported and personal essays that explore what it's like to live at the intersection of racism and queerness.

12 Los Angeles Almanac, n.d.–a.

13 Molina 2010, 157.

14 Ochoa 2013.

15 Muñoz 2009, 68.

16 Fauci 1999. According to Fauci, up through 1998, there were 410,800 AIDS-related deaths reported by the Centers for Disease Control and Prevention.

17 Dutta 2020; Fauci 1999. Fauci notes that between 1996 and 1997, the death rate for HIV/AIDS declined by 48 percent.

18 Krutzsch 2019.

19 Badgett 2010.

20 Machado 2019, 126.

21 Liptak 2015.

22 Ball 2015.

23 Robinson 2020; Rojas and Swales 2019.

24 Pew Research Center 2019.

25 Perry 2019.

26 Du Bois (1903) 1989; Itzigsohn and Brown 2020; Morris 2015.

27 Taylor 2017, "Introduction," Kindle.

28 Ferguson 2019.

29 Ferguson 2019, 39–40.

CHAPTER 2. LESSONS IN MANHOOD AND MORALITY

1 Thorne 1995.

2 Maglaty 2011.

3 Butler 1990; West and Zimmerman 1987.

4 Kane 2006.

5 Levine 1998.

6 Carrillo 2017; Carrillo, a sociologist at Northwestern University and a renowned expert on the intersections between sexuality and migration, coined the term "sexual schemas" to describe "the publicly available and partially internalized understandings from which individuals draw sexual meanings." The latter half of this chapter will focus on how growing up in a gendered, multigenerational, and transnational social context can lead second-generation gay men to develop a sexual schema that frames being gay as immoral and wrong.

7 Manalansan 2003. *Bakla* is the Tagalog word for "gay," a portmanteau of *babae* (woman) and *lalake* (man). *Bakla* is often, though not always, used as a pejorative.

8 Nadal 2013, 119. While there are certainly more LGBTQ television shows and films than when my interviewees were children and teenagers, LGBTQ characters of color remain underrepresented. For example, researchers at the University of Southern California conducted a content analysis of films and TV shows on Netflix, generally considered more "LGBTQ-friendly" than network television.

Out of more than twelve thousand *speaking* characters, only 135 were LGBTQ
people of color; see Smith et al. 2021.

9 Gonzalez 2009.

10 Menjívar 2003.

11 Gonzalez 2009.

12 Menjívar 2003; Ransford, Carrillo, and Rivera 2010.

13 Kim 2004.

14 Menjívar 2003.

15 Cantú, Naples, and Vidal-Ortiz 2009.

16 Carrillo 2017.

17 In a previous study (Ocampo 2014), I termed this process "moral management."
Moral management entails the hyperconscious monitoring of gender
presentation—which includes behaviors and mannerisms, voice inflections,
clothing choices, cultural tastes, and even friendship networks—in the effort to
maintain rapport and social support from family members.

CHAPTER 3. SURVIVING SCHOOL

1 Kosciw et al. 2019.

2 Pascoe 2007.

3 Snyder and Broadway 2004.

4 Pascoe 2007, 27.

5 Kumashiro 2000.

6 D'Augelli et al. 2005.

7 *Anak* is the Tagalog word for "child." It is gender neutral.

8 Goffman (1963) 1986, 102.

9 Conchas 2006; Kasinitz et al. 2008.

10 Zhou and Bankston 1998.

11 This is a pattern that emerged in the educational narratives of Filipinos I
interviewed for an earlier study, *The Latinos of Asia* (Ocampo 2016).

12 Lee and Zhou 2015, 116.

13 Ochoa 2013. See also Portes and Fernández-Kelly 2008; and Portes and Rumbaut
2001; and Portes and Rumbaut 2014.

14 Kumpchik 2010; G. Rodriguez 2020.

15 Rios 2011.

16 Ocampo and Soodjinda 2016.

17 Rios 2011.

18 Carter 2005; Rios 2011.

19 Hinojosa 2008; Rios 2011; Skiba et al. 2011.

20 Ochoa 2013; Rios 2011.

21 G. Flores 2017.

22 Rios 2011, 82

23 Rios 2011, 145.

24 Pedulla 2014. Armando's Asian American friends diffused their parents' negative stereotypes of Latinos by bringing up his queer sexuality. This echoes Pedulla's research findings, which indicate that gay Black men are seen as less threatening and aggressive because of the stereotypes people held about gay men as effeminate and weak.

CHAPTER 4. ESCAPING TO COLLEGE

1 D. Moore 2018, 129.
2 Carrillo 2017. Carrillo's book, *Pathways of Desire*, influenced me to think of the college pathways of second-generation gay men through the frame of migration.
3 Kastanis and Gates 2013.
4 Dhingra 2020; Espiritu 2003; Ocampo 2016; Ochoa 2013.
5 Robinson and Roska 2016. According to Robinson and Roska, a college-going culture is a social and cultural environment in which educators and peers are providing social support and promoting the value of higher education.
6 Price 2016.
7 Morales 2014. As Morales argues, a university may have a large number of students of color (e.g., the UC campuses), but may be considered a historically White university if the power structures remain in the hands of White faculty, administrators, staff, and students.
8 Camacho 2016.
9 Ray 2019.
10 University of California–Los Angeles, n.d.
11 Robinson 2020.
12 Buenavista 2009.
13 Morales 2021, 74; Ocampo 2016.
14 Zidani 2020.
15 Maldonado, Rhoads, and Buenavista 2005.
16 Reyes 2018.
17 Mabalon 1995.
18 Mabalon 1995.
19 Hunter 2010, 87.
20 Gonzalves 2009.
21 Hunter 2010.
22 Terriquez 2015.
23 Rhoads 2016; Zimmerman 2011.
24 Davis 2016, 118.
25 Gunckel 2009.
26 Bidell 2013.
27 Gates 2002, 514.
28 Hoang 2018.

29 Irwin 2000.

30 Reyes 2018.

CHAPTER 5. BECOMING BROWN AND GAY IN LA

1 Alter 2016.

2 Keller et al. 2016; McKay 2016b.

3 McKay 2016b.

4 Munzenrieder 2016.

5 McKay 2016a.

6 V. B. Flores 2016.

7 González 2016.

8 Los Angeles Conservancy 2017.

9 Manalansan 2003, 70.

10 madison moore 2018.

11 Greene 2014.

12 AOL stands for America Online.

13 Arce 2016.

14 Simón 2017.

15 During the course of my interviews, respondents referred to other people I had previously interviewed who also frequented the T-party scene. At no point during any interview did I signal to a respondent that I had interviewed any of the persons they named.

16 Avant-Mier 2010.

17 DeHaan et al. 2013.

18 Harper, Serrano, and Bruce 2016.

19 Tolentino 2019. The wonderful opening essay in Tolentino's book, "The I in Internet," addresses the interconnectedness of online and real-life personhood.

20 Manalansan 2003; Ocampo 2012.

21 Ocampo 2012.

22 Manalansan 2003; Yoshino 2006.

23 Ocampo 2012.

24 Cantú, Naples, and Vidal-Ortiz 2009; Ward 2008.

25 Barangay Los Angeles 2012; Mangaoang 1994.

26 In Los Angeles, there were Latino gay clubs and Latin night themed parties. During the time of this research, there were also weekly parties in WeHo that catered to Asian American and Black gay patrons. For additional scholarly discussions of these LA-based queer POC parties, see Cantú, Naples, and Vidal-Ortiz 2009; Hunter and Winder 2019; Ng 2004; and Rodríguez 2006.

27 Davis and Jurgenson 2014.

28 Davis and Jurgenson 2014.

29 Davis and Jurgenson 2014.

30 Silver, Clark, and Yanez 2010.

31 Ocampo 2012; Rodríguez 2006.

32 Mabalon, De Leon, and Ramos 1997; Macias 2014.

33 Unfortunately, Rage closed its doors in 2020 due to the COVID-19 pandemic.

34 A. I. Green 2008; Ocampo 2012.

35 While I do not use pseudonyms for bars and clubs in other parts of this chapter, I use one here because I include a story from a respondent, AJ, who still has a working relationship with this bar.

36 Chiland 2017; WEHOville 2020. Around the time of my interviews, the average cost of a one-bedroom apartment rental was just over $2,000. Since then the average cost has risen to nearly $3,000. By comparison, rentals in East LA or South Central LA are about $1,100–$1,500 per month.

37 Mitchell 2018.

38 Nadal 2013; Sue et al. 2002. While psychologists have popularized the term "racial microaggression" in the early 2000s, the term was first coined in 1970 by Chester Pierce, an African American psychiatrist at Harvard University.

39 Sue et al. 2002, 271.

40 Mignon Moore 2011.

41 Han et al. 2017.

42 Nichols 2015.

43 Han 2015, 63.

44 A. I. Green 2011; Han et al. 2017; Ng 2004.

45 Green 2011; Orne 2017.

46 Pachankis et al. 2020. As much as they provided community, these sites were also a source of what public health scholar John Pachankis and his colleagues have described as "gay community stress."

CHAPTER 6. NOT THAT GAY

1 Dewaele et al. 2011. Within queer communities, "the chosen family" refers to non-blood-related kin who step in as the social support for LGBTQ individuals unable to rely on traditional kin networks.

2 Thompson 2016, emphasis in the original.

3 Decena 2011.

4 Battle, Pastrana, and Daniels 2013.

5 Will & Grace, season 1, episode 19, "Will Works Out," directed by Ivan Kohan, Max Mutchnick, and James Burrows; written by Michael Michael Patrick King, Tracy Poust, and Jon Kinnally; featuring Eric McCormack and Sean Hayes, aired April 22, 1999, on NBC, www.nbc.com/will-and-grace-original/video/will-works -out/3557742

6 Ferguson 2019.

7 Talusan 2019.

8 Robinson 2020.

9 Nadal 2013. See also Robinson 2020.
10 Higbee, Wright, and Roemerman 2020.
11 Higbee, Wright, and Roemerman 2020; Mallory, Brown, and Conron 2019.

CHAPTER 7. BEYOND ACCEPTANCE

1 Machado 2019, 228.
2 Machado 2019, 228.
3 Vargas 2018, 117.
4 Washington and Vuong 2020.
5 Washington and Vuong 2020.
6 Muñoz 2009, 1.

APPENDIX

1 Vidal-Ortiz 2015, 3.
2 Luibhéid and Cantú 2005. Luibhéid and Cantú's excellent edited volume addresses how queer immigrants of color make their way within immigrant communities in US metropolitan cities. Some of the scholars included in the volume argue that immigrants, by virtue of their transient and liminal existence across contexts and countries, are, in many respects, queer. Much of the conversation here focuses on immigrants, though, and not specifically on the second generation.
3 For examples, see Collins 2008; Cooper 2018; Cottom 2019; Crenshaw 2017; hooks 2000; Perry 2018; and Taylor 2017.
4 Portes and Rumbaut 2001.
5 Fuligni 2001; Guevarra 2012; E. Rodriguez 2006, 2013.
6 Ochoa 2013; Portes and Rumbaut 2014.
7 *Los Angeles Almanac*, n.d.–a, n.d.–b.
8 Mignon Moore 2011.
9 Small 2009.

BIBLIOGRAPHY

Alter, Charlotte. 2016. "Orlando Shooter Bought Gun Legally, Store Owner Says." *Time*, June 13, 2016. www.time.com.

Arce, Virginia. 2016. "Splendid Intensity, Splendid Subversion: Transgression on the Dance Floor." *Western Humanities Review* 70 (3). www.westernhumanitiesreview .com.

Avant-Mier, Roberto. 2010. *Rock the Nation: Latin/o Identities and the Latin Rock Diaspora*. New York: Bloomsbury.

Badgett, M. V. Lee. 2010. *When Gay People Get Married: What Happens When Societies Legalize Same-Sex Marriage*. New York: New York University Press.

Ball, Molly. 2015. "What Other Activists Can Learn from the Fight for Gay Marriage." *Atlantic*, July 14, 2015. www.theatlantic.com.

Barangay Los Angeles. 2012. "Barangay Los Angeles Celebrates Filipino LGBTQ Pride." *Bakit Why*, July 17, 2012. www.bakitwhy.com/.

Barrett, Kay Ulanday, Karen Buenavista Hanna, and Anang Palomar. 2021. "In Defense of the X: Centering Queen, Trans, and Non-binary Pilipina/x/os, Queer Vernacular, and the Politics of Naming." *Alon: Journal for Filipinx American and Diasporic Studies* 1 (2): 125–47. https://escholarship.org/.

Battle, Juan, Antonio Jay Pastrana, and Jessie Daniels. 2013. *Social Justice Sexuality Project: 2010 National Survey, including Puerto Rico*. Ann Arbor, MI: Inter-university Consortium for Political and Social Research. https://doi.org/10.3886/ICPSR34363.v1.

Bidell, M. P. 2013. "Addressing Disparities: The Impact of a Lesbian, Gay, Bisexual, and Transgender Graduate Counselling Course." *Counselling and Psychotherapy Research* 13 (4): 300–307.

Brown, Brené. 2018. *Dare to Lead: Brave Work. Tough Conversations. Whole Hearts.* New York: Random House.

Buenavista, Tracy Lachica. 2009. "Examining the Postsecondary Experiences of Pilipino 1.5-Generation College Students." *ASHE/Lumina Policy Briefs and Critical Essays*, no. 8, 1–12.

———. 2007. "Movement from the Middle: Pilipina/o 1.5-Generation College Student Access, Retention, and Resistance." PhD diss., University of California–Los Angeles.

Butler, Judith. 1990. *Gender Trouble: Feminism and the Subversion of Identity*. New York: Routledge.

Cabangun, Anthony Benjamin. 2016. "Power, Identity, and Sex among Gay Filipino Men in San Francisco." Master's thesis, San Francisco State University.

Camacho, Trace. 2016. "Navigating Borderlands: Gay Latino Men in College." PhD diss., Michigan State University.

Cantú, Lionel, Jr., Nancy A. Naples, and Salvador Vidal-Ortiz. 2009. *The Sexuality of Migration: Border Crossings and Mexican Immigrant Men*. New York: New York University Press.

Carrillo, Héctor. 2017. *Pathways of Desire: The Sexual Migration of Mexican Gay Men*. Chicago: University of Chicago Press.

Carruthers, Charlene. 2018. *Unapologetic: A Black, Queer, and Feminist Mandate for Radical Movements*. Boston: Beacon.

Carter, Prudence L. 2005. *Keepin' It Real: School Success beyond Black and White*. New York: Oxford University Press.

Centers for Disease Control and Prevention. n.d. "Risk for COVID-19 Infection, Hospitalization, and Death by Race/Ethnicity." Retrieved February 10, 2021. www .cdc.gov.

Chee, Alexander. 2018. *How to Write an Autobiographical Novel*. Boston: Mariner Books.

Cheves, Alexander. 2019. "9 LGBTQ+ People Explain How They Love, Hate, and Understand the Word 'Queer.'" Them, June 4, 2019. www.them.us.

Chiland, Elijah. 2017. "Here's How Much It Costs to Rent All Across LA." Curbed Los Angeles, December 18, 2017. https://la.curbed.com.

Collins, Patricia Hill. 2008. *Black Feminist Thought*. New York: Routledge.

Conchas, Gilberto Q. 2006. *The Color of Success: Race and High-Achieving Urban Youth*. New York: Teachers College Press.

Cooper, Brittney. 2018. *Eloquent Rage: A Black Feminist Discovers Her Superpower*. New York: St. Martin's.

Cottom, Tressie McMillan. 2019. *Thick: And Other Essays*. New York: New Press.

Craven, Julia. 2020. "Capitalizing *White* Won't Fix the Media's Racism Problem." *Slate*, August 5, 2020. https://slate.com.

Crenshaw, Kimberlé. 2017. *On Intersectionality: Essential Writings*. New York: New Press.

Cross, Erin, and Amy Hillier. 2021. "Respecting Pronouns in the Classroom." Educator's Playbook. www.gse.upenn.edu.

D'Augelli, Anthony, Arnold H. Grossman, Nicholas P. Salter, Joseph J. Vasey, Michael T. Starks, and Katerina O. Sinclair. 2005. "Predicting the Suicide Attempts of Lesbian, Gay, and Bisexual Youth." *Suicide and Life-Threatening Behavior* 35 (6): 646–68.

David, E. J. R. 2013. *Brown Skin, White Minds: Filipino American Postcolonial Psychology*. Charlotte, NC: Information Age.

Davis, Danné. 2016. "Queering Children's Literature: Rationale and Resources." In *Voices of LGBTQ Students and Teachers: Problematizing the Culture of Schooling*, edited by Veronica E. Bloomfield and Marni E. Fisher, 117–31. Boulder, CO: Paradigm.

Davis, Jenny L., and Nathan Jurgenson. 2014. "Context Collapse: Theorizing Context Collusions and Collisions." *Information, Communication, and Society* 17 (4): 476–85.

Decena, Carlos Ulises. 2011. *Tacit Subjects: Belonging and Same-Sex Desire among Dominican Immigrant Men*. Durham, NC: Duke University Press.

DeHaan, Samantha, Laura E. Kuper, Joshua C. Magee, Lou Bigelow, and Brian S. Mustanski 2013. "The Interplay between Online and Offline Explorations of Identity, Relationships, and Sex: A Mixed-Methods Study with LGBT Youth." *Journal of Sex Research* 50 (5): 421–34.

Dewaele, Alexis, Nele Cox, Wim Van den Berghe, and John Vincke. 2011. "Families of Choice? Exploring the Supportive Networks of Lesbians, Gay Men, and Bisexuals." *Journal of Applied Social Psychology* 41 (2): 312–331.

Dhingra, Pawan. 2020. *Hypereducation: Why Good Schools, Good Grades, and Good Behavior Are Not Enough*. New York: New York University Press.

Dinco, Dino. 2017. "Loving and Partying at Chico: 'The Best Latino Gay Bar' in Montebello." KCET, February 15, 2017. www.kcet.org.

Dry, Jude. 2020. "As Trans 'Pose' Stars Are Shut Out of Emmys Once Again, Another Milestone Is Reached." IndieWire, July 30, 2020. www.indiewire.com.

Du Bois, W. E. B. (1903) 1989. *The Souls of Black Folk*. New York: Penguin.

Dutta, Sanchari Sinha. 2020. "Advancements in Treating HIV." News Medical Life Sciences. www.news-medical.net.

Ellis, Mark, and Gunnar Almgren. 2009. "Local Contexts of Immigrant and Second Generation Integration in the United States." *Journal of Ethnic and Migration Studies* 35 (7): 1059–76.

Eng, David, and Alice Hom, eds. 1998. *Q&A: Queer in Asian America*. Philadelphia: Temple University Press.

Espiritu, Yen Le. 2003. *Home Bound: Filipino American Lives across Cultures, Communities, and Countries*. Berkeley: University of California Press.

Ewing, Eve L. 2020. "I'm a Black Scholar Who Studies Race. Here's Why I Capitalize 'White.'" *Zora*, July 1, 2020. https://zora.medium.com.

Faderman, Lillian, and Stuart Timmons. 2006. *Gay L.A.: A History of Sexual Outlaws, Power Politics, and Lipstick Lesbians*. New York: Basic Books.

Fauci, Anthony S. 1999. "The AIDS Epidemic: Considerations for the 21st Century." *New England Journal of Medicine*, no. 341, 1046–50.

Ferguson, Roderick A. 2018. *One-Dimensional Queer*. Cambridge: Polity Press.

Flores, Glenda M. 2017. *Latina Teachers: Creating Careers and Guarding Culture*. New York: New York University Press.

Flores, Veronica Bayetti. 2016. "The Pulse Nightclub Shooting Robbed the Queer Latinx Community of a Sanctuary." Remezcla, June 13, 2016. https://remezcla.com.

Fuligni, Andrew J. 2001. "Family Obligation and the Academic Motivation of Adolescents from Asian, Latin American, and European Backgrounds." *New Directions for Child and Adolescent Development*, no. 94, 61–76.

Gates, Henry Louis, Jr. 2002. "Integrating the American Mind." In *Racial and Ethnic Diversity in Higher Education*, edited by Caroline S. Turner, Anthony Lising Antonio,

Mildred García, Berta Vigil Laden, Amaury Nora, and Cheryl Presley, 513–19. Boston: Pearson.

Gay, Roxane. 2014. *Bad Feminist: Essays*. New York: Harper Perennial.

Goffman, Erving. (1963) 1986. *Stigma: Notes on the Management of Spoiled Identity*. Greenwich, CT: Touchstone.

Gonzalez, Joaquin Jay, III. 2009. *Filipino Faith in Action: Immigration, Religion, and Civic Engagement*. New York: New York University Press.

González, Rigoberto. 2006. *Butterfly Boy: Memories of a Chicano Mariposa*. Madison: University of Wisconsin Press.

———. 2016. "I Found a Home in Clubs like Pulse in Cities like Orlando." BuzzFeed, June 16, 2016. www.buzzfeednews.com.

Gonzalves, Theodore S. 2009. *The Day the Dancers Stayed: Performing in the Filipino/American Diaspora*. Philadelphia: Temple University Press.

Grady, Constance. 2020. "Why the Term 'BIPOC' Is So Complicated, Explained by Linguists." Vox, June 30, 2020. www.vox.com.

Green, Adam Isaiah. 2008. "The Social Organization of Desire: The Sexual Fields Approach." *Sociological Theory* 26 (1): 25–50.

———. 2011. "Playing the (Sexual) Field: The Intersectional Basis of Systems of Sexual Stratification." *Social Psychological Quarterly* 74 (3): 244–66.

Green, David, Jr. 2019. "Hearing the Queer Roots of Black Lives Matter." Medium, February 6, 2019. https://medium.com/.

Greene, Theodore. 2014. "Gay Neighborhoods and the Rights of Vicarious Citizen." *City and Community* 13 (2): 99–118.

Groom, Nichola. 2016. "UCLA Murder-Suicide Gunman Had Planned Third Killing, Police Say." Reuters, June 2, 2016. www.reuters.com.

Guevarra, Rudy P. 2012. *Becoming Mexipino: Multiethnic Identities and Communities in San Diego*. New Brunswick, NJ: Rutgers University Press.

Gunckel, Kristin. 2009. "Queering Science for All: Probing Queer Theory in Science Education." *Journal of Curriculum Theorizing* 25 (2): 62–75.

Hamad, Ruby. 2020. *White Tears / Brown Scars: How White Feminism Betrays Women of Color*. New York: Catapult.

Hames-García, Michael, and Ernesto Martínez, eds. 2011. *Gay Latino Studies: A Critical Reader*. Durham, NC: Duke University Press.

Han, C. Winter. 2015. *Geisha of a Different Kind: Race and Sexuality in Gaysian America*. New York: New York University Press.

Han, Chong-Suk, George Ayala, Jay P. Paul, and Kyung-Hee Paul. 2017. "West Hollywood Is Not Big on Anything but White People: Constructing 'Gay Men of Color.'" *Sociological Quarterly* 58 (4): 721–37.

Harper, Gary W., Pedro A. Serrano, and Douglas Bruce. 2016. "The Internet's Multiple Roles in Facilitating the Sexual Orientation Identity of Gay and Bisexual Male Adolescents." *American Journal of Men's Health* 10 (5): 359–76.

Higbee, Madison, Eric R. Wright, and Ryan M. Roemerman. 2020. "Conversion Therapy in the Southern United States: Prevalence and Experience of the Survivors."
Journal of Homosexuality, November 2020. https://pubmed.ncbi.nlm.nih.gov.

Hinojosa, Melanie. 2008. "Black-White Differences in School Suspension: Effect of
Student Beliefs about Teachers." *Sociological Spectrum* 28 (2): 175–93.

Hoang, Kimberly Kay. 2018. "Are Public Sociology and Scholar-Activism Really at
Odds?" *Contexts*, August 9, 2018. www.contexts.org.

hooks, bell. 2000. *Feminist Theory: From Margin to Center*. Boston: South End Press.

Hunter, Marcus. 2010. "All the Gays Are White and All the Blacks Are Straight: Black
Gay Men, Identity, and Community." *Sexuality Research and Social Policy*, no. 7,
81–92.

Hunter, Marcus Anthony, and Terrell J. A. Winder. 2019. "Visibility Is Survival: The
Chocolate Maps of Black Gay Life in Urban Ethnography." *Urban Ethnography*,
no. 16, 131–42.

Irwin, Robert. 2000. "The Famous 41: The Scandalous Birth of Modern Mexican
Homosexuality." *GLQ: A Journal of Lesbian and Gay Studies* 6 (3): 353–76.

Itzigsohn, José, and Karida L. Brown. 2020. *The Sociology of W. E. B. Du Bois: Racialized Modernity and the Global Color Line*. New York: New York University Press.

Jamero, Peter. 2006. *Growing Up Brown: Memoirs of a Filipino American*. Seattle:
University of Washington Press.

Johnson, E. Patrick. 2008. *Sweet Tea: Black Gay Men of the South*. Chapel Hill: University of North Carolina Press.

Jones, Saeed. 2019. *How We Fight for Our Lives: A Memoir*. New York: Simon &
Schuster.

Kababayan Weekly. 2016. "P-Grad 2016 Commencement Speaker Dr. Anthony Ocampo."
YouTube, June 26, 2016. www.youtube.com.

Kane, Emily. 2006. "No Way My Boys Are Going to Be like That!" *Gender and Society*
20 (2): 149–76.

Kasinitz, Philip, Mary C. Waters, John H. Mollenkopf, and Jennifer Holdaway. 2008.
Inheriting the City: The Children of Immigrants Come of Age. New York: Russell Sage
Foundation.

Kastanis, Angliki, and Gary Gates. 2013. *LGBT Asian and Pacific Islander Individuals and
Same-Sex Couples*. Los Angeles: Williams Institute, UCLA School of Law. https://
williamsinstitute.law.ucla.edu.

Keller, Josh, Iaryna Mykhyalyshyn, Adam Pearce, and Derek Watkins. 2016. "Why the
Orlando Shooting Was So Deadly." *New York Times*, June 12, 2016. www.nytimes.com.

Kim, Rebecca Y. 2004. "Second-Generation Korean American Evangelicals: Ethnic,
Multiethnic, or White Campus Ministries?" *Sociology of Religion* 65 (1): 19–34.

Kosciw, Joseph, Caitlin M. Clark, Nhan L. Truong, and Adrian D. Zongrone. 2019.
*The 2019 National School Climate Survey: The Experiences of Lesbian, Gay, Bisexual,
Transgender, and Queer Youth in Our Nation's Schools*. New York: GLSEN.

Krutzsch, Brett. 2019. *Dying to Be Normal: Gay Martyrs and the Transformation of American Sexual Politics.* New York: Oxford University Press.

Kumashiro, Kevin. 2000. "Toward a Theory of Anti-Oppressive Education." *Review of Education Research* 70 (1): 25–53.

Kumpchik, Aaron. 2010. *Homeroom Security: School Discipline in an Age of Fear.* New York: New York University Press.

Lambe, Stacy. 2020. "Emmys: Laverne Cox, Rain Valdez on Being Nominated Together and Why a Win Matters." *Entertainment Tonight*, August 27, 2020. www.etonline.com.

Levine, Martin P. 1998. *Gay Macho: The Life and Death of the Homosexual Clone.* New York: New York University Press.

Liptak, Adam. 2015. "Supreme Court Ruling Makes Same-Sex Marriage a Right Nationwide." *New York Times*, June 27, 2015. www.nytimes.com.

Lee, Jennifer and Min Zhou. 2015. *The Asian American Achievement Paradox.* New York: Russell Sage Foundation.

Lee, Tony, and Maya Eaglin. 2021. "Social Media Star Bretman Rock Vows to Be Unapologetically Queer in MTV Show." *NBC News*, February 11, 2021. www.nbcnews.com.

Lopez, German. 2017. "A New FBI Report Says Hate Crimes—Especially against Muslims—Went Up in 2016." Vox, November 13, 2017. www.vox.com.

Los Angeles Almanac. n.d.–a. "Asian Ethnic Origin, Los Angeles County." Retrieved January 20, 2021. www.laalmanac.com.

———. n.d.–b. "Hispanic or Latino Ethnic Origin (of Any Race), Los Angeles County." *Los Angeles Almanac.* Retrieved January 20, 2021. www.laalmanac.com.

Los Angeles Conservancy. 2017. "Circus Disco: Issue Overview." Last updated April 6, 2017. www.laconservancy.org.

Los Angeles Times. n.d. "Mapping L.A." Map database. Retrieved September 17, 2020. www.latimes.com.

Luibhéid, Eithne, and Lionel Cantú Jr. 2005. *Queer Migrations: Sexuality, US Citizenship, and Border Crossings.* Minneapolis: University of Minnesota Press.

Mabalon, Dawn, Lakan de Leon, and Jonathan Ramos, dirs. 1997. *Beats, Rhymes, and Resistance: Pilipinos and Hip Hop in Los Angeles.* DVD. Los Angeles: independently produced.

Machado, Carmen Maria. 2019. *In the Dream House: A Memoir.* Minneapolis: Graywolf.

Macias, Anthony. "Black and Brown Get Down: Cultural Politics, Chicano Music, and Hip Hop in Racialized Los Angeles." In *Sounds and the City: Popular Music, Place, and Globalization*, edited by Brett Lashua, Karl Spracklen, and Stephen Wagg, 55–75. London: Palgrave Macmillan.

Maglaty, Jeanne. 2011. "When Did Girls Start Wearing Pink?" *Smithsonian*, April 7, 2011. www.smithsonianmag.com.

Maldonado, David, Robert Rhoads, and Tracy Lachica Buenavista. 2005. "The Student-Initiated Retention Project: Theoretical Contributions and the Role of Self-Empowerment." *American Educational Research Journal* 42 (4): 605–38.

Mallory, Christy, Taylor N. T. Brown, and Kerith J. Conron. 2019. "Conversion Therapy and LGBT Youth." Los Angeles: Williams Institute, UCLA School of Law. https://williamsinstitute.law.ucla.edu.

Manalansan, Martin F. 2003. *Global Divas: Filipino Gay Men in the Diaspora.* Durham, NC: Duke University Press, 2003.

Mangaoang, Gil. 1994. "From the 1970s to the 1990s: Perspective of a Gay Filipino American Activist." *Amerasia* 20 (1): 33–44.

McKay, Tom. 2016a. "Donald Trump Issues Appalling Statement on Pulse Nightclub Massacre in Orlando." Mic, June 12, 2016. www.mic.com.

———. 2016b. "These Are the Names of the Victims of the Pulse Nightclub Shooting in Orlando." Mic, June 12, 2016. www.mic.com.

Meadow, Tey. 2018. *Trans Kids: Being Gendered in the Twenty-First Century.* Berkeley: University of California Press.

Menjívar, Cecilia. 2003. "Religion and Immigration in Comparative Perspective: Salvadorans in Catholic and Evangelical Communities in San Francisco, Phoenix, and Washington D.C." *Sociology of Religion* 64 (1): 21–45.

Mitchell, Koritha. 2018. "Identifying White Mediocrity and Know-Your-Place Aggression: A Form of Self-Care." *African American Review* 51 (4): 253–62.

Molina, Natalia. 2010. "The Power of Racial Scripts: What the History of Mexican Immigration to the United States Teaches Us about Relational Notions of Race." *Latino Studies* 8 (2): 156–75.

Moore, Darnell L. 2018. *No Ashes in the Fire: Coming of Age Black and Free in America.* New York: Bold Type Books.

moore, madison. 2018. *Fabulous: The Rise of the Beautiful Eccentric.* New Haven, CT: Yale University Press.

Moore, Mignon R. 2011. *Invisible Families: Gay Identities, Relationships, and Motherhood among Black Women.* Berkeley: University of California Press.

Morales, Erica. 2014. "Intersectional Impact: Black Students and Race, Gender, and Class Microaggressions in Higher Education." *Race, Gender, and Class* 21 (3–4): 48–66.

———. 2021. "'Beasting' at the Battleground: Black Students Respondent to Racial Microaggressions in Higher Education." *Journal of Diversity in Higher Education* 14 (1): 72–83.

Morris, Aldon. 2015. *The Scholar Denied: W. E. B. Du Bois and the Birth of Modern Sociology.* Berkeley: University of California Press.

Muñoz, José Esteban. 2009. *Cruising Utopia: The Then and There of Queer Futurity.* New York: New York University Press.

———. 2020. *The Sense of Brown.* Edited by Joshua Chambers-Letson and Tavia Nyong'o. Durham, NC: Duke University Press.

Munzenrieder, Kyle. 2016. "Rick Scott Has Refused to Say the Words 'Gay' and 'LGBT' since Orlando Attack." *Miami New Times*, June 13, 2016. www.miaminewtimes.com.

Nadal, Kevin L. 2013. *That's So Gay! Microaggressions and the Lesbian, Gay, Bisexual, and Transgender Community.* Washington, D.C.: American Psychological Association.

Ng, Mark Tristan. 2004. "Searching for Home: Voices of Gay Asian American Youth in West Hollywood." In *Asian American Youth: Culture, Identity, and Ethnicity*, edited by Jennifer Lee and Min Zhou, 269–84. New York: Routledge.

Nichols, James. 2015. "What Happens When Modern Queer Men See 'Queer As Folk' for the First Time." *HuffPost*, November 6, 2015. www.huffpost.com.

Ocampo, Anthony Christian. 2012. "Making Masculinity: Negotiations of Gender Presentation among Latino Gay Men." *Latino Studies* 10 (4): 448–72.

———. 2014. "The Gay Second Generation: Sexual Identity and the Family Relations of Filipino and Latino Gay Men." *Journal of Ethnic and Migration Studies* 40 (1): 155–73.

———. 2016. *The Latinos of Asia: How Filipino Americans Break the Rules of Race*. Stanford, CA: Stanford University Press.

Ocampo, Anthony, and Daniel Soodjinda. 2016. "Invisible Asian Americans: The Intersection of Sexuality, Race, and Education among Gay Asian Americans." *Race, Ethnicity, and Education* 19 (3): 480–99.

Ochoa, Gilda. 2013. *Academic Profiling: Latinos, Asian Americans, and the Achievement Gap*. Minneapolis: University of Minnesota Press.

Orne, Jason. 2017. *Boystown: Sex and Community in Chicago*. Chicago: University of Chicago Press.

Ortile, Matt. 2020. *The Groom Will Keep His Name: And Other Vows I've Made about Race, Resistance, and Romance*. New York: Bold Type Books, 2020.

Pachankis, John E., Kirsty A. Clark, Charles L. Burton, Jaclyn M. White Hughto, Richard Bränström, and Danya E. Keene. 2020. "Sex, Status, Competition, and Exclusion: Intraminority Stress from within the Gay Community and Gay and Bisexual Men's Mental Health." *Journal of Personality and Social Psychology* 119 (3): 713–40.

Pascoe, C. J. 2007. *Dude You're a Fag: Masculinity and Sexuality in High School*. Berkeley: University of California Press.

Passell, Jeffrey, and D'Vera Cohn. 2008. "US Population Projections: 2005–2050." Pew Research Center, February 11, 2008. www.pewresearch.org.

Peay, Austin, and Sam Kmack 2019. "Why Students at LA's Richest Public Schools Are Far More Likely to Get Extra Time on the SAT." LAist, August 29, 2019. https://laist.com.

Pedulla, David S. 2014. "The Positive Consequences of Negative Stereotypes: Race, Sexual Orientation, and the Job Application Process." *Social Psychology Quarterly* 77 (1): 75–94.

Perry, Imani. 2018. *Looking for Lorraine: The Radiant and Radical Life of Lorraine Hansberry*. Boston: Beacon.

———. 2019. *Breathe: A Letter to My Sons*. Boston: Beacon.

Pew Research Center. 2019. "Majority of Public Favors Same-Sex Marriage, but Divisions Persist." Pew Research Center, May 14, 2019. www.pewresearch.org.

Phillips, Steve. 2016. *Brown Is the New White: How the Demographic Revolution Has Created a New American Majority*. New York: The New Press.

Pimentel, Benjamin. 2013. "Why Filipino Americans Say Pilipino, not Filipino." *Inquirer*, July 17, 2013. https://globalnation.inquirer.net.

Portes, Alejandro, and Patricia Fernández-Kelly. 2008. "No Margin for Error: Educational and Occupational Achievement among Disadvantaged Children of Immigrants." *Annals of the American Academy of Political and Social Science* 620 (1): 12–36.

Portes, Alejandro, and Rubén G. Rumbaut. 2001. *Legacies: The Story of the Immigrant Second Generation*. Berkeley: University of California Press.

———2014. *Immigrant America: A Portrait*. Berkeley: University of California Press.

Portes, Alejandro, and Min Zhou. 1993. "The New Second Generation: Segmented Assimilation and Its Variants." *Annals of the American Academy of Political and Social Science* 530: 74–96.

Price, Robert. 2016. "Greetings from the Rural Village of Bakersfield." Bakersfield.com, September 28, 2016. www.bakersfield.com.

Quesada, Uriel, Letitia Gomez, and Salvador Vidal-Ortiz. 2015. *Queer Brown Voices: Personal Narratives of Latina/o LGBT Activism*. Austin: University of Texas Press.

Ransford, Edward, Frank Carrillo, and Yessenia Rivera. 2010. "Health Care-Seeking among Latino Immigrants: Blocked Access, Use of Traditional Medicine, and the Role of Religion." *Journal of Health Care for the Poor and Underserved* 21 (3): 862–78.

Ray, Victor. 2019. "A Theory of Racialized Organizations." *American Sociological Review* 84 (1): 26–53.

Reyes, Daisy. 2018. *Learning to Be Latino: How Colleges Shape Identity Politics*. New Brunswick, NJ: Rutgers University Press.

Rhoads, Robert. 2016. "Student Activism, Diversity, and the Struggle for a Just Society." *Journal of Diversity in Higher Education* 9 (3): 189–202.

Rios, Victor. 2011. *Punished: Policing the Lives of Black and Latino Boys*. New York: New York University Press.

Robertson, Mary. 2019. *Growing Up Queer: Kids and the Remaking of LGBTQ Identity*. New York: New York University Press.

Robinson, Brandon Andrew. 2020. *Coming Out to the Streets: LGBTQ Youth Experiencing Homelessness*. Berkeley: University of California Press.

Robinson, Karen, and Josipa Roska. 2016. "Counselors, Information, and High School College-Going Culture: Inequalities in the College Application Process." *Research in Higher Education* 57 (7): 845–68.

Rodriguez, Evelyn Ibatan. 2006. "Primerang Bituin: Philippines-Mexico Relations at the Dawn of the Pacific Rim Century." *Asia Pacific Perspectives* 6 (1): 4–12.

———. 2013. *Celebrating Debutantes and Quinceañeras: Coming of Age in American Ethnic Communities*. Philadelphia: Temple University Press.

Rodriguez, Gabriel. 2020. "From Troublemakers to Pobrecitos: Honoring the Complexities of Survivorship of Latino Youth in a Suburban High School." *Journal of*

Latinos and Education, July 2020. www.tandfonline.com/doi/full/10.1080/15348431 .2020.1796672.

Rodríguez, Richard T. 2006. "Queering the Homeboy Aesthetic." *Aztlán: A Journal of Chicano Studies* 31 (2): 127–37.

Rojas, Rick, and Vanessa Swales. 2019. "18 Transgender Killings This Year Raise Fears of an 'Epidemic.'" *New York Times*, September 27, 2019. www.nytimes.com.

Rubin, Joel, Hailey Branson-Potts, Zahira Torres, and Frank Shyong. 2016. "Man with Weapons Was Headed to L.A. Gay Pride Parade." *Los Angeles Times*, June 12, 2016. www.latimes.com.

Rumbaut, Rubén G., and Alejandro Portes, eds. 2001. *Ethnicities: Children of Immigrant in America.* Berkeley: University of California Press.

Salinas, Cristobal, Jr, and Adele Lozano. 2017. "Mapping and Recontextualizing the Evolution of the Term *Latinx*: An Environmental Scanning in Higher Education." *Journal of Latinos and Education* 18 (4): 302–15.

Santora, Marc. 2016. "Last Call at Pulse Nightclub, and Then Shots Rang Out." *New York Times*, June 12, 2016. www.nytimes.com.

Shoichet, Catherine. 2020. "COVID-19 Is Taking a Devastating Toll on Filipino American Nurses." CNN, December 11, 2020. www.cnn.com.

Silver, Daniel, Terry Nichols Clark, and Clemente Jesus Navarro Yanez. 2010. "Scenes: Social Context in an Age of Contingency." *Social Forces* 88 (5): 2293–324.

Simón, Yara. 2017. "This Instagram Is an Archive of SoCal's 90s Ditch Party Scene and the Latino Teens Behind It." Remezcla, April 25, 2017. https://remezcla.com.

Skiba, Russell, Robert H. Horner, Choong-Geun Chung, M. Karega Rausch, Seth L. May, and Tary Tobin. 2011. "Race Is Not Neutral: A National Investigation of African American and Latino Disproportionality in School Discipline." *School Psychology Review* 40 (1): 85–107.

Small, Mario Luis. 2009. "'How Many Cases Do I Need?' On Science and the Logic of Case Selection in Field-Based Research." *Ethnography* 10 (1): 5–38.

Smith, Stacy, Katherine Pieper, Marc Choueiti, Kevin Yao, Ariana Case, Karla Hernandez, and Zoe Moore. 2021. *Inclusion in Netflix Original US Scripted Series and Film.* Los Angeles: USC Annenberg Inclusion Initiative / Netflix, February 2021. https:// assets.uscannenberg.org.

Snyder, Vicky, and Francis Broadway. 2004. "Queering High School Biology Textbooks." *Journal of Research in Science Teaching* 41 (6): 617–34.

Solnit, Rebecca. 2018. *Call Them by Their True Names: American Crises (and Essays).* Chicago: Haymarket Books.

Sue, Derald Wing, Christina M. Capodilupo, Gina C. Torino, Jennifer M. Bucceri, Aisha M. B. Holder, Kevin L. Nadal, and Marta Esquilin. 2002. "Racial Microaggressions in Everyday Life: Implications for Clinical Practice." *American Psychologist* 62 (4): 271–86.

Talusan, Meredith. 2019. "Celebrate Your Kid's Transition. Don't Grieve It." *New York Times*, October 18, 2019. www.nytimes.com.

Taylor, Keeanga-Yamahtta, ed. 2017. *How We Get Free: Black Feminism and the Combahee River Collective*. Chicago: Haymarket Books. Kindle.

Terriquez, Veronica. 2015. "Intersectional Mobilization, Social Movement Spillover, and Queer Youth Leadership in the Immigrant Rights Movement." *Social Problems* 62 (3): 343–62.

Thompson, Matt. 2016. "To Be Outed in the Worst Possible Way." *Atlantic*, June 14, 2016. www.theatlantic.com.

Thorne, Barrie. 1995. *Gender Play: Girls and Boys in School*. New Brunswick, NJ: Rutgers University Press.

Tolentino, Jia. 2019. *Trick Mirror: Reflections on Self-Delusion*. New York: Penguin Random House.

University of California–Los Angeles. n.d. *2011–12 Undergraduate Profile*. Los Angeles: University of California–Los Angeles. Retrieved September 17, 2020. www.ucla.edu.

Valencia, Misha. 2020. "The Challenges of the Pandemic for Queer Youth." *New York Times*, June 29, 2020. www.nytimes.com.

Vargas, Jose Antonio. 2018. *Dear America: Notes of an Undocumented Citizen*. New York: Dey Street Books.

Vidal-Ortiz, Salvador. 2015. "Introduction: Brown Writing Queer; A Composite of Latina/o LGBT Activism." In *Queer Brown Voices: Personal Narratives of Latina/o LGBT Activism*, edited by Uriel Quesada, Letitia Gomez, and Salvador Vidal-Ortiz, 1–28. Austin: University of Texas Press.

Ward, Jane. 2008. *Respectably Queer: Diversity Culture in LGBT Activist Organizations*. Nashville: Vanderbilt University Press.

Washington, Bryan, and Ocean Vuong. *All the Ways to Be with Bryan Washington and Ocean Vuong*, podcast, A24 Films, December 21, 2020. https://a24films.com/notes /2020/12/all-the-ways-to-be-with-bryan-washington-ocean-vuong.

WEHOville. 2020. "The Third Most Expensive City for Renters in SoCal, WeHo Also Sees Rents Drop." *WEHOville*, April 3, 2020. www.wehoville.com.

West, Candace, and Don Zimmerman. 1987. "Doing Gender." *Gender and Society* 23 (1): 112–122.

Yoshino, Kenji. 2006. *Covering: The Hidden Assault on Our Civil Rights*. New York: Random House.

Zhou, Min, and Carl L. Bankston. 1998. *Growing Up American: How Vietnamese Children Adapt to Life in the United States*. New York: Russell Sage Foundation.

Zhou, Min, and Yang Sao Xiong. 2005. "The Multifaceted American Experiences of the Children of Asian Immigrants: Lessons for Segmented Assimilation." *Ethnic and Racial Studies* 28 (6): 1119–52.

Zidani, Sulafa. 2020. "Whose Pedagogy Is It Anyway? Decolonizing the Syllabus through a Critical Embrace of Difference." *Media, Culture, & Society* 43 (5): 970–78. https://journals.sagepub.com/.

Zimmerman, Arely. 2011. "A Dream Detained: Undocumented Latino Youth and the DREAM Movement." *NACLA Report on the Americas*, no. 38: 14–17, 38.

INDEX

Page numbers in italics indicate tables

ABOUT THE AUTHOR

ANTHONY CHRISTIAN OCAMPO is Professor of Sociology at California State Polytechnic University–Pomona and the author of *The Latinos of Asia: How Filipino Americans Break the Rules of Race*, which has been featured on NPR, NBC News, BuzzFeed, Literary Hub, and in the *Los Angeles Times*. His writing has appeared in numerous publications, including *GQ, Catapult, Colorlines, Gravy, Life & Thyme*, and the *Chronicle of Higher Education*, among others. He has received fellowships from the Ford Foundation, Jack Jones Literary Arts, Tin House, and the Voices of Our Nations Arts Foundation. Raised in Northeast Los Angeles, he earned his BA and MA from Stanford University and his MA and PhD in sociology from UCLA. Say hi to him on Twitter: @anthonyocampo.